LISTS TO LIVE BY

THE BIG BOOK OF LISTS TO LIVE BY®
published by Multnomah Publishers, Inc.

Compilation of:
Lists to Live By, The First Collection © 1999 by Alice Gray, Steve Stephens, John Van Diest 1-57673-478-1
Lists to Live By, The Second Collection © 2001 by Alice Gray, Steve Stephens, John Van Diest 1-57673-685-7

International Standard Book Number: 1-59052-701-1

The lists in this book are not substitutes for obtaining professional advice
from qualified persons and organizations. Consult the appropriate
professional advisor for complete and updated information.

Every effort has been made to provide proper and accurate source attributions for
selections in this volume. If any attribution is incorrect, the publisher welcomes written
documentation supporting correction for subsequent printings. The publisher gratefully
acknowledges the cooperation of publishers and individuals granting permission
for use of selections. Please see the acknowledgements for full attribution of these sources.

Unless otherwise indicated, Scripture quotations are from:

The Holy Bible, New International Version (NIV) © 1973, 1984
by International Bible Society, used by permission of Zondervan Publishing House

The Holy Bible, King James Version (KJV)

The New Testament in Modern English, Revised Edition (Phillips)
1958, 1960, 1972 by J. B. Phillips

Holy Bible, New Living Translation (NLT) © 1996.
Used by permission of Tyndale House Publishers, Inc. All rights reserved.

The Message by Eugene H. Peterson © 1993, 1994, 1995, 1996, 2000
Used by permission of NavPress Publishing Group
All rights reserved.

For information:
MULTNOMAH PUBLISHERS, INC.
601 N. LARCH ST.
SISTERS, OR 97759

06 07 08 09 10 11— 10 9 8 7 6 5 4 3 2 1

1

Lists
to live by

FOR EVERYTHING
THAT REALLY MATTERS

COMPILED BY

ALICE GRAY

STEVE STEPHENS

JOHN VAN DIEST

Multnomah® Publishers *Sisters, Oregon*

CONTENTS

FOR EVERYTHING THAT REALLY MATTERS

You name it and this book has it—well, almost!
It's more than trivia—it is life changing.
It's more than opinions—it is timeless truth.
It's more than words—it is motivating.
It's more than a collection—it is a treasure.

L ists are a great way of wrapping up powerful thoughts in an easy and accessible package. You can read them one at a time, pondering and reflecting on each point. Or you can read them in bunches. Start at the beginning and work your way through to the treasures at the end, or jump around to your favorites. Read them when you're on the run, or curl up with a steaming cup of hot chocolate.

Within these pages are dynamic ideas covering a gamut of topics from contentment to friendship, from family to virtue. The lists are brief and usable, and at the same time, valuable and thought provoking. However you approach it, Lists to Live By is so full of good concepts and ideas that you will likely come back to it over and over again. And you'll find yourself sharing the practical wisdom in conversation with your business associates, family, and friends.

We have carefully selected two hundred lists which we hope will impact you in such a way that your life will be easier and richer and truer. Some will cause you to reflect. Some will bring excitement. Some will make you smile. Some will move you to action. Some might even change your life.

ALICE GRAY   DR. STEVE STEPHENS   JOHN VAN DIEST

1
Success

Growing through learning and creativity

THREE SECRETS TO SUCCESS

1.
Be willing to learn new things.

2.
Be able to assimilate new information quickly.

3.
Be able to get along with and work with other people.

SALLY RIDE
ASTRONAUT

FIVE REASONS IT'S EASIER TO SUCCEED

1.

*It's easier to succeed because failure exacts a high price
in terms of time when you have to do a job over.*

2.

*It's easier to succeed because success
eliminates the agony and frustration of defeat.*

3.

*It's easier to succeed because money spent to fail
must be spent again to succeed.*

4.

*It's easier to succeed because a person's
credibility decreases with each failure, making it
harder to succeed the second time.*

5.

*And it's easier to succeed because joy and expressions of
affirmation come from succeeding, whereas feelings
of discouragement and discontent accompany failure.*

CATHY S. TRUETT, FOUNDER, CHICK-FIL-A COMPANY
FROM "IT'S EASIER TO SUCCEED THAN TO FAIL"

SIX WAYS TO BURY A GOOD IDEA

1.
It will never work.

2.
We've never done it that way before.

3.
We're doing fine without it.

4.
We can't afford it.

5.
We're not ready for it.

6.
It's not our responsibility.

AUTHOR UNKNOWN
AS CITED IN "MORE OF...THE BEST OF BITS & PIECES," ROB GILBERT, PH.D., ED.

TAKING CONTROL OF YOUR TIME

1.
Remember who's in charge. Time is something you manage, not something that manages you. Learn to think through each time commitment in its entirety. Buy yourself time to think by asking, "Can I let you know tomorrow?"

2.
Decide what is truly urgent. Rather than think, "I must get this done now!" Try putting it off. Surprise! Most "urgent" needs aren't really that urgent.

3.
Schedule in reverse. Put the *real* priorities on the calendar first—family picnic or date night. Then write in everything else.

4.
Drop one thing from your schedule. You'll probably let someone down, but look who benefits. Spending two less days a month as a lunch monitor at your son's school frees you up for a lunch date with your spouse.

5.

Be, rather than do. Try it for an evening. Think. Pray. Relax in a lawn chair.

6.

Get your spouse's perspective. Ask your mate to comment on how you're using your time and what seems to be robbing you of time.

7.

Be honest about your limitations. Do you find yourself saying "yes" to a project in the hopes that a weekend will suddenly hold the ten extra hours you'd need to complete it? You can't manufacture time.

8.

Make a list of your commitments. Post the list next to the phone or your calendar. A visual reminder of all that you're involved with will make you think twice before tacking on something else.

LOUISE A. FERREBEE, ASSOCIATE EDITOR
FROM "MARRIAGE PARTNERSHIP" MAGAZINE

25 TRAITS OF ENTREPRENEURS

DRIVE	*a high degree of motivation*
COURAGE	*tenacity and persistence*
GOALS	*a sense of direction*
KNOWLEDGE	*and a thirst for it*
GOOD HEALTH	*taking care of one's body*
HONESTY	*especially intellectual*
OPTIMISM	*positive attitude*
JUDGMENT	*knowing the wise from the foolish*
ENTHUSIASM	*excitement about life*
CHANCE TAKING	*willingness to risk failure*
DYNAMISM	*energy*
ENTERPRISE	*willingness to tackle tough jobs*
PERSUASION	*ability to sell*
OUTGOINGNESS	*friendly*

PATIENT YET IMPATIENT	*patient with others, yet*
	impatient with the status quo
ADAPTABILITY	*capable of change*
PERFECTIONISM	*desire to achieve excellence*
HUMOR	*ability to laugh at self and others*
VERSATILITY	*broad interests and skills*
CURIOSITY	*interested in people and things*
SELF-IDENTITY	*self-esteem and self-sufficiency*
REALISM/IDEALISM	*occupied by reality*
	but guided by ideals
IMAGINATION	*seeking new ideas, combinations,*
	and relationships
COMMUNICATION	*articulate*
RECEPTIVE	*alert*

EARL NIGHTINGALE
CO-FOUNDER OF NIGHTINGALE AND CONANT CORPORATION

HOW TO GIVE
CONSTRUCTIVE CRITICISM

1.
CONSIDER YOUR MOTIVE FIRST.

What do you desire to accomplish? Is it selfish?
Is it from anger or hurt feelings? Will what you say benefit others?

2.
WRITE DOWN WHAT YOU WILL SAY.

Begin with any affirmations that are sincere about the other person.
Use facts, opinions, intuitions, and feelings.
Read it over several times and rewrite until it sounds like what you
want to convey. Practice saying it out loud in front of a mirror.

3.
ASK FOR AN APPOINTMENT TO SPEAK
WITH THE OTHER PERSON.

Be amiable to his or her schedule. Say, "I have something I have
been thinking about, and I want to share it with you."

4.
SET ASIDE ALL EXPECTATIONS AND ACCUSATIONS.

Be open to hearing the other's reasoning. Don't argue.
Knowing your motives as suggested above will
help you communicate without arguing.

5.
THANK THE OTHER PERSON FOR LISTENING.

GLENDA HOTTON
MARRIAGE AND FAMILY THERAPIST

WHY WE PROCRASTINATE

We feel overwhelmed.

We overestimate the amount of time needed.

We would rather be doing something else.

We think that if we wait long enough, the task will go away.

We fear failure.

We fear success.

We enjoy the last-minute adrenaline rush.

BOB AND EMILIE BARNES
FROM "THE 15-MINUTE MONEY MANAGER"

EIGHT THINGS YOU NEED
TO KNOW ABOUT FAILURE

1.
TO FAIL IS NOT THE SAME AS BEING A FAILURE.

One may have many failings and yet still be far from being a failure.

2.
TO FAIL IS NOT THE DISGRACE EVERYONE THINKS IT IS.

To err is to do nothing more than to join the human race.

3.
FAILURE IS ONLY A TEMPORARY SETBACK.

*Failure is never the final chapter of the book of your life
unless you give up and quit.*

4.
NOTHING WORTHWHILE IS EVER ACHIEVED
WITHOUT RUNNING THE RISK OF FAILURE.

*The man who risks everything to try to achieve something truly
worthwhile and fails is anything but a disgraceful failure.*

5.

FAILURE IS A NATURAL PREPARATION FOR SUCCESS.

*Strange as it may seem to some of you, success
is much more difficult to live with successfully than is failure.*

6.

EVERY FAILING BRINGS WITH IT THE POSSIBILITIES OF SOMETHING GREATER.

*Analyze failure under whatever circumstances you choose, and you will
discover some seeds for turning failure into success.*

7.

WHAT YOU DO WITH FAILURES IN YOUR LIFE IS UP TO YOU.

*Failure is either a blessing or a curse, depending upon the
individual's reaction or response to it.*

8.

FAILINGS ARE OPPORTUNITIES TO LEARN HOW TO DO THINGS BETTER THE NEXT TIME— TO LEARN WHERE THE PITFALLS ARE AND HOW TO AVOID THEM.

The best possible thing to do with failure is to learn all you can from it.

DALE GALLOWAY, DEAN, SCHOOL OF CHURCH LEADERSHIP AND BIBLICAL PREACHING,
ASBURY THEOLOGICAL SEMINARY, WILMORE, KY, FROM "HOW TO FEEL LIKE A SOMEBODY AGAIN!"

COMMONLY ASKED
INTERVIEW QUESTIONS

1.
TELL ME ABOUT YOURSELF.

Keep your answer brief. He or she is interested in your goals, experience, interests, and communication skills.

2.
WHAT ARE YOUR STRENGTHS/WEAKNESSES?

Emphasize your good traits and those that relate to the job for which you are interviewing. You can mention an area that you're working to improve or one in which you have recently made great strides.

3.
WHY DO YOU WANT TO WORK HERE?

This is a good chance to mention how you can apply your skills, interests, and goals to the job.

4.
WHY SHOULD WE HIRE YOU?

Take this opportunity to highlight the unique qualities you can bring to the job.

5.
WHAT WOULD YOU DO IN (A PARTICULAR SITUATION)?

Don't be afraid to say that you would ask questions of your supervisor and approach each challenge as a learning opportunity.

SELECTED FROM "ABOUT...GETTING YOUR FIRST JOB" A "LIFE ADVICE®" PAMPHLET
PUBLISHED BY METLIFE'S CONSUMER EDUCATION CENTER

WHAT TO INCLUDE ON A RESUME

A HEADER

Located at the top, this should include your name, address, and phone number.

EDUCATION

List the most recent diploma or degree you have earned or are working toward, the date of graduation, and your field of study.

WORK EXPERIENCE

List employers, job titles, the dates worked, and a brief description of your duties, starting with the most recent. You may also want to include volunteer work or part-time jobs.

SKILLS

This is optional. List computer and language skills or other skills that may be relevant to the job for which you are applying.

HONORS AND ACTIVITIES

List awards you have earned, clubs or organizations to which you belong, and activities in which you participate.

REFERENCES

Include the notation, "References will be provided upon request." You should be prepared to provide the names of at least three people who can attest to your ability and personality. (Be sure to tell your references ahead of time that you may be using them, so they are not caught off guard when an employer calls to ask about you.)

SELECTED FROM "ABOUT...GETTING YOUR FIRST JOB," A "LIFE ADVICE®" PAMPHLET
PUBLISHED BY METLIFE'S CONSUMER EDUCATION CENTER

TOP 10 LIST FOR INTERVIEWEES

1.
COME PREPARED.

Do research in advance about the company. Interviewees who do their homework find themselves more confident and better prepared to answer questions about the responsibilities of a current open position.

2.
BRING A CLEAN COPY OF AN UP-TO-DATE RESUME.

Resumes should list major accomplishments and results achieved. Resumes should be no more than two pages. Bring a separate folder to the interview containing examples of your work, reference letters, etc.

3.
DRESS THE PART.

At least one day prior to your interview, examine the outfit you plan to wear to the interview (including shoes). Leave strong perfume and cologne at home. It's better to be conservative than flashy during interviews.

4.
PLAN TO ARRIVE TEN MINUTES EARLY.

Make sure you know how to get where you are going and allow for enough time to collect your thoughts before your appointment.

5.
KNOW WHY YOU WANT THE JOB.

Be prepared to answer the questions, whether asked directly or indirectly, why you want this particular job and why you would be the best choice for it.

6.
LISTEN TO YOUR INTERVIEWER'S QUESTIONS CAREFULLY.

Be prepared to answer difficult questions under pressure. If you need an extra few seconds to prepare your answer, it is okay to ask the interviewer to repeat and/or clarify the question.

7.
ANSWER WITH ENTHUSIASM AND PROFESSIONAL VOCABULARY.

Avoid slang. Highlight appropriate aspects of your education, work experience, and continuing education (seminars, training, etc.). Convey enthusiasm. Body language is important. Make eye contact with your interviewer.

8.
BE PREPARED TO DISCUSS AREAS YOU NEED TO STRENGTHEN IN YOUR WORK EXPERIENCE AND KNOWLEDGE.

It's hard to trust an interviewee who expresses no limitations in his or her performance. Avoid trying to present a perfect image.

9.
BRING QUESTIONS OF YOUR OWN.

The interviewee who asks informed questions about the company and the position is set apart from the crowd. Don't be afraid to ask information about what the company has to offer you.

10.
FOLLOW UP AFTER THE INTERVIEW WITH A THANK-YOU.

Within twenty-four hours, send a postcard or brief letter thanking the interviewer for the opportunity to interview for the job. Include something specific that was discussed during your time together. Call five to ten days later and let the interviewer know you are still interested in the job.

LANI WILLIAMS
DIRECTOR OF ADVANCEMENT, WESTERN SEMINARY

10 QUALITIES OF SUCCESSFUL BOSSES

1.
Cheerfully greets all employees with a
smile regardless of their job status.

2.
Properly calls people by name
(and title when appropriate).

3.
Never considers himself or herself "above" doing
menial tasks or helping someone.

4.
Delegates but does not dump his or her tasks on others.

5.
Privately and constructively critiques an employee who
has made an error, no matter how insignificant or egregious.

6.
Displays an appropriate sense of humor
in the proper circumstances.

7.
Is self-deprecating, always willing to take responsibility
for errors, never placing blame on others.

8.
Is not self-absorbed, but interested in
others—an attentive listener.

9.
Never expects employees to keep rules
he or she is unwilling to observe.

10.
Treats employees of the opposite sex as business
professionals and does not require females to do
the traditionally "old-fashioned female chores."

JUNE HINES MOORE, MOORE THAN MANNERS CONSULTING
FROM "THE ETIQUETTE ADVANTAGE"

12 QUALITIES OF SUCCESSFUL EMPLOYEES

1.
Always introduce people in a manner that
makes the two of them comfortable.

2.
Always write a note or letter to acknowledge a gift or favor.

3.
Be able to converse intelligently on a variety
of subjects. Don't pretend to be a "know-it-all"
on any topic of conversation. Don't brag.

4.
Know how to dress properly on and off the
job and in keeping with the company image.

5.
Never discuss private company matters with outsiders.

6.
Maintain the appearance of dignity but not superiority.

7.
Keep promises, obligations, and appointments. Always be on time. If detained, notify the host or guest.

8.
Return telephone calls within twenty-four hours or ask assistance in doing so.

9.
Don't procrastinate or neglect your duties and conse quently burden someone else's schedule.

10.
Return "borrowed" property quickly and in good condition.

11.
Don't engage in office gossip, but attempt to stop rumors.

12.
Give recognition, and don't take credit for someone else's work.

JUNE HINES MOORE, MOORE THAN MANNERS CONSULTING
FROM "THE ETIQUETTE ADVANTAGE"

14 WAYS TO SHOCK YOUR BOSS

1.
Show up to work early.

2.
Take the initiative to ask questions.

3.
Ask for advice, use it, then thank your boss.

4.
Speak well of your boss behind his or her back.

5.
When necessary, willingly stay late to finish an important project.

6.
Do more than your share of work.

7.
Be willing to work odd shifts.

8.
Every morning, come prepared to work hard.

9.
Continue to grow professionally.

10.
Read whatever you can about your field.

11.
Suggest new ideas that will save the company time and money.

12.
Stick around—don't always look for greener pastures.

13.
Pray for your boss.

14.
Invite your boss to church.

DAVID SANFORD, SENIOR DIRECTOR OF PUBLISHING,
LUIS PALAU EVANGELISTIC ASSOCIATION

12 STEPS TO CREATIVE THINKING

1.
RIGHT AWAY, WRITE IT DOWN.
Record ideas as soon as you think of them. Keep paper and pen handy at all times—in your car, by your television, on your nightstand.

2.
LISTEN TO MUSIC.
Listen to whatever sparks your imagination, whether it's Bach, the Beatles, or something you've never heard before.

3.
EXERCISE.
Go for a run, shoot some hoops, do jumping jacks—anything that starts your blood pumping and keeps your mind sharp.

4.
BRAINSTORM WITH A FRIEND, CO-WORKER, OR SIX-YEAR-OLD.
Talk with someone who looks at the world a little differently than you do. Chances are he or she will inspire a new approach.

5.
DO IT POORLY.
If you're a perfectionist, don't be. Create something that isn't necessarily your best work, but that gets the job done. Then go back later to fix it or redo it.

6.
WATCH PEOPLE.
Go downtown or to the mall, sit on a bench, and observe the passersby. Imagine what kind of life they lead.

7.
KEEP A JOURNAL.
*Write about your life and what's important to you, then
revisit your old thoughts when you need new ideas.*

8.
PRAY OR READ THE BIBLE.
*Putting life into spiritual perspective can take the
pressure off and jump-start the creative juices.*

9.
FREE-WRITE.
*Sit down at the computer or with pen and paper and write whatever
comes into your mind. You might be surprised at what comes out.*

10.
CHANGE YOUR LOCALE.
*Find a new quiet place—a park, the beach, a library, or
just a different room—and let your mind wander.*

11.
WASH THE DISHES OR MOW THE LAWN.
*It's easy and it gives you a feeling of
accomplishment while you're trying to think.*

12.
SLEEP ON IT.
*If nothing is working, your best bet may be to give up for now. Let your
subconscious create overnight and you'll have fresh ideas tomorrow.*

JAMES LUND
MARKETING COPY EDITOR

HOW TO BECOME
A LIFELONG LEARNER

1.
START WITH YOUR ATTITUDE.

Lifelong learning begins with a heart that desires change, wisdom, and application.

2.
ASK QUESTIONS.

Learners ask good questions. They possess an insatiable curiosity—a longing to know, discover, inquire. Ask questions that get below the surface.

3.
JOIN OTHERS.

Collaborative learning—in classes, small groups, with friends and colleagues—allows us to benefit from diverse perspectives and approaches. People are a gold mine of learning that is tapped through conversation.

4.
CHECK OUT THE OTHER SIDE.

Take time to examine and understand another point of view, even if it radically contradicts yours. You may see things in a new light, or you may have your old convictions strengthened. Personal convictions that have never been tested remain flabby.

5.
READ BROADLY.

Include a diversity of books, authors, and topics. Resist the temptation to read only those books that reinforce what you already believe.

6.
KEEP A JOURNAL.

Recording what we learn captures our growth in wisdom.

7.
EXPERIMENT.

Try new approaches and ideas. Age does not affect your ability to learn. An eighty-year-old can learn to surf the net like an eighteen-year-old.

8.
APPLY WHAT YOU KNOW.

Our depth of understanding is often directly related to our ability to apply what we've learned. Application takes knowledge from the head to the heart.

BILL MOWRY
FROM "DISCIPLESHIP JOURNAL"

SUCCESS

YOUR FUTURE DEPENDS ON...

Who you will be in the next five years
depends on three things:

the books you read

the people you meet

the choices you make

Choose today to live a transformed life!

BOB AND EMILIE BARNES
FROM "THE 15-MINUTE MONEY MANAGER"

WHAT IS SUCCESS?

To laugh often and love much;

To win the respect of intelligent people and the affection of children;

To earn the approval of honest critics and
endure the betrayal of false friends;

To appreciate beauty;

To find the best in others;

To give of one's self;

To leave the world a bit better, whether by a healthy child,
a garden patch, or a redeemed social condition;

To have played and laughed with enthusiasm
and sung with exultation;

To know even one life has breathed easier because you have lived...

This is to have succeeded.

RALPH WALDO EMERSON
POET, ESSAYIST, AND PHILOSOPHER

2
Friendship

A heart for others

HINTS FOR A HAPPY FRIENDSHIP

1.
Make friends even if you don't think you need them.

2.
Seek out quiet people. They have a lot to say, if you say something first.

3.
Don't establish a friendship based on mutual dislikes.

4.
Call if you're running late.

5.
Look people in the eye when you talk to them.

6.
Be one who says positive things about others.

7.
Learn to tell a good story.

8.
Ask other people about themselves.

9.
Be happy for others in their good fortune.

10.
Make sure your caring includes doing.

11.
Know when to say good-bye.

BRUCE & CHERYL BICKEL AND STAN & KARIN JANTZ
FROM "LIFE'S LITTLE HANDBOOK OF WISDOM"

HOW TO GET ALONG WITH PEOPLE

1.

LIKE. *If you genuinely like people, enjoy being with them, talking with them, and like being helpful to them, you will find that people generally will like you. And when mutual liking exists, people get along with one another.*

2.

INTEREST. *Become interested in the other person's ideas and activities. Direct conversation to the other individual's interests, rather than talking about yourself. As you become absorbed in his interests, he will become attentive to yours, and you will have a pleasant time together.*

3.

LIKABLE. *To be liked and to get along with people, it is necessary to be a likable person. Practice the old saying: "To have friends, be friendly."*

4.

NAMES. *Practice the art of remembering names. Focus on the other person, so that the name will register. Remember that a person's name is important to him. Knowing it will help you get along with him.*

5.

EASY. *Be easy to get along with. Be a comfortable sort of person, so that there is no strain in being with you. Be an "old shoe" kind of individual. Be homey, down to earth.*

6.

STIMULATING. *Cultivate the quality of being stimulating. If being with you makes people feel better and more alive, you will be sought after; people will want to be with you; your personal relations will be excellent.*

7.

SCRATCHY. *Personal relations deteriorate when a person has scratchy elements in his personality. That is to say, do not rub people the wrong way. Be untense and affable.*

8.

SENSITIVE. *Avoid being on edge and sensitive, so that you are easily hurt; for people instinctively shy off from the super-sensitive, fearing to arouse an unpleasant reaction. Avoid the temptation to react with hurt feelings, and you will get along with people.*

9.

HEAL. *Sincerely attempt to heal on an honest basis every misunderstanding that you may have with other individuals. Mentally and spiritually drain off your grievances, and maintain an attitude of goodwill with every human being.*

10.

DO. *Love people and do things for them. Perform unselfish and outgoing acts of friendship. Such sincere self-giving inevitably leads to pleasant personal relations. It is all summed up in a familiar Scripture admonition: "Do for others what you want them to do for you." (See Matthew 7:12; Luke 6:31.)*

NORMAN VINCENT PEALE
FROM "HELP YOURSELF WITH GOD'S HELP"

FRIENDSHIP

CELEBRATE YOUR DIFFERENCES

10 AREAS IN WHICH PEOPLE ARE DIFFERENT

1.

Extrovert or Introvert: Extroverts love crowds while introverts would rather spend time in solitude or with a close friend. Extroverts are energized by people and introverts are worn out by people.

2.

Leaper or Looker: Leapers take risks; when they see an opportunity they want to jump on it before it's too late. Lookers are more cautious. They like to carefully check everything out before making a decision.

3.

Outliner or Detailer: Outliners have a general focus and look at the big picture. They think in terms of direction and getting things done. Detailers look at the nuts and bolts. Their concern is *how* to get things done.

4.

Spender or Saver: If spenders have extra money, they want to spend—on themselves, on others, on worthy causes, on anything. If savers have extra money, they want to put it away for a rainy day. They do not like to spend unless it's very important.

5.

Planner or Flexer: Planners love structure with everything organized and neatly packaged. They like schedules and deadlines. Flexers bend with the flow of life and take things as they come. They tend to be spontaneous and laid back. Loose ends don't bother them because they believe everything will work out.

6.

Scurrier or Ambler: Scurriers are always busy. Speed and efficiency are their watchwords—accomplish as much as you can as fast as you can. Amblers take their time and set their own pace. They might not do as much, but they enjoy what they do.

7.

Thinker or Feeler: Thinkers focus on facts and principles. They base decisions on objective data and tend to be task oriented. Feelers focus on people and emotions. They base decisions on subjective data and tend to be relationship oriented.

8.

Dreamer or Worker: Dreamers are creative people who love to come up with ideas. They are optimistic and oriented toward the future. Workers are practical. They like to take other people's ideas and make them happen. They tend to be realistic and focus on the present.

9.

Collector or Tosser: Collectors gather things. They hate to throw anything away because they know they just might need it sometime. Tossers get rid of things. They hate clutter and they insist that if you haven't used something recently, you probably never will.

10.

Juggler or Holder: Jugglers are multichanneled and can deal with many things simultaneously. Holders are singlechanneled and can only deal with one, maybe two, things at a time. If they try to do more, they become stressed and overwhelmed.

We are all different and unique.
That creates balance, variety, and challenges in relationships.
Celebrate your differences; talk about them too.

DR. STEVE STEPHENS
FROM "MARRIAGE: EXPERIENCE THE BEST"

RATING YOURSELF AS A FRIEND

1.
*Do you reach out to others rather than always expect
that they will call or come to see you?
Do you reciprocate?*

2.
*When you meet others, are you open to the possibility that they may
become future allies, confidantes, best friends?*

3.
Do you approach others with an attitude of acceptance and interest?

4.
*Are you a good listener,
or do you claim more than your share of the airtime?*

5.
Do you refuse to become the only nurturer in the relationship?

6.
Are you loyal, and do you guard your friends' secrets?

7.
Do you practice unsolicited acts of kindness?

8.
Do you live an authentic life based on your values and beliefs?

9.
Can you ask for and grant forgiveness?

10.
*Can you listen when a friend tells you that you've hurt her,
or do you withdraw or get defensive?*

11.
*Do you encourage other people to develop their strengths
and graciously help them overcome weaknesses?*

12.
*Can you enjoy a friend's good fortune—whether in marriage,
motherhood, or career—even if you aren't on a parallel track?*

BRENDA HUNTER AND HOLLY LARSON
FROM "IN THE COMPANY OF FRIENDS"

TO BE A GOOD FRIEND

1.
Smile often; laugh aloud now and then; giggle, even.

2.
Become aware of several things that you especially enjoy.
Watch for others who enjoy those same things.

3.
Identify an acquaintance who has a need you can supply.
Offer yourself.
(Hint: Start with the obvious—your sister, spouse, neighbor...)

4.
Learn to enjoy being alone with yourself.
Identify what elements of living enrich your life.
Incorporate them in your daily routines. If you are happy being
with you, it's likely others will enjoy your company too!

5.
Forget what you give, and remember what you receive.

6.
Be the one who is there doing when others are saying,
"Is there anything I can do?"

7.
Listen—even in the silence.

GLORIA GAITHER, SUE BUCHANAN, PEGGY BENSON, AND JOY MACKENZIE
FROM "FRIENDS THROUGH THICK AND THIN"

WATCH WHAT YOU SAY

1.
Never tell jokes that slander.

2.
Never criticize in public unless you:
have already expressed your disappointment with
the other person in private, have already taken
someone with you to discuss the grievance
with the person, and are absolutely convinced
that public reprimand is necessary and will be helpful.

3.
Never say anything about anyone in their absence
that you wouldn't say in their presence.

MAX LUCADO
FROM "GOD CAME NEAR"

FRIENDSHIP

HOW TO FORGIVE AND FORGET

TO FORGIVE ANOTHER IS THE GREATEST FAVOR
YOU CAN DO—FOR YOURSELF.

1.

Take the initiative. Don't wait for the other person to apologize.

2.

If the forgiven person wants to reenter your life, it is fair to demand truthfulness. He or she should be made to understand, to feel the hurt you've felt. Then you should expect a sincere promise that you won't be hurt that way again.

3.

Be patient. If the hurt is deep, you can't forgive in a single instant.

4.

Forgive "retail," not "wholesale." It is almost impossible to forgive someone for being a bad person. Instead, focus on the particular act that hurt you. (It might help to write it down.)

5.

Don't expect too much. To forgive doesn't mean you must renew a once-close relationship.

6.

Discard your self-righteousness. A victim is not a saint. You, too, will need forgiveness some day.

7.

Separate anger from hate. To dissolve your hate: Face your emotion and accept it as natural. Then discuss it, either with the object of your hatred (if you can do so without escalating the hatred) or with a trusted third party.

8.

Forgive yourself. This may be the hardest act of all. Candor is critical. Admit your fault. Relax your struggle to be perfect. Then be concrete and specific about what is bothering you. Your deed was evil. You are not.

LEWIS B. SMEDES
CONDENSED FROM "FORGIVE AND FORGET"

FRIENDSHIP

12 TIMES TO SAY "I'M SORRY"

When you...

1.
Are wrong

2.
Are rude

3.
Are defensive

4.
Are impatient

5.
Are negative

6.
Are hurtful

7.
Are insensitive

8.
Are forgetful

9.
Are confused or confusing

10.
*Have neglected, ignored, or overlooked
something important to one you love*

11.
*Have damaged or misused something that
is not yours (even if it was an accident)*

12.
*Have not said "I'm sorry" as sincerely
and quickly as the situation needed*

DR. STEVE STEPHENS
PSYCHOLOGIST AND SEMINAR SPEAKER

MENDING A FRIENDSHIP

1
LOCATE THE TROUBLE SPOT.

This is the diagnosis step. Look back and try to assess what has gone wrong. Where did the misunderstanding begin? How did we get into this vicious circle of put-downs?

2.
APOLOGIZE WHEN YOU'RE WRONG.

All of us are wrong—plenty of times. It is foolish to let pride and insecurity keep us from saying so and patching up the friendship. Norman Vincent Peale writes, "A true apology is more than just acknowledgment of a mistake. It is recognition that something you have said or done has damaged a relationship—and that you *care* enough about the relationship to want it repaired and restored."

3.
CHECK TO SEE IF YOUR NEUROSES ARE SPOILING YOUR FRIENDSHIPS.

If a large number of your close friendships go sour, you might do well to ask if your neurotic patterns of relating are causing the problem.

4.
CHECK TO SEE IF YOU EMPLOY OLD METHODS
OF RELATING THAT NO LONGER WORK.

Each of us has emotional needs, and along the way each of us has acquired a bagful of tricks for getting those needs met. Unfortunately, we can learn some very neurotic ways of meeting those needs, and those neurotic patterns can get us into trouble again and again.

5.
CHECK TO SEE IF YOU HAVE EXCESSIVE NEED FOR APPROVAL.

The better a man's self-image, the better friends he is likely to choose, hence the better the relationship, and hence his self-esteem is enhanced. The worse a man's self-image, the more likely he is to choose jerks for friends, hence the relationship is likely to go bad, and his self-image is further lowered because of this failure. So the lesson is obvious: You cannot depend on others for your sense of self-worth. It must come from within you.

ALAN LOY MCGINNIS
CONDENSED FROM "THE FRIENDSHIP FACTOR"

FRIENDSHIP

IF YOU'RE GOING TO FIGHT...

Fight for the relationship—not against it!

Fight for reconciliation—not for alienation.

Fight to preserve the friendship—not to destroy it.

Fight to win your spouse—not to lose him/her.

Fight to save your marriage—not to cash it in.

Fight to solve the problem—not to salve your ego.

If you're going to fight, fight to win...not to lose!

DR. RICHARD C. HALVERSON, FORMER CHAPLAIN TO THE UNITED STATES SENATE
FROM "SOMEHOW INSIDE ETERNITY"

HOW TO BUILD A FRIENDSHIP WITH SOMEONE YOU'RE DATING

1.
Keep physical contact to a minimum.

2.
Explore new interests and hobbies.

3.
Do activities that are fun.

4.
Be yourself—don't put on an act just to get the person to like you.

5.
Ask open-ended questions.

6.
Listen to the other person's heart, not just to the words.

7.
*Talk with a godly older couple and discover
how they built their friendship.*

8.
*Read a good book together, and discuss how its content
can help you foster your relationship.*

9.
Seek to understand the other person's viewpoint.

REMEMBER THAT THE MORE YOU KNOW ABOUT EACH OTHER BEFORE
MARRIAGE, THE FEWER NEGATIVE SURPRISES THERE WILL BE AFTER THE WEDDING

DICK PURNELL
FROM "DECISION" MAGAZINE

FINDING A LISTENING EAR

IN CHOOSING A CONFIDANT, YOU SHOULD LOOK FOR:

someone you trust

someone who can keep a confidence

someone who will respect your boundaries

someone who will give you perspective

someone who will pray for you

someone who is wise and has more experience than you

someone who values commitment in marriage

*someone who will keep you accountable
without unjustly condemning you*

someone of the same sex, or a married couple

someone who will not be negatively affected by your confidences.

JANIS LONG HARRIS
FROM "MARRIAGE PARTNERSHIP" MAGAZINE

KEEPING A CONFIDENCE

When you're making progress toward developing an intimate friendship, it's crucial that you keep a confidence. Nothing will ruin a potential relationship quicker than a loose tongue. The only information you should be revealing to a third party is the type that passes the following criteria:

1.
Is it true?

2.
Is it kind?

3.
Is it necessary to tell?

4.
Is it beneficial to all concerned?

5.
Do you have the other person's permission to share the story?

Use these five questions as your rule of thumb when you're tempted to divulge someone else's business. If the answer to any or all of these five questions is no, you're just asking for trouble if you pass it along.

JOANNA WALLACE AND DEANNA WALLACE
FROM "ESPECIALLY FOR A WOMAN"

10 WAYS TO WELCOME
A NEW NEIGHBOR

1.

Acknowledge that you see them moving in, whether it is a wave of your hand from your yard or a quick "Welcome to the neighborhood. I'm looking forward to getting to know you."

2.

Resist the urge to stand at your window while they unload.

3.

A plate of cookies or a pot of stew can be most appreciated at their front door but don't go in unless invited. Then stay only a few minutes unless your help is welcome.

4.

When you finish with it, leave your copy of the newspaper in their box or on their porch for the first week.

5.

If the new neighbors are from out of town, a packet made up of a city map, a list of local events, museums, concerts, etc., might be really welcome. Or, with their permission, give their name and address to a local welcoming service.

6.

Blending kindness with firmness, make your boundaries known if the new neighbor's children or pets begin to violate your space. If you don't complain about their dog pottying in your yard when it first begins, the habit will become difficult to break.

7.

Tell neighbors to let you know if they need recommendations for shopping, a dentist, dry cleaners, etc., rather than just volunteering them.

8.

Never be critical of the people who used to live there.

9.

After two weeks, a neighborhood dessert or potluck dinner can introduce newcomers to other people who live nearby.

10.

If your offer of help or friendship is refused, don't push. Wait until your neighbors have time to get settled and look *you* over. In the meantime, smile.

BARBARA BAUMGARDNER
AUTHOR AND SPEAKER

FRIENDSHIP

NURTURING LONG-DISTANCE FRIENDSHIPS

*Choose a specific time of day when you can commit to
praying for each other.*

*Send photos! Not just the kids' school pictures, but
photos of anything important in your life—
a new hairstyle, your latest gardening or remodeling project,
your children's everyday antics, new friends.*

*Create a code between the two of you that says,
"I'm thinking of you—you're special."
Maybe it's a particular greeting or closing to your letters.*

*Always send a birthday card—unless
you've agreed ahead of time not to do cards.*

*Make it a habit to hit that reply button on the e-mail,
even if it's just a short note.
Don't wait so long between letters
that it takes a novel to catch up on your life.*

Never underestimate the effectiveness of the oft-maligned
Christmas newsletter to keep friends up-to-date.
Just don't send the newsletter to everyone.

Talk about your friend to others.
Saying her name out loud and "introducing" her to
others keeps your friendship alive.

If you're on e-mail, send a "real letter" every once in a while—
something pretty or a funny card or even a comic from
the newspaper that made you laugh.

Create your own traditions.
My mom and her best friend sent each other the same birthday card
for years. They added a personal letter each birthday and
kept that special card in a safe place the rest of the year.

Embrace when you finally see each other again!

RENÉE S. SANFORD
RENÉE LIVES IN THE UNITED STATES—HER BEST FRIEND LIVES IN EUROPE

WHAT IS LOVE?

1.
Love delights in giving attention rather than attracting it.

2.
Love finds the element of good and builds on it.

3.
Love does not magnify defects.

4.
Love is a flame that warms but never burns.

5.
Love knows how to disagree without becoming disagreeable.

6.
Love rejoices at the success of others instead of being envious.

FATHER JAMES KELLER, FOUNDER, THE CHRISTOPHERS
AS CITED IN "MORE OF...THE BEST OF BITS & PIECES," ROB GILBERT, PH.D., ED.

3
Virtue
Marks of character

DESTINY

Watch your thoughts; they become words.

Watch your words; they become actions.

Watch your actions; they become habits.

Watch your habits; they become character.

Watch your character; it becomes your destiny.

FRANK OUTLAW
AS CITED IN "MORE OF...THE BEST OF BITS & PIECES," ROB GILBERT, PH.D., ED.

20 GIFTS TO GIVE

1.
Mend a quarrel.

2.
Seek out a forgotten friend.

3.
Hug someone tightly and whisper, "I love you so."

4.
Forgive an enemy.

5.
Be gentle and patient with an angry person.

6.
Express appreciation.

7.
Gladden the heart of a child.

8.
Find the time to keep a promise.

9.
Make or bake something for someone else. Anonymously.

10.
Speak kindly to a stranger.

11.
Enter into another's sorrow.

12.

Smile. Laugh a little. Laugh a little more.

13.

Take a walk with a friend.

14.

Kneel down and pat a dog.

15.

Lessen your demands on others.

16.

Apologize if you were wrong.

17.

Turn off the television and talk.

18.

Pray for someone who helped you when you hurt.

19.

Give a soft answer even though you feel strongly.

20.

Encourage an older person.

CHARLES R. SWINDOLL
CONDENSED FROM "THE FINISHING TOUCH"

VIRTUE

ACTIONS THAT TAKE COURAGE

Admitting you are wrong.

Doing what is right when everyone else isn't.

Speaking to someone you don't know.

*Saying "no" when people are trying to get you to do
something you know you shouldn't.*

Telling the truth and accepting the consequences.

*Standing up for something you believe in even though
it might mean rejection or ridicule or even physical harm.*

Defending someone who is considered unpopular or unacceptable.

*Facing a limitation and giving it your very best
regardless of pain or discomforts.*

Confronting a fear without running away.

*Giving sacrificially to protect or promote either
someone you love, someone who has been wronged,
or someone who is in need.*

Being the only one.

Taking a risk.

*Sharing your heart honestly
(including your feelings and fears and failures).*

*Living your faith with all your heart, mind, soul, and
strength regardless of the cost.*

DR. STEVE STEPHENS
PSYCHOLOGIST AND SEMINAR SPEAKER

VIRTUE

BENJAMIN FRANKLIN'S 13 VIRTUES

1.
TEMPERANCE

Eat not to dullness; drink not to elevation.

2.
SILENCE

Speak not but what may benefit others or yourself;avoid trifling conversation.

3.
ORDER

Let all your things have their places; let each part of your business have its time.

4.
RESOLUTION

Resolve to perform what you ought; perform without fail what you resolve.

5.
FRUGALITY

Make no expense but to do good to others or yourself; i.e., waste nothing.

6.
INDUSTRY

Lose no time; be always employed in something useful; cut off all unnecessary actions.

7.
SINCERITY

Use no hurtful deceit; think innocently and justly; and, if you speak, speak accordingly.

8.
JUSTICE

Wrong none by doing injuries, or omitting the benefits that are your duty.

9.
MODERATION

Avoid extremes; forbear resenting injuries so much as you think they deserve.

10.
CLEANLINESS

Tolerate no uncleanliness in body, clothes, or habitation.

11.
TRANQUILLITY

Be not disturbed by trifles or at accidents common or unavoidable.

12.
CHASTITY

*Rarely use venery but for health or offspring, never to dullness, weakness,
or the injury of your own or another's peace or reputation.*

13.
HUMILITY

Imitate Jesus and Socrates.

PETER SHAW, ED.
FROM "THE AUTOBIOGRAPHY AND OTHER WRITINGS BY BENJAMIN FRANKLIN"

WHAT I BELIEVE IN AND VALUE

GRACE
Treasure life as a gift from God.

STRENGTH/FORTITUDE
Fight the good fight, hard.

LOVE
Embrace people with openness and acceptance.

HOPE
Facilitate the growth and success of others.

HUMAN DIGNITY
Seek first to understand before passing judgment.

BEING REAL (INTEGRITY)
Acquire enough wisdom to be humble.

FUN
Have at least one hearty laugh each day.

IMPACT
Practice the courage to take risks.

CHARLIE HEDGES
CONDENSED FROM "GETTING THE RIGHT THINGS RIGHT"

PEOPLE WITH CHARACTER

They walk with integrity.

They do what is right.

They tell the truth.

They don't gossip.

They don't mistreat people.

They side with those who are right.

They keep their word.

They lend money to those in need without interest.

They don't take advantage of people for financial gain.

ADAPTED FROM THE PSALMS
COMPILED BY ANDREW STANLEY FROM "A DIAMOND IN THE ROUGH"

10 REASONS FOR GOING TO CHURCH

Teddy Roosevelt offered his reasons for going to church in
Ladies' Home Journal *in 1917:*

1.

In this actual world a churchless community, a community where men have abandoned and scoffed at or ignored their religious needs, is a community on the rapid downgrade.

2.

Church work and church attendance mean the cultivation of the habit of feeling some responsibility for others and the sense of braced moral strength which prevents a relaxation of one's own moral fiber.

3.

There are enough holidays for most of us which can quite properly be devoted to pure holiday making... Sundays differ from other holidays—among other ways—in the fact that there are fifty-two of them every year.... On Sunday, go to church.

4.

Yes, I know all the excuses. I know that one can worship the Creator and dedicate oneself to good living in a grove of trees, or by a running brook, or in one's own house, just as well as in church. But I also know as a matter of cold fact the average man does not thus worship or thus dedicate himself. If he stays away from church he does not spend his time in good works or in lofty meditation. He looks over the colored supplement of the newspaper.

5.

He may not hear a good sermon at church. But unless he is very unfortunate he will hear a sermon by a good man who, with his good wife, is engaged all the week long in a series of wearing and humdrum and important tasks for making hard lives a little easier.

6.

He will listen to and take part in reading some beautiful passages from the Bible. And if he is not familiar with the Bible, he has suffered a loss....

7.

He will probably take part in singing some good hymns.

8.

He will meet and nod to, or speak to, good, quiet neighbors.... He will come away feeling a little more charitably toward all the world, even toward those excessively foolish young men who regard church-going as rather a soft performance.

9.

I advocate a man's joining in church works for the sake of showing his faith by his works.

10.

The man who does not in some way, active or not, connect himself with some active, working church misses many opportunities for helping his neighbors, and therefore, incidentally, for helping himself.

THEODORE ROOSEVELT
TWENTY-SIXTH PRESIDENT OF THE UNITED STATES

A PRAYER FOR EVERYONE

From the cowardice that shrinks from new truth,

From the laziness that's content with half-truth,

From the arrogance from the one who thinks he knows all truth,

Oh God of truth,

Deliver me!

AN ANCIENT PRAYER

EXTREME VIRTUES

Truth, if it becomes a weapon against persons.

Beauty, if it becomes a vanity.

Love, if it becomes possessive.

Loyalty, if it becomes blind, careless trust.

Tolerance, if it becomes indifference.

Self-confidence, if it becomes arrogance.

Faith, if it becomes self-righteousness.

ASHLEY COOPER, COLUMNIST
AS CITED IN "MORE OF...THE BEST OF BITS & PIECES," ROB GILBERT, PH.D., ED.

THE ADVENTURE OF GIVING

ANONYMOUS GIVING

Listen for specific needs people have and then
figure out a way to meet them undetected.

PLANNING FOR ANNUAL GIFTS

Every spring I anticipate several one-time gift appeals
for summer missions opportunities.
I set aside money so that I can respond to as many as possible.

TAKING SOMEONE SHOPPING

Rather than just handing someone money, take them shopping.

HIRING FOR SERVICES

I know a talented single mom on a meager income.
I "commission" her to make floral arrangements for me.
She earns extra money with dignity, and I get hand-crafted decorations.

FOOTING THE BILL

*Pay some of the tuition, or cover for the textbooks, or supply
the paper and pens, for someone going back to school.*

RECYCLING THINGS YOU DON'T NEED

*A friend of mine recently upgraded to a new computer system.
Rather than selling her old system, she gave it to a high school student
with the promise of tutoring her in word processing skills.*

GIVING AS A FAMILY

*Many families have rediscovered the joy of the holidays by
pooling the money they'd normally spend on each other
and getting gifts for people less fortunate.*

JUST 'CUZ GIFTS

*Giving gifts for no apparent reason is a creative way to express
care and love, especially when you give them in unusual ways.*

BECKY BRODIN
FROM "DISCIPLESHIP JOURNAL"

KINDNESS

Be kind and merciful.

Let no one ever come to you

without leaving better and happier.

Be a living expression of God's kindness.

Kindness in your face,

Kindness in your eyes,

Kindness in your smile,

Kindness in your warm greeting.

MOTHER TERESA
FOUNDER OF MISSIONARIES OF CHARITY

RULES FOR CHRISTIAN LIVING

Do all the good you can,

By all the means you can,

In all the ways you can,

In all the places you can,

At all the times you can,

To all the people you can,

As long as ever...

...you can!

JOHN WESLEY
EVANGELIST AND THEOLOGIAN

VIRTUE

MORAL GUIDANCE
FOR YOUR FAMILY

YOU CAN MAKE A DIFFERENCE!

1.
Do what is morally right.
Be a role model, and act with authority.

2.
Choose good, and reject the mediocre and evil.
Now is the time to rid your household of any reading or viewing
material you know to be vulgar, offensive, or morally confusing.

3.
Bring into your home only things you know to be interesting, educational,
entertaining, AND edifying. Leave magazines and books around
where your child will be enticed to pick them up and browse.

4.
The TV and remote belong to you.
You hold the power! Get your children accustomed to
asking permission before watching TV or selected videos.

5.
Your home is your castle.
What you have on display or allow to be viewed
represents *you*. "Would God be pleased?" is a good
guide in judging material allowed in the home.

6.
Don't let teens or young adults bully you.
Gently but firmly remind them that until they are in their own home,
they have no right to air a program you consider objectionable.

7.
Don't allow TV sets in children's bedrooms.
They cause isolation and can promote unlimited
or unhealthy viewing habits.

8.
Be consistent.
Don't confuse a child with changed minds or plea bargaining
in the area of material you know to be vulgar or immoral.

9.
Set the tone.
Viewing graphically violent or sexually explicit material invades
a youngster's imagination and may confuse his or her thinking.

10.
Be fair.
Tell your youngster beforehand, then stick to your rules.

11.
Don't give in or give up.
If setting media standards is new at your house, be patient, yet firm.

MARY ANN KUHARSKI, FREELANCE WRITER, HOMEMAKER, AND MOTHER OF 13
CONDENSED FROM "HOMELIFE" MAGAZINE

THE 10 COMMANDMENTS

1.

Do not worship any other gods besides me.

2.

Do not make idols of any kind.

3.

Do not misuse the name of the Lord your God.

4.

Remember to observe the Sabbath day by keeping it holy.

5.

Honor your father and mother.

6.

Do not murder.

7.

Do not commit adultery.

8.

Do not steal.

9.

Do not testify falsely against your neighbor.

10.

Do not covet your neighbor's house or anything else your neighbor owns.

FROM "THE HOLY BIBLE"
NEW LIVING TRANSLATION

SEVEN DEADLY WRONGS

1.

Wealth without work

2.

Pleasure without conscience

3.

Knowledge without character

4.

Science without humanity

5.

Commerce without morality

6.

Worship without sacrifice

7.

Politics without principle

AUTHOR UNKNOWN

FAITH

I believe in the sun, even though it doesn't shine,

I believe in love, even when it isn't shown,

I believe in God, even when he doesn't speak.

FOUND ON THE WALL OF A CONCENTRATION CAMP

4
Life's
Transitions
Passages through the years

THINGS TO FEEL NOSTALGIC ABOUT

A barefoot walk along a sandy beach.

A quiet visit to the place you were raised.

Listening to a rippling brook running over the rocks

through a forest of autumn leaves.

Singing the song of your alma mater.

Looking over childhood photos in the family album.

Watching your now-grown "child" leave home.

Standing silently beside the grave of a close,

personal friend or relative.

The smell and sounds of a warm fireplace.

An old letter, bruised with age, signed by one who loved you.

Climbing to the top of a wind-swept hill.

Getting alone—all alone—and reading aloud.

Christmas Eve, late at night.

Certain poems...certain melodies.

Weddings...graduations...diplomas.

Snow...sleds...toboggans.

Saying good-bye.

CHARLES R. SWINDOLL
FROM "GROWING STRONG IN THE SEASONS OF LIFE"

LIFE'S LESSONS

WISDOM THROUGH THE AGES

I've learned that I like my teacher because she cries when we sing "Silent Night." (Age 6)

I've learned that you can't hide a piece of broccoli in a glass of milk. (Age 7)

I've learned that when I wave to people in the country, they stop what they are doing and wave back. (Age 9)

I've learned that if you want to cheer yourself up, you should try cheering someone else up. (Age 14)

I've learned that although it's hard to admit it, I'm secretly glad my parents are strict with me. (Age 15)

I've learned that silent company is often more healing than words of advice. (Age 24)

I've learned that if someone says something unkind about me, I must live so that no one will believe it. (Age 39)

I've learned that the greater a person's sense of guilt, the greater his need to cast blame on others. (Age 46)

I've learned that singing "Amazing Grace" can lift my spirits for hours. (Age 49)

I've learned that you can tell a lot about a man by the way he handles these three things: a rainy day, lost luggage, and tangled Christmas tree lights. (Age 52)

I've learned that regardless of your relationship with your parents, you miss them terribly after they die. (Age 53)

I've learned that if you want to do something positive for your children, try to improve your marriage. (Age 61)

I've learned that life sometimes gives you a second chance. (Age 62)

I've learned that if you pursue happiness, it will elude you. But if you focus on your family, the needs of others, your work, meeting new people, and doing the very best you can, happiness will find you. (Age 65)

I've learned that whenever I decide something with kindness, I usually make the right decision. (Age 66)

I've learned that everyone can use a prayer. (Age 72)

I've learned that even when I have pains, I don't have to be one. (Age 82)

I've learned that every day you should reach out and touch someone. People love human touch—holding hands, a warm hug, or just a friendly pat on the back. (Age 85)

I've learned that I still have a lot to learn. (Age 92)

SELECTED

DON'T LET YOUR NEW
BABY DRIVE YOU APART

1.

"The greatest thing parents can do for their children is to love each other," advises Dr. Benjamin Salk, family psychologist.

2.

While giving your baby as much love as you can, be careful about protecting your own privacy. At times you'll want to let your baby share your bed, but be cautious as to how often. If space allows, let the baby sleep in a separate room as soon as possible.

3.

Have conversations that are not dominated by the latest in baby foods and teething rings.

4.

Realize how easy it is for the father to feel both unneeded and excluded.

5.

Share as many tasks as possible, even if this means they are not done to perfection. The baby will survive with a crooked diaper.

6.

Recognize how physically shattered many women become with the sheer effort of looking after a small baby.

7.

If sex is not at the top of the agenda for a while, make sure this is not confused with rejection, and try to show intimacy in other ways.

8.

Don't lose touch with your friends.

9.

Don't refuse to let trusted friends look after your child for a few hours.

10.

As the child grows, keep a sense of moderation in terms of his involvement in extra activities. You can exhaust yourselves and your child quite easily.

ROB PARSONS
CONDENSED FROM "THE 60-MINUTE MARRIAGE BUILDER"

COUNTDOWN TO COLLEGE

DEFINE EXPECTATIONS

• Talk honestly about the temptation of putting new interests and friends ahead of studies. Be encouraging but firm about the importance of time management.

• Holidays and vacation times in the year ahead will no doubt offer opportunities for new cultural experiences. Discuss which holidays you expect your child to spend at home. Don't forget to talk about opportunities for your child to bring friends home to visit.

DETERMINE A BUDGET

• Whether your freshman will be working or receiving a monthly allowance, sit down together and determine a livable budget. As you're crunching numbers, don't forget to include the phone bill, clothing and personal items, as well as gas and maintenance for a vehicle (if applicable).

• Open a checking account early in the summer to foster familiarity with banking processes. Make sure your child understands how to balance a checkbook.

KEEP THE LINES OF COMMUNICATION OPEN

• A college post-office box can be the loneliest spot on campus. Try to keep your freshman's box filled by sending cards and letters as often as possible. Why not surprise him or her with a favorite magazine subscription?

• Decide how often you will communicate by telephone. Once your freshman is settled on campus, let him or her set a regular time for calling home—and then make sure you're 100 percent available when he or she calls.

KATHY CHAPMAN SHARP AND REBEKAH D. SHARP
FROM "HOMELIFE" MAGAZINE

WHEN YOUR ADULT CHILDREN WANT TO MOVE BACK HOME

1.
BE IN AGREEMENT.

Before you take anyone into your home, agree with your mate to stand together on decisions. If one partner is strongly opposed to the return of the adult child (with or without a family), the situation will never work.

2.
ESTABLISH CONTROL.

If your children come back home, clearly spell out whose home it is. When your kids show the first sign of bucking for control, both parents must take quick action.

3.
SET A TIME LIMIT RIGHT FROM THE START.

Don't let anyone move in for an indefinite time.

4.
ASSIGN JOBS.

Don't start doing their laundry and making their beds. You already raised your family once; you don't need to do it a second time.

5.
KEEP YOUR REGULAR MEALTIMES.

If your guests want to eat at separate times or don't like what you cook, make it clear they can buy their own food, cook it, and clean up afterwards.

6.
LET THEM KNOW THIS ISN'T A HOTEL.

Not only should mealtimes be established and cleanup assigned, but guests must not expect hotel services. You should not be in charge of their business calls, their dry cleaning, or their change of linens.

7.
MAKE THEM CONTRIBUTE FINANCIALLY.

Granting family members a week or two of hospitality can be considered a kind gift, but if signs reveal this visit will be longer, establish a time frame and ask them to share the expenses.

8.
DON'T LET THEM CRITICIZE.

Right from the start, let them know that if they don't like your home, your lifestyle, or your friends, they can leave.

9.
DON'T USE THE CHILDREN AS A DUMPING GROUND.

Often when grandchildren move in, Grandma and Grandpa use them to express the feelings they don't dare say to the parents.

10.
DON'T ASSUME GUILT.

One young couple complained when their parents didn't always want to babysit so they could go out more. The parents stated calmly but clearly, "We did not have these babies; you did. We love them, but we are not responsible for their care. When we babysit, it is a gift of love."

FLORENCE LITTAUER
ADAPTED FROM "WAKE UP, WOMEN!"

PREPARING FOR RETIREMENT

1.
Speak to people who are already retired.

2.
Reevaluate priorities.

3.
Determine what legacy you wish to leave.

4.
Reassess finances and plan your future.

5.
Begin downsizing if necessary.

6.
Develop new hobbies.

7.
Do more things with your spouse.

8.
Look for volunteer activities.

9.
Plan future vacations.

10.
Think of classes you might want to take.

11.
Set up an exercise program.

12.
Increase time with special friends and start developing new friends with similar interests.

ALICE GRAY, DR. STEVE STEPHENS, AND JOHN VAN DIEST

FOUR WAYS TO GROW
OLD GRACEFULLY

1.
Fear less; hope more.

2.
Eat less; chew more.

3.
Talk less; say more.

4.
Hate less; love more.

ABIGAIL VAN BUREN
FROM "THE OREGONIAN"

STAY YOUNG WHILE GROWING OLD

1.

Applaud others' successes.

2.

Exercise daily.

3.

Keep a positive attitude.

4.

Read widely and often.

5.

Play with children.

6.

Enjoy nature.

7.

Laugh heartily.

8.

Take a class.

9.

Plant a garden.

10.

Count your blessings.

11.

Take risks.

12.

Sing from your heart.

13.

Get a pet.

14.

Eat healthy.

15.

Give generously to others.

IF I HAD IT TO DO OVER AGAIN

I would love my wife more in front of my children.

I would laugh with my children more—at our mistakes and our joys.

I would listen more—even to the youngest child.

I would be more honest about my own
weaknesses and stop pretending perfection.

I would pray differently for my family.

I would do more things with my children.

I would be more encouraging and bestow more praise.

I would pay more attention to little things,
deeds, and words of love and kindness.

Finally, if I had to do it all over again, I would share God
more intimately with my family. I would use ordinary
things that happened in every ordinary day to point them to God.

AUTHOR UNKNOWN

TOUGH QUESTIONS TO ASK ELDERLY PARENTS

1.

Do you have up-to-date wills?

2.

Do you have hidden assets or liabilities?

3.

Where do you keep your important financial documents?

4.

Who will handle your affairs if you become incapacitated?

5.

Do you have a living will and a medical power of attorney?

6.

Do you have sufficient medical insurance?

7.

Do you have long-term care insurance?

8.

Have you made funeral plans?

9.

Will your estate owe taxes, and do you have money to pay them?

FINANCIAL LITERACY CENTER
FROM "NEW MAN" MAGAZINE

HOW ADULT CHILDREN
CAN HELP THEIR PARENTS

1.
COMMUNICATE OFTEN.

Keep in touch by telephone, visits, and letters.
Remember holidays, birthdays, and anniversaries.

2.
RESPECT INDEPENDENCE.

As long as possible, your parents need to make their
own decisions about where and how to live.

3.
SUPPORT "LETTING GO."

Help them find constructive ways to dispose of possessions by alerting
them to thrift stores or mission programs that can benefit from
their contributions. Listen to them and weep with them when they must
give up their homes, their driver's licenses, or their leadership positions.

4.
EMPATHIZE WITH THEM.

If you were in their place, how would you act and feel?

5.
ENCOURAGE REMINISCING.

Draw forth memories of the past and help them
fit together the pieces of their experiences.

6.
LISTEN TO THEM.

Hear the accounts of their past disappointments, accomplishments, and satisfactions—even if told repeatedly—as well as the accounts of their current worries and fears, joys and hopes and delights.

7.
ENCOURAGE SPIRITUAL GROWTH.

Help them find large-print Bibles, enriching TV and radio programs, and transportation to attend church. Encourage them to join a prayer chain or a service group.

8.
SUPPORT USEFULNESS.

Seek their counsel, praise their hobbies, and encourage their giving service to others.

9.
STIMULATE THEIR SOCIAL LIFE.

Encourage them to maintain old social relationships and to make new ones. "For none of us lives to himself alone and none of us dies to himself alone."

10.
PRAY FOR THEM AND WITH THEM.

Their physical, mental, social, and material well-being is interconnected with their spiritual health.

DAVID O. MOBERG
FROM "DECISION MAGAZINE"

QUESTIONS PARENTS SHOULD ASK BEFORE MOVING IN WITH THEIR CHILDREN

1.

Do you really want to live with your son or daughter? Do they want you to live with them?

2.

Can your family afford to have you live with them? Can you help with household expenses?

3.

How easily can you adapt to your family's lifestyle and they to yours? Will you feel like a visitor in their home?

4.

What are the strengths and weaknesses of your relationship with your children (and their spouses)?

5.

Can you continue to pursue hobbies you enjoy? Can you keep in touch with your friends?

6.

How much time do you expect your family to spend with you? If you are home alone during the day, will you feel isolated or depressed?

7.

Will you have your own room? Can you bring along a favorite chair? Are there stairs to climb?

8.

Can you keep your car and driver's license? Are you willing and able to ride a bus or do you need to depend on your family for transportation?

9.

Can you help with the cooking and cleaning? Do you want to? Will your family let you?

10.

Will you need help with your personal care? If you will, can your family accommodate your needs?

11.

If you can't manage your own financial affairs, who will assume this responsibility?

NURSING HOME CHECKLIST

1.
What are the facility's admission requirements?

2.
Are the staff kind and do they show respect to the residents?

3.
Are most residents dressed for the season and time of day?

4.
Do the staff know the residents by name?

5.
Do the staff respond quickly to resident calls for assistance?

6.
Are activities tailored to residents' individual needs and interests?

7.
Does the home use care in selecting roommates?

8.
Does the home have enough help on weekends and night shifts?

9.
Does the facility have contact with community groups,
such as churches, pet therapy programs, or Scouts?

10.
Does the resident or his or her family participate in
developing the resident's care plan?

11.
Does the home offer on-sight programs to restore lost physical functioning (for
example, physical therapy, occupational therapy, speech and language therapy)?

12.
Does the home have the special services that meet your needs? For example, special care units for residents with dementia or with respiratory problems?

13.
Is a registered nurse available for nursing staff and do they have an arrangement with a nearby hospital?

14.
Is the facility certified for government health insurance?

15.
Are there outdoor areas accessible for resident use?

16.
Is the inside of the nursing home clean and free from unpleasant odors?

17.
Are there private areas for residents to visit with family, visitors, or physicians?

18.
Does the nursing home have a good reputation in the community?

19.
Is the facility close for family or friends to visit?

20.
Does the home have a staff physician who systematically calls on the residents?

DAN GRADY, CHAPLAIN
NURSING HOME MINISTRIES

A ROAD MAP THROUGH GRIEF

1.

Pace yourself.

2.

Lean into the pain.

3.

Get ready for a second wave of grief.

4.

Trust the recovery process.

5.

Welcome help from those who love you.

6.

Protect your physical health.

7.

Refuse to live with regrets.

8.

Avoid major changes.

9.

Look beyond people's words.

10.

Let your grief benefit others.

MARY A. WHITE
FROM "HARSH GRIEF, GENTLE HOPE"

RECOVERY FROM GRIEF

YOU WILL KNOW YOU'RE BEGINNING TO RECOVER WHEN:

Taking care of yourself is not only okay, but it feels good.

The future is not so frightening.

You can handle "special days" without falling apart.

You want to reach out to others in need or in pain.

Your emotional roller coaster is slowing down.

You skip or forget a ritual, such as visiting the cemetery, without grief.

SISTER TERESA MCINTIER, CSI, RNM, MB
FROM "YOU'LL KNOW YOU ARE RECOVERING WHEN..."

HEAVEN IS A PLACE...

With no hunger.

With no thirst.

With no tears.

With no death.

With no sadness.

With no pain.

With no hard labor.

That is beautiful.

That is magnificent.

JAY CARTY
CONDENSED FROM "PLAYING THE ODDS"

5

Marriage

Experiencing the best

18 ATTRIBUTES TO LOOK FOR IN A MARRIAGE PARTNER

1. Positive attitude

2. Spiritual values

3. Sense of humor

4. Faithfulness

5. Honesty

6. Respect

7. Good communication skills

8. Hard working

9. Compassionate

10. Playful

11. Generous

12. Forgiving

13. Flexible

14. Confident

15. Sensitive

16. Understanding

17. Common sense

18. Money-wise

AL AND ALICE GRAY
MARRIED 32 YEARS AND MORE IN LOVE EVERY DAY

MARRIAGE

WHAT KEEPS A MARRIAGE STRONG?

IN MY TWENTY YEARS OF FAMILY COUNSELING,
HERE ARE THE TOP REASONS COUPLES
HAVE GIVEN ME FOR STAYING TOGETHER:

My spouse is my best friend.

We enjoy our time together.

I like my spouse as a person.

Marriage is a lifelong commitment.

My spouse is interested in me as a person.

Marriage is sacred.

We have common dreams and goals.

Children need a stable home.

My spouse is positive and builds me up.

I want the relationship to succeed.

We respect and appreciate each other.

My spouse encourages my personal growth.

We laugh together.

I trust my spouse.

We have a positive sexual life.

We have built a secure and comfortable life together.

My spouse accepts me for who I am.

We have similar beliefs and interests.

We communicate well.

I respect my spouse.

DR. STEVE STEPHENS
PSYCHOLOGIST AND SEMINAR SPEAKER

MARRIAGE

HIS NEEDS, HER NEEDS

THE MAN'S MOST BASIC NEEDS:	THE WOMAN'S MOST BASIC NEEDS:
1. Sexual fulfillment	1. Affection
2. Recreational companionship	2. Conversation
3. An attractive spouse	3. Honesty and openness
4. Domestic support	4. Financial support
5. Admiration	5. Family commitment

Time and again these ten needs have surfaced as I have helped literally thousands of couples improve their troubled marriages. Although each individual may perceive his or her needs differently, the consistency with which these two sets of five categories have surfaced to explain marital problems impresses me.

WILLARD HARLEY
CONDENSED FROM "HIS NEEDS, HER NEEDS"

SPRINGBOARDS TO DEEPER CONVERSATION

1.

What is the happiest thing that has ever happened to you?

2.

What has been the hardest experience of your life?

3.

What are your secret ambitions, your goals for your life?

4.

What are your deep fears?

5.

What about me do you appreciate the most?

6.

What traits of mine would you like to see changed?

7.

What people do you most admire?

CAROLE MAYHALL
CONDENSED FROM "LORD, TEACH ME WISDOM"

THINGS **NOT** TO SAY TO YOUR SPOUSE

"I told you so."

"I can do whatever I like."

"You're just like your mother."

"If you don't like it, you can just leave."

"You're always in a bad mood."

"Can't you do anything right?"

"You just don't think."

"That was stupid."

"It's your fault."

"All you ever do is think of yourself."

"What's wrong with you?"

"If you really loved me, you'd do this."

"All you ever do is complain."

"You're such a baby."

"I can't do anything to please you."

"Turnabout's fair play."

"You get what you deserve."

"Why don't you ever listen to me?"

"What's your problem?"

"Can't you be more responsible?"

"I can never understand you."

"What were you thinking?"

"Do you always have to be right?"

"You're impossible!"

"I don't know why I put up with you."

"You deserve a dose of your own medicine."

DR. STEVE STEPHENS
FROM "MARRIAGE: EXPERIENCE THE BEST"

THINGS TO SAY TO YOUR SPOUSE

"I love you."

"I was wrong."

"Good job!"

"What would you like?"

"You are wonderful."

"What is on your mind?"

"That was really great."

"Let me just listen."

"You are so special."

"I missed you today."

"What can I do to help?"

"I couldn't get you off my mind today."

"I appreciate all the things you've done for me all these years."

"Pray for me."

"I'm praying for you today."

"As always, you look good today."

"Thank you for loving me."

"I trust you."

"I can always count on you."

"Thank you for accepting me."

"You make me feel good."

"You make every day brighter."

"I prize every moment we spend together."

"I'm sorry."

"I love to see your eyes sparkle when you smile."

DR. STEVE STEPHENS
FROM "MARRIAGE: EXPERIENCE THE BEST"

HOW TO MAKE YOUR
MARRIAGE HEALTHY

1.
COMMITMENT

*True commitment means much more than simply committing
to staying married. Genuine commitment involves being committed
to the growth and best interest of your partner.*

2.
TEAMWORK

*Use the five most important words in marriage:
"Let's try it your way."*

3.
COMMUNICATION

*Without exception, every couple I have ever worked with
struggles with effective communication.
Part of the reason is that two people with the exact same
communication style rarely marry each other.*

4.
MEETING EMOTIONAL NEEDS

*Discover and then meet the emotional needs
of your partner. How? Simple. Just ask!*

5.
RESOLVING CONFLICT

Conflict in marriage is inevitable. Fighting is optional.

6.
APOLOGY AND FORGIVENESS

On a regular basis, practice the three A's of successful relationships:
Apologize for something from the past,
Appreciate something in the present,
Anticipate something in the future.

7.
CREATING A RELATIONSHIP VISION

Ask yourself and each other this question:
"If we knew we couldn't fail, and we could design our relationship
any way that we wanted it,
how would we like to be?"

JEFF HERRING
FROM "THE OREGONIAN"

20 WAYS TO MAKE
YOUR WIFE FEEL SPECIAL

1.
Ask her to dance when you hear your love song.

2.
Polish her shoes for special occasions.

3.
Have good conversation when you'd rather read the paper.

4.
Give her a back rub with no expectations of lovemaking.

5.
Buy and plant a rose bush as a surprise.

6.
Keep your home repaired and in good order.

7.
Make sure the car has good tires and is in good running condition.

8.
Hold her hand when you lead the family in prayer.

9.
Write out a list of all your important documents and where you keep them.

10.
Find a way to save something from every paycheck.

11.
Ask her input before making decisions.

12.
Hold her tenderly when she cries and tell her it's okay.

13.
Ask her out and plan the complete date yourself—
including making the reservations.

14.
Occasionally, eat quiche and dainty desserts
with her at a Victorian restaurant.

15.
Understand when she forgets to enter a check in the ledger.

16.
Shave on your day off.

17.
Call if you're going to be more than fifteen minutes late.

18.
Encourage her to take time out with her friends.

19.
Remember to carry Kleenex or a clean handkerchief
when you go to a romantic movie.

20.
Tell her she will always be beautiful when she worries about getting older.

AL GRAV
MARRIED 32 YEARS

MARRIAGE

20 WAYS TO MAKE YOUR
HUSBAND FEEL SPECIAL

1.
Don't interrupt or correct him when he is telling a story.

2.
*Compliment him in front of his children,
your parents, his parents, and friends.*

3.
Be as concerned about your looks as you were when you were dating.

4.
Let him have some time to relax when he first gets home.

5.
Develop a genuine interest in his work and hobbies.

6.
Admire him for his strength and significance.

7.
If he wants to take a lunch to work, pack it for him.

8.
*Try to be home (and off the phone) when he gets home
from work, and up in the morning when he leaves.*

9.
Help your kids be excited about dad coming home.

10.
*Buy him new socks and underwear on ordinary days instead
of giving these as gifts on holidays and birthdays.*

11.
Keep your bedroom tastefully decorated and clutter free.

12.
*Understand when he wants to spend time
enjoying sports or hobbies with his friends.*

13.
Keep his favorite snack on hand.

14.
Stick to your budget.

15.
Watch his favorite TV sporting events with him.

16.
*Try to go to bed at the same time he does;
understand if he falls asleep in the recliner after a hard day.*

17.
Trade babysitting with friends so you have some nights at home alone.

18.
*Keep lovemaking fresh and exciting, and remember
he probably has more frequent desires than you have.*

19.
Bake homemade cookies for him to take to work.

20.
Ask yourself one question every day: "What's it like being married to me?"

ALICE GRAY
FROM HER SEMINAR "THREE TREASURES FOR EVERY MARRIAGE"

TOGETHERNESS

When husbands focus only on their interests and wives focus only on their interests, the bonds of marriage break. Building togetherness in each of the following areas will strengthen your marriage and increase your love.

1.

Emotional togetherness—being tuned into each other's feelings.

2.

Intellectual togetherness—sharing thoughts, ideas, opinions, and beliefs.

3.

Aesthetic togetherness—enjoying the beauty and artistry of life.

4.

Recreational togetherness—having fun and excitement as a couple.

5.

Work togetherness—doing common, everyday tasks and chores as a team.

6.

Crisis togetherness—leaning on each other when times are hard.

7.

Sexual togetherness—bonding through physical closeness.

8.

Spiritual togetherness—drawing closer to God and encouraging each other's faith.

DR. STEVE STEPHENS
PSYCHOLOGIST AND SEMINAR SPEAKER

50 GIFTS FOR MARRIAGE

1. Start each day with a kiss. 2.. Wear your wedding ring at all times. 3. Date once a week. 4. Accept differences. 5. Be polite. 6. Be gentle. 7. Give gifts. 8. Smile often. 9. Touch. 10. Talk about dreams. 11. Choose a song that can be "your song." 12. Give back rubs. 13. Laugh together. 14. Send a card for no reason. 15. Do what your spouse wants before being asked. 16. Listen. 17. Encourage. 18. Do it the other's way. 19. Know your mate's needs. 20. Fix his (or her) favorite breakfast. 21. Compliment your partner twice a day. 22. Call just to say "I love you." 23. Slow down. 24. Hold hands. 25. Cuddle. 26. Ask your spouse's opinion. 27. Show respect. 28. Welcome each other home. 29. Look your best for your mate. 30. Wink at each other. 31. Celebrate birthdays in a big way. 32. Apologize. 33. Forgive. 34. Set up a romantic getaway. 35. Ask, "What can I do to make you happier?" 36. Be positive. 37. Be kind. 38. Be vulnerable. 39. Respond quickly to your mate's requests. 40. Talk about your love. 41. Reminisce about your favorite times together. 42. Treat his (or her) friends and relatives with courtesy. 43. Send flowers every Valentine's Day and anniversary. 44. Admit when you are wrong. 45. Be sensitive to your mate's sexual desires. 46. Pray for him (or her) daily. 47. Watch sunsets together. 48. Say "I love you" frequently. 49. End each day with a hug. 50. Seek outside help when you need it.

DR. STEVE STEPHENS
FROM "UNDERSTANDING THE ONE YOU LOVE"

BEING A REAL MAN

1.
A real man includes his wife in envisioning the future.

2.
A real man accepts spiritual responsibility for his family.

3.
A real man is willing to say "I'm sorry" and "Forgive me" to his family.

4.
*A real man discusses household responsibilities with his
wife and makes sure they are fairly distributed.*

5.
*A real man seeks the consultation of his wife
on all major financial decisions.*

6.
A real man follows through with commitments he has made to his wife.

7.
A real man frequently tells his wife what he likes about her.

8.
A real man provides financially for his family's basic living expenses.

9.
*A real man deals with distractions so he
can unite with his wife and family.*

10.
A real man prays with his wife on a regular basis.

11.
A real man initiates meaningful family traditions.

12.

A real man initiates family outings for the family on a regular basis.

13.

A real man takes the time to give his children practical instruction
about life, which in turn gives them confidence with their peers.

14.

A real man manages the schedule of the home and anticipates any pressure points.

15.

A real man keeps his family financially sound and out of harmful debt.

16.

A real man makes sure he and his wife have drawn up a will and
arranged a well-conceived plan for their children in case of death.

17.

A real man lets his wife and children into the interior of his life.

18.

A real man honors his wife often in public.

19.

A real man encourages his wife to grow as an individual.

20.

A real man provides time for his wife to pursue
her own personal interests.

DR. ROBERT LEWIS, PASTOR, FELLOWSHIP BIBLE CHURCH
LITTLE ROCK, ARKANSAS

MARRIAGE

BONDS OF INTIMACY

Physical touching of an affectionate, nonsexual nature

Shared feelings

Closeness without inhibitions

Absence of psychological defenses

Open communication and honesty

Intellectual agreement on major issues

Spiritual harmony

Sensitive appreciation of the mate's physical and emotional responses

Similar values held

Imparted secrets

Genuine understanding

Mutual confidence

A sense of warmth, safety, and realization when together

Sensuous nearness

Sexual pleasures lovingly shared

Signs of love freely given and received

Mutual responsibility and caring

Abiding trust

ED WHEAT, M.D.
CONDENSED FROM "LOVE LIFE FOR EVERY MARRIED COUPLE"

REIGNITING ROMANCE
AFTER AGE 50

In our national survey on long-term marriage, we discovered
that sexual satisfaction actually goes up, not down, for those married
thirty-plus years. So how can you reignite the spark?

BE AFFECTIONATE.

*Romance isn't reserved just for the bedroom. Being affectionate, thoughtful and
kind at other times will spill into your love life. Phone calls, notes, holding hands,
a peck on the cheek, a wink across the room will add romance to your relationship.*

BE A LISTENER.

*Two of the most important lovemaking skills and romance enhancers
are listening with your heart and talking to your spouse.*

BE ADVENTURESOME.

Try a little spontaneity. Explore.

BE PLAYFUL.
Romance depends on your attitude and perspective.

GET IN SHAPE.

*Get enough exercise. Eat right and get enough sleep. An annual
physical is a good investment in the health of your marriage.*

BE A LITTLE WACKY.

*What can you do to jolt your old patterns? Plan a getaway and kidnap your wife. Or
surprise her by coming home early or by taking off a morning and staying home together.*

CLAUDIA AND DAVID ARP
FROM "NEW MAN" MAGAZINE

20 CREATIVE, ROMANTIC IDEAS THAT COST UNDER $20

1.

Dress up for a meal you bring home from your favorite fast-food restaurant. Take out a tablecloth, centerpiece, and a tape recorder of your favorite romantic music and dine to a "Golden Arches" delight.

2.

Buy a half gallon of your favorite ice cream, go to the most beautiful park in town, throw a blanket on the ground, and eat the whole thing.

3.

Visit a museum or art gallery. Talk with each other about the art you like and dislike. Use the "twenty questions" method to learn all you can about why your spouse likes or dislikes what you see. Concentrate on listening to the other person and learning all you can from what he or she says.

4.

Go to a driving range together. Cheer each other's good shots.

5.

Go bowling together. Come up with prizes you can give each other for winning games; i.e., a massage, a week's worth of doing dishes, a promise to paint the fence, etc.

6.

Go on a hayride with four other couples, singing camp songs from a tape recorder or guitar. Plan a cookout under the stars afterward.

7.

Write love notes to one another and hide them in unusual places like the freezer, a shoe, the car's glove box, the bathtub, her makeup kit, or under the bed covers.

8.

Go snorkeling in a lake.

9.

Collect leaves and pine cones together on an autumn day. Take them home and make fall ornaments for the house.

10.
Attend a free outdoor concert.

11.
Buy a pass from the Forest Service, go to a National Forest, and cut your own Christmas tree.

12.
Buy a modern paraphrase of the Song of Solomon and read it to one another.

13.
Walk hand in hand along a nature trail.

14.
Watch a sunset together.

15.
Make "dough" ornaments together, bake them, and then color them with the kids.

16.
Rent each other's all-time favorite movies and play a double feature at home.

17.
Go to your favorite restaurant for dessert. Bring a child's baby book or your wedding album and relive some memories together.

18.
Throw a party commemorating your spouse's graduation date.

19.
Get the children together and make a "Why I Love Mom" and "Why I Love Dad" book, complete with text and illustrations.

20.
Take your spouse out for an afternoon in her favorite store. Note the items under twenty dollars she likes best. Return to the store the next day and buy one of these items as a gift.

GARY SMALLEY WITH JOHN TRENT
FROM "LOVE IS A DECISION"

MARRIAGE

10 SUGGESTIONS FOR TOUCHING

1.

Show each other where you like to be touched and the kind of touch that pleases you. Usually, a light touch is the most thrilling. Be imaginative in the way you caress.

2.

Demonstrate to each other how you prefer to be held. Kiss your partner the way you would like to be kissed—not to criticize past performances, but to communicate something your partner has not sensed before.

3.

To learn the art of expressing warm, sensual feelings, you will have to slow down. If what you are doing feels good, take the time to enjoy it.

4.

Caress each other's back. Pay special attention to the back of the neck at the hairline and the area just above the small of the back.

5.

Make sure that both of you are having equal opportunity to give and to receive. Take turns giving pleasure to each other.

6.

Have a period of fifteen to thirty minutes every night to lie in each other's arms in the dark before you drift off to sleep. Whisper together, sharing private thoughts and pleasant little experiences of the day. This is the time to build intimacy and wind down for sleep.

7.

Establish the cozy habit of staying in some sort of physical contact while you are going to sleep—a hand or a leg touching your partner's, for instance.

8.

Begin every day with a few minutes of cuddling and snuggling before you get out of bed. A husband can tell his wife how nice she feels and how glad he is to be close to her. A wife can nestle in her husband's arms and tell him she wishes they didn't have to leave each other that morning. Just be close and savor gentle physical contact for awhile.

9.

Hold hands often. Think of all the different ways you can enjoy just touching with your hands and all the different feelings that can be conveyed.

10.

Become aware of the many ways you can have physical contact in the course of a week. Touch when you are talking and maintain eye contact. Sit close to each other in church. Kiss each other when there is no occasion for it. Add variety to your kisses, your touches, and your love pats.

ED WHEAT, M.D.
CONDENSED FROM "LOVE LIFE FOR EVERY MARRIED COUPLE"

WEDDING ANNIVERSARY GIFTS

1st	Paper or clocks	13th	Lace or textiles
2nd	Cotton or china	14th	Ivory or gold jewelry
3rd	Leather or glass	15th	Crystal or watches
4th	Flowers or small appliances	20th	China or platinum
5th	Wood or silverware	25th	Silver
6th	Iron or candy	30th	Pearl
7th	Wool or copper	35th	Coral or jade
8th	Bronze or linen	40th	Ruby
9th	Pottery or leather	45th	Sapphire
10th	Aluminum or diamond	50th	Gold
11th	Steel or jewelry	55th	Emerald
12th	Silk or pearls	60th	Diamond

6
Home

Where life gets organized

ORGANIZING MAIL

HANDLE EACH PIECE OF MAIL ONLY ONCE BY PRACTICING THE FOUR D'S:

Do it now *(pay the bill, answer the letter).*

Delegate *(pass on for someone else to handle).*

Delay it *(put it in project file to deal with).*

Dump it *(into the trash can).*

AUTHOR UNKNOWN

OVERCOMING CLUTTER

1.
MINIMIZE YOUR BELONGINGS.

Every few months go through clothes, toys, books, games, and even furnishings. Give away things you don't use.

2.
CAREFULLY CONSIDER YOUR PURCHASES.

The more you have, the more time, space, and energy is required from you to maintain those purchases. Whenever you purchase something new, discard an old item.

3.
CREATE A RECYCLE CENTER.

You can purchase a variety of systems or create your own. Locate an easily accessible space to put paper sacks—one sack for each type of recyclable material.

4.
GO THROUGH YOUR MAIL RIGHT AWAY.

Use an accordion file folder labeled with your various household bills. Include a "To Be Paid" section. When you pay your bills move receipts to correct category. Include a "Tax Info" section to file tax information and receipts.

5.
RECYCLE JUNK MAIL.

Don't waste time opening it. Tear or shred credit card opportunities to avoid theft. Request that catalog companies not sell or rent your name.

6.
RECYCLE MAGAZINES.

If you are saving magazines because of good articles, file the articles in a three-ring notebook by category and recycle the magazines.

7.
ORGANIZE CHILDREN'S SCHOOLWORK.

Purchase large three-ring notebooks with a clear cover and spine. Let each child design their own notebook. Include grade level, school year, and other pertinent information. Divide the notebook by subjects.

8.
CREATE AN "INFORMATION CENTER."

Install some cork on the inside of one of your upper kitchen cabinets to keep all your "notes and loose paper" information.

9.
IMPLEMENT "THE BOX."

Find a box that will fit in a closet or some other enclosed space. At the end of each day collect items your family chooses to leave lying around and put them in "The Box." Items can be earned back by doing extra chores. If they are not redeemed within a week, the items are yours to do with as you please.

10.
GIVE TO CHARITY.

What is extra or unused might be needed by someone else. Teach children to give away extra toys. Let them choose the charity and go with you to drop them off.

ALLISON ALLISON
INTERIOR DESIGNER

HINTS FOR
KITCHEN ORGANIZATION

1.

Do not store cookies, cereal, or other "bait" by the stove. Children can get burned climbing on the stove to reach an item overhead.

2.

Use glass or ceramic pans for baking; you can reduce your oven temperature by twenty-five degrees.

3.

I've found an easy way to clean the cheese grater: before using it, spray it with no-stick vegetable spray.

4.

Put a decorative hook by the sink. Hang your watch and rings on it while you work.

5.

Glue a twelve-inch square of cork to the inside of the cabinet door over your kitchen work area. On the cork tack the recipe card you are using and newspaper clippings of recipes you plan to try within a few days. It keeps them at eye level and they stay spatter-free.

6.

Increase your efficiency with an extra-long phone cord or a cordless phone, to reach to all corners of your kitchen. Instead of wasting time while on the phone, you can cook, set the table, or clean out a drawer.

7.

Meat slices easier if it's partially frozen.

8.

Want to mix frozen juice in a hurry without using the blender? Use your potato masher on the concentrate.

9.

You can peel garlic cloves faster if you mash them lightly with the side of the blade of a chef's knife.

10.

To keep bugs out of your flour canister, put a stick of spearmint gum in the flour, and it will be bug-free.

EMILIE BARNES
CONDENSED FROM "MORE HOURS IN MY DAY"

HOW LONG TO KEEP IT

Bank statements and canceled checks: Six years*

Birth or adoption certificates: Forever

Contracts: Until updated

Credit card account numbers: Until updated

Marriage or divorce papers: Forever

Home purchase and improvement records:

Even with new tax law, keep until you sell

Life insurance policies: Forever

Car, home insurance: Until updated

Investment records: Six years after tax deadline for year of sale

Loan agreements: Until updated

Military service records: Forever

Real estate deeds: As long as you own property

Receipts for large purchases: Until sale or discard

Service contracts and warranties: Until sale or discard

Social Security card: Forever

Tax returns: Forever

Vehicle titles: Until sale or disposal

Will: Until updated

*The IRS may audit returns up to three years after filing. But it has six years to challenge a return if it thinks gross income was underreported by at least 25 percent. No time limit applies to fraudulent returns.

EXCERPTED FROM "YOUR FINANCIAL ORGANIZER"
TEACHERS INSURANCE & ANNUITY ASSOCIATION

TIME MAKERS

CONTROL PHONE USAGE.

Limit phone conversations to fifteen minutes or less. Turn the ringer off your phone once in a while. If you have a message recorder, return calls at your convenience.

PLAN FOR CHILDREN'S BOREDOM.

Make space in a cupboard and fill it with prepared activities.

DO MAJOR GROCERY SHOPPING AT ONE STORE.

It saves time and energy that may be better used somewhere else.

PREPARE GROCERY LIST AHEAD OF TIME.

Organize your list by store aisles, including brand names you prefer.

COOK MEALS IN BULK.

Double recipes and freeze half to use later.

SCHEDULE YOUR TASKS.

Do routine tasks, such as laundry, on a specific day of the week.

DESIGNATE A BILL DAY.

*Pay bills at the same time each month to avoid missing
due dates. If you don't have the money to pay all
your bills at once, do this twice a month.*

MAKE A "REFERENCE BINDER."

*Create a three-ring "reference binder" with takeout
menus, phone lists, birthdays, emergency information
and whatever else you frequently need.*

ENJOY YOUR LIFE.

*With the extra time you've saved, visit a friend,
take a walk, read a good book, or just relax.*

ALLISON ALLISON
INTERIOR DESIGNER

HOME

BABYSITTER CHECKLIST

Write out instructions for all of the following information:

Emergency Information

✓ Emergency phone numbers for police, fire, and poison control

✓ Street address and phone number at residence

✓ Nearest cross streets

✓ Parent(s) names

✓ Where to reach parent(s)

✓ Phone numbers of available neighbors

✓ Instructions regarding medications and allergies

✓ Location of first aid kit

✓ Fire escape route

General Information

✓ Names and ages of children

✓ Feeding routines

✓ Bedtime routines

✓ Discipline preferences

✓ Guidelines for television, computer, telephone, food

✓ Visitor restrictions for children and sitter

✓ Expectations for kitchen cleanup or other chores
  for children and sitter

ALICE GRAY
SEMINAR SPEAKER

FOUR AXIOMS OF SPENDING

1
The more shopping we do,
the more we spend.

2
The more we watch television,
the more we spend.

3
The more time we spend looking
through catalogs, the more we spend.

4
The more we read magazines and newspaper
advertisements, the more we spend.

HOWARD L. DAYTON, JR.
FROM "GETTING OUT OF DEBT POCKET GUIDE"

SIMPLE WAYS TO CUT EXPENSES

1.

USE A FIFTEEN-YEAR INSTEAD OF A THIRTY-YEAR
MORTGAGE ON YOUR HOME.

2.

REFINANCE YOUR MORTGAGE.

*If interest rates have dropped substantially, check with your bank or
mortgage company about the cost of refinancing.*

3.

SET YOUR THERMOSTAT FIVE DEGREES WARMER IN THE SUMMER
AND FIVE DEGREES COOLER IN THE WINTER.

Your utility savings will be dramatic.

4.

KEEP DRIVING THE CAR YOU HAVE
INSTEAD OF PURCHASING A NEW ONE.

*Ron Blue says it best when he observes, "The cheapest
car to own is the one you are driving."*

5.

USE A SELF-SERVICE INSTEAD OF FULL-SERVICE GAS STATION, IF POSSIBLE.

*The savings can result in several hundred dollars a year. The only
item you really need to check once a week is the oil.*

6.

REFUSE TO SHOP FOR GROCERIES WHEN YOU ARE HUNGRY.

Waiting until after you have eaten can prevent wasteful spending.

7.

USE A LIST WHEN YOU SHOP FOR GROCERIES.

Impulse buying can destroy your food budget.

8.

POSTPONE CLOTHES PURCHASES UNTIL MAJOR SALES.

You will be amazed at how much money you can save.

9.

SPLIT ENTREES WHEN YOU EAT OUT.

Most restaurants serve more food than you'll ever want to eat.

10.

PLAN YOUR TRAVEL AHEAD OF TIME.

Airlines and hotels penalize those who make last-minute travel plans.

ROBERT JEFFRESS
CONDENSED FROM "SAY GOODBYE TO REGRET"

PLANNING AHEAD FOR
HOLIDAY SHOPPING

Shopping Lists

- Make a list of everyone receiving gifts.
- Determine total budget for Christmas shopping.
- Try to spend less than the previous year.
- Decide early what gifts you will make.
- Figure out the maximum you will spend on each person.
- Record favorite colors and correct sizes.
- Write down ideas you come across during the year.
- Keep current with kids' fads and trends.
- Choose a ministry or needy family and include some outreach gifts.
- Never go shopping without your list.

Shopping Days

- Order from catalogs and mail directly to recipient's home.
- Don't wait until Thanksgiving weekend to begin shopping.
- Finish by December 15.
- Avoid carrying a big purse, heavy coat, or umbrella.
- Use a small purse with strap that crosses over your shoulder to free hands.

- Only take checkbook, cash, credit cards, I.D., Kleenex, car keys, shopping list, paper, and pencil.
- Trade babysitting with a friend and leave the children at home.
- If children go with you, shorten your shopping time.
- Ask for gift boxes or use free wrapping service when provided.
- Enjoy a treat from the espresso or juice bar.
- Don't forget where you parked the car.
- Take time to enjoy the lights, the people, and *the season*.

After Shopping

- Make a wrapping center at home and wrap gifts as you buy.
- Consider enclosing receipts for easy returns.
- Keep all other receipts in a separate envelope.
- Mail out-of-town gifts early.
- When family or friends visit, send packages home with them.
- Light a fragrant candle and play Christmas music.
- Enjoy the *Reason for the season*.

BECKY MCCLURE
SEMINAR SPEAKER

HOLIDAY ENTERTAINING
WITH LESS STRESS

Food Preparation

- Write out complete menus in advance.
- Select simple menus and use the same menu more than once.
- Bake cookies, breads, and rolls in advance and keep in the freezer.
- Make frozen salads and desserts in advance.
- Include other family members in the planning and responsibilities.
- Make out a list and purchase all nonperishable items at one time.
- Purchase perishable items weekly.
- Every night look over your calendar and make a list for the next day.

Home Preparation

- Clean your house thoroughly the first week in December.
- Spot clean your house weekly.
- Put up outside lights the first week in December.
- Decorate inside your house (except for the tree) the first week in December.
- Use artificial greens so they will not need to be replaced.
- Put up and decorate your tree the second week in December.

Time Out for Your Family

- Plan some family nights.
- Drive to see the Christmas lights.
- Attend a musical or play.
- Gather around the tree and roast marshmallows in the fireplace.
- Entertain with less stress and greater pleasure.
- Keep a candle burning and enjoy the fragrance…but don't burn your candle at both ends.

BECKY MCCLURE
SEMINAR SPEAKER

HOME

MAKE YOUR OLD HOME
FEEL LIKE NEW

1.

See the potential. Look beyond the chipped paint and the worn and cracked linoleum to the charm of the architecture and don't be afraid of what it will take to make this "find" your dream home.

2.

First room to redecorate. Decide which room you will spend a lot of time in.

3.

Complete one room at a time. This will encourage you to keep going. You will be better able to see results when an entire room is redone than if you do one or two small things in several rooms. This can be discouraging.

4.

Paint. The cheapest way to decorate is with paint. It is amazing how a couple coats of paint will transform the drabbest of rooms. Paint the walls a different shade than the woodwork if you have painted woodwork.

5.

Wallpaper. My absolute favorite way to decorate is with wallpaper. Pick high-quality paper; though it is more costly, it will last for years. Try papering the top half of the room with a border, or perhaps just one wall in the room (this will cut costs). Rooms that are papered need fewer decorative items on the walls as your wallpaper is part of the decorating. *Nothing* transforms a room like wallpaper.

6.

Big budget items. Carpet, linoleum, counter tops, etc. Tackle these items as your budget allows. Paint and wallpaper will transform enough of your house until you can afford to replace the more costly items.

7.

Color. Pick two or three main colors and use these same colors and their various shades to decorate the entire house. Too many colors make a house look chopped up; you want your house to "flow" from room to room. You don't have to use only these three colors in every room—you can add one or two accent colors with your three primary colors.

8.

Decorating ideas. If you are at a loss as to how to decorate your home, decorating magazines and wallpaper books are full of great ideas. Visit some model homes as well.

9.

Most of all, have fun making your home your own personal "haven."

NANCY LARSON
HOME MAKEOVER CONSULTANT TO FRIENDS

HOME SAFETY TIPS

1.

*Keep stairs and surrounding areas well-lit,
unobstructed, and in good repair.*

2.

*Use nonslip mats in the tub and on the bathroom floor,
along with wall-mounted grab bars, to help prevent falls.*

3.

*Keep household chemicals and medicines locked up.
Some common products containing alcohol, such as
mouthwash, can be harmful to children.*

4.

*Test smoke detectors once each month,
and change batteries every six months.*

5.

Sleep with bedroom doors closed to keep toxic gases out in case of fire.

6.

Douse smoking materials with water before discarding.

7.

*Install a carbon monoxide detector to monitor
furnaces, dryers, and space heaters.*

8.

Make it a rule to never leave a child unattended at a pool.

9.

Install fencing with self-closing and self-latching gates around pools.

10.

*Remember that small children can fall into
toilets, even five-gallon buckets, and drown.*

11.

Make your kitchen "off-limits" to children while you are cooking.

12.

Install anti-scalding devices on tubs and showers.

13.

Use ground-fault circuit interrupters in outlets near water to prevent shocks.

TOM PHILBIN, FROM "PARADE" MAGAZINE
REPRINTED WITH PERMISSION FROM "PARADE MAGAZINE" © 1988

CRIME STOPPERS' CHECKLIST

✔ *Do you have a dog?* Barking dogs attract the kind of attention a burglar doesn't need.

✔ *Do you leave a radio or television set on when you're out?* The sound of voices will send an intruder elsewhere.

✔ *Do you refuse to open doors to strangers?* Always ask for identification or check the driveway for a repair or delivery truck. If in doubt, call the utility or business in question to ask if they have sent someone to your home.

✔ *Do you have peepholes in all solid doors?* Don't rely on chain locks to see who is at the door. They can easily be forced once a door is ajar.

✔ *Do you keep your garage door locked?* Thieves like attached garages because, once inside, they can unobtrusively force the door to the house.

✔ *Are your basement windows secure?* These are another popular point of entry for intruders.

✔ *Do you keep trees and shrubbery trimmed?* Overgrown vegetation gives a burglar more privacy.

✔ *Do you have neighbors collect your mail and newspapers while you're away?* You can also ask the post office and paper carrier to hold deliveries until you return.

✔ *Have you familiarized babysitters and other outsiders with your safety measures?* Show them escape routes and familiarize them with any locks and alarm systems.

✔ *Does your neighborhood have a watch program?* If not, check with your local police for information about starting one.

SELECTED FROM "ABOUT...KEEPING YOUR HOME SAFE," A LIFE ADVICE® PAMPHLET
PUBLISHED BY METLIFE'S CONSUMER EDUCATION CENTER

FIRE SAFETY CHECKLIST

✓ *Are your smoke detectors working?* There should be at least one on every floor of your home. Test each detector monthly and replace batteries annually.

✓ *Do you hold regular fire drills?* Several times a year, have your family practice exiting your home safely and quickly in the event of an emergency. Designate a meeting place for all family members to gather once they are out of the house.

✓ *Have you taught your children to "stop, drop and roll"?* In the event their clothing catches fire, kids (and adults) should stop, drop to the floor, cover their faces, and roll over and over or back and forth to put out the fire. Keep rolling until the fire goes out.

✓ *Have you planned an alternate escape route?* It's important to have at least two escape routes from each room in your home, often a door and a window. Practice using them now to be sure you could get out in an emergency.

✓ *Can you safely exit from the second floor?* A chain ladder or other easily accessible ladder can help you escape from the upper stories of your home in the event of a fire.

✓ *Do you know how to use your fire extinguishers?* Know where your fire extinguishers are kept, and read the instructions for use before you need them.

✓ *Do you know the phone number for your local fire department and the location of the nearest phone outside your house?* In case of fire, always evacuate your home first, then call for help from a cellular or other nearby phone.

SELECTED FROM "ABOUT...KEEPING YOUR HOME SAFE," A LIFE ADVICE® PAMPHLET
PUBLISHED BY METLIFE'S CONSUMER EDUCATION CENTER

PREPARE FOR DISASTERS

1.
Discuss the disasters most likely to happen in your area and their impact on your family's safety. Hazards include home fires, harsh winter weather, earthquakes, flooding, and hazardous materials threats.

2.
Train all family members. Enroll all members of your household in first aid classes. Learn to use a fire extinguisher and how to shut off utilities. Don't take a chance that the only person who knows first aid or how to turn off the natural gas will be at home when needed. Learn how to respond safely to earthquakes and other disasters.

3.
Assemble emergency supplies including food, water, a flashlight, a battery-powered radio, extra batteries, a first aid kit, extra prescription medications, and emergency tools. Store enough supplies to last your family at least three days following a disaster.

4.
Identify emergency names and numbers. Choose an out-of-state friend or relative to be your emergency contact. Give this person's name and number to all members of your household so when local phones are down, they can use their out-of-state contact to relay messages to one another.

5.
Maintain your readiness. Review your plan at least once a year to determine what training, equipment, and supplies are needed. Commit to a day or weekend to update phone numbers, hold fire and earthquake drills, and check supplies.

FROM THE AMERICAN RED CROSS
OREGON TRAIL CHAPTER

7

Health

A long and satisfying life

DANGER SIGNALS OF STRESS

YOU MAY BE UNDER TOO MUCH STRESS IF YOU...

...find yourself irritable or impatient with things you normally tolerate.

...have difficulty getting to sleep and feel exhausted when you awake.

...sense you are one step away from falling apart.

...suffer from frequent headaches or stomach pains.

...get distracted easily and have trouble concentrating.

...talk more negatively than usual.

...become forgetful and absentminded.

...don't laugh as much as you used to.

...use alcohol, non-prescription drugs, or food to help you relax.

...postpone what is truly important, to accomplish what isn't that important.

CAROL CLIFTON, PH.D.
LICENSED PSYCHOLOGIST

21 FACTORS FOR A LONG, HEALTHY LIFE

IN ORDER OF IMPORTANCE:

1.
Not smoking.

2.
Not smoking in bed, if you do smoke.

3.
Wearing your seat belt.

4.
Not drinking and driving

5.
Having a smoke detector in your home.

6.
Socializing regularly.

7.
Getting frequent strenuous exercise.

8.
Drinking alcohol moderately. *

9.
Avoiding home accidents.

10.
Limiting fat in your diet.

11.
Maintaining your proper weight.

12.
Obeying the speed limit.

*EDITORIAL COMMENT...IF AT ALL

13.
Getting an annual blood pressure test.

14.
Controlling stress.

15.
Consuming fiber.

16.
Limiting cholesterol in your diet.

17.
Getting adequate vitamins and minerals.

18.
Having an annual dental exam.

19.
Limiting sodium in your diet.

20.
Limiting consumption of sugar and sweets.

21.
Getting seven to eight hours sleep each night.

FROM THE "PREVENTION INDEX"

HEALTH

DO YOU NEED MORE SLEEP?

TAKE THE FOLLOWING TRUE/FALSE QUIZ AND SEE FOR YOURSELF.

1.

I need an alarm clock to wake up at the appropriate time.

2.

It's a struggle for me to get out of bed in the morning.

3.

*Weekday mornings I hit the snooze button several
times to get more sleep.*

4.

I feel tired, irritable, and stressed-out during the week.

5.

I have trouble concentrating and remembering.

6.

I feel slow in critical thinking, problem solving, and being creative.

7.

I often fall asleep watching TV.

8.

I often fall asleep in meetings, in lectures, or in warm rooms.

9.

I often fall asleep after heavy meals or after a low dose of alcohol.

10.

I often fall asleep while relaxing after dinner.

11.

I often fall asleep within five minutes of getting into bed.

12.

I often feel drowsy while driving.

13.

I often sleep extra hours on weekend mornings.

14.

I often need a nap to get through the day.

15.

I have dark circles around my eyes.

IF YOU ANSWERED "TRUE" TO THREE OR MORE OF THE
FIFTEEN ITEMS, YOU PROBABLY ARE NOT GETTING ENOUGH SLEEP.
UNFORTUNATELY, YOU ARE NOT ALONE.

PATRICIA ANSTETT
FROM "THE OREGONIAN"

HEALTH

SEVEN WAYS TO KEEP YOUR BRAIN CELLS WORKING

1.
Play complex puzzles and games such as Scrabble or chess.

2.
Learn a foreign language.

3.
Study music.

4.
Solve math problems without using a calculator.

5.
Write letters or poetry.

6.
Engage in thought-provoking discussions.

7.
Study and memorize Scripture.

AUTHOR UNKNOWN

KEYS TO A LIFETIME OF FITNESS

TIPS TO MAKE EXERCISE A HABIT

Choose an activity you enjoy.

Tailor your program to your own fitness level.

Set realistic goals.

Choose an exercise that fits your lifestyle.

Give your body a chance to adjust to your new routine.

Don't get discouraged if you don't see immediate results.

Don't give up if you miss a day; just get back on track the next day.

Find a partner for a little motivation and socialization.

Build some rest days into your exercise schedule.

Listen to your body. If you have difficulty breathing or

experience faintness or prolonged weakness

during or after exercise, consult your physician.

~~~

CONDENSED FROM "ABOUT...FITNESS AND EXERCISE," A LIFE ADVICE® PAMPHLET
PUBLISHED BY METLIFE'S CONSUMER EDUCATION CENTER

BENEFITS OF EXERCISE

IMPROVED HEALTH

Increased efficiency of heart and lungs
Reduced cholesterol levels
Increased muscle strength
Reduced blood pressure
Reduced risk of major illnesses
such as diabetes and heart disease
Weight loss

IMPROVED SENSE OF WELL-BEING

More energy
Less stress
Improved quality of sleep
Improved ability to cope with stress
Increased mental acuity

IMPROVED APPEARANCE

Weight loss
Toned muscles
Improved posture

ENHANCED SOCIAL LIFE

Improved self-image
Increased opportunities to make new friends
Increased opportunities to share an
activity with friends or family members

INCREASED STAMINA

Increased productivity
Increased physical capabilities
Less frequent injuries
Improved immunity to minor illnesses

CONDENSED FROM "ABOUT...FITNESS AND EXERCISE," A LIFE ADVICE® PAMPHLET
PUBLISHED BY METLIFE'S CONSUMER EDUCATION CENTER

10 SIMPLE WAYS TO BUILD
EXERCISE INTO YOUR DAY

1.

Use the stairs instead of the elevator. Set a rule for yourself that any time you are going up or down fewer than five floors, you take the stairs.

2.

If you take the bus, train, or subway to work or school, don't board it at the closest stop to your home. Instead, make it a habit to walk to a stop twenty to thirty minutes away.

3.

If it is practical, ride your bike to work instead of taking a car or other transportation. If this is not practical, ride your bike or walk on errands or when going to the market.

4.

Take an exercise break instead of a coffee break. Keep a pair of tennis shoes at your office and walk around the block a couple of times.

5.

Leave your car parked at the farthest end of a parking lot and walk vigorously to your destination. Walk completely around a mall before you start shopping.

6.

While at home watching television, ride an exercise bike or use a rowing machine. If you don't have either, do ten situps during every commercial break of any one-hour program you watch. Build up to twenty situps, then thirty, and finally fifty.

7.

While doing simple chores around the home, wear ankle and wrist weights.

8.

Next time you have to drive the kids to work, band practice, or Little League, walk them there instead.

9.

Perhaps there is no way you can find fifty minutes a day for regular exercise, so do the next best thing. Find five ten-minute intervals throughout the day to get your exercising done.

10.

Set your alarm fifteen minutes early each day and take a short walk to a special place near your home.

CARL DREIZLER AND MARY E. EHEMANN
FROM "52 WAYS TO LOSE WEIGHT"

BACK SAVERS

Bend at your hips, not at your waist.

Avoid lying on your stomach.

Lift heavy objects no higher than your waist.

Sit down to put on socks, shoes, pants—don't bend over.

*Get down on one knee before picking up
a small child or infant from the floor.*

*When reading, don't bend your neck and shoulders—bring
your book up to your eyes by placing two pillows on your lap
and propping the book on top of them.*

FROM "THE BACK ALMANAC"

12 REASONS TO KEEP YOUR CHILD HOME FROM SCHOOL

1.
A high temperature

2.
Lice or scabies (until treated)

3.
A cold with a fever

4.
A sore throat with fever

5.
An earache or headache

6.
Diarrhea and/or abdominal cramps

7.
Nausea and/or vomiting

8.
Any skin injury or burn that may become infected

9.
Any infectious disease

10.
Conjunctivitis (pinkeye)

11.
Your own judgment that your child isn't well

12.
Your child is overly tired

PAT VAN DIEST
REGISTERED NURSE

10 WAYS TO HELP
PREVENT HEART DISEASE

1.

*Know your risk factors (high
cholesterol, bad diet, smoking,
obesity, lack of exercise, other diseases
such as diabetes and hypertension).*

2.

*Ask your doctor about
taking an aspirin a day.*

3.

Have regular medical checkups.

4.

*Get your blood pressure and
cholesterol under control.*

5.

*Replace a bad habit such as smoking
with a good one like swimming.*

6.

*Eat five servings of fruit
and vegetables a day.*

7.

Cut the fat.

8.

Eat fiber and whole grains.

9.

Walk and swim.

10.

Slow down.

TERRY SHINTANI AND J.M.T. MILLER
FROM "52 WAYS TO PREVENT HEART DISEASE"

RECOGNIZE A HEART ATTACK!

When a heart attack occurs, there's no time for delay.
The symptoms of a heart attack vary, but the usual warning signs are:

1.
*Uncomfortable pressure, fullness, squeezing, or pain in the center of
the chest lasting more than a few minutes.*

2.
Pain spreading to the shoulders, neck, or arms.

3.
*Chest discomfort with lightheadedness, fainting, sweating,
nausea, or shortness of breath.*

Not all of these signs occur in every attack. In some cases, the symptoms
subside and then return. If you notice one or more of these signs, don't wait.
Get medical help right away!

AMERICAN HEART ASSOCIATION

RECOGNIZE A STROKE!

1.
*Sudden weakness or numbness of the face,
arm, or leg on one side of the body.*

2.
Sudden dimness or loss of vision, particularly in one eye.

3.
Loss of speech or trouble talking or understanding speech.

4.
Sudden, severe headaches with no apparent cause.

5.
*Unexplained dizziness, unsteadiness, or sudden falls, especially
along with any of the previous symptoms.*

YOU ARE PARTICULARLY AT RISK FOR STROKE IF YOU HAVE:

1.
Diagnosed high blood pressure.

2.
Diagnosed heart disease.

The warning signs listed above may be temporary, lasting anywhere from a few minutes to almost twenty-four hours. If any of these symptoms occur, get medical help right away!

AMERICAN HEART ASSOCIATION

HEALTH

14 WARNING SIGNS FOR CANCER

KEY WARNING SIGNS

1.
Change in bowel or bladder habits

2.
A sore that does not heal

3.
Unusual bleeding or discharge

4.
Thickening or lump in the breast or elsewhere

5.
Indigestion or difficulty swallowing

6.
Obvious change in a wart or mole

7.
Nagging cough or hoarseness

SECONDARY WARNING SIGNS

8.
Chronic fatigue

9.
Prolonged depression

10.
Sudden loss of appetite

11.
Unexplained and chronic pain

12.
Any other unusual and troublesome changes in your body

13.
Long-term paleness

14.
Unexplained bruising

THE AMERICAN CANCER SOCIETY

WHAT CANCER CANNOT DO

CANCER IS LIMITED—

It cannot cripple love

It cannot shatter hope

It cannot corrode faith

It cannot destroy peace

It cannot kill friendship

It cannot suppress memories

It cannot silence courage

It cannot invade the soul

It cannot steal eternal life

It cannot conquer the spirit.

AUTHOR UNKNOWN

8

Contentment

Finding peace and fulfillment

A BETTER LIFE

Feel positive emotions

Think positive thoughts

Focus on the positive in people

Offer positive prayers

Speak positive words

Practice positive actions

RON JENSON
FROM "TAKING THE LEAD"

CHOICES

If you want to be rich...GIVE!

If you want to be poor...GRASP!

If you want abundance...SCATTER!

If you want to be needy...HOARD!

JOHN LAWRENCE
FROM "THE SEVEN LAWS OF THE HARVEST"

THE MYSTERY OF ANSWERED PRAYER

I asked God for strength, that I might achieve;

I was made weak, that I might learn humbly to obey.

I asked for health, that I might do greater things;

I was given infirmity, that I might do better things.

I asked for riches, that I might be happy;

I was given poverty, that I might be wise.

I asked for power, that I might have the praise of men;

I was given weakness, that I might feel the need of God.

I asked for all things that I might enjoy life;

I was given life, that I might enjoy all things.

I got nothing I asked for but everything I had hoped for.

Almost despite myself, my unspoken prayers were answered.

I am, among men, most richly blessed.

AT THE END OF THE CIVIL WAR, THIS PRAYER WAS FOUND FOLDED
IN THE POCKET OF A CONFEDERATE SOLDIER

NINE ESSENTIALS FOR
CONTENTED LIVING

1.

Health enough to make work a pleasure

2.

Wealth enough to support your needs

3.

Strength enough to battle difficulties and overcome them

4.

Grace enough to confess your sins and forsake them

5.

Patience enough to toil until some good is accomplished

6.

Clarity enough to see some good in your neighbor

7.

Love enough to move you to be useful and helpful to others

8.

Faith enough to make real the things of God

9.

Hope enough to remove all anxious fears confronting the future

GOETHE
POET, PLAYRIGHT, AND NOVELIST

A PRAYER OF MOTHER TERESA

DELIVER ME...

From the desire of being loved,

From the desire of being extolled,

From the desire of being honored,

From the desire of being praised,

From the desire of being preferred,

From the desire of being consulted,

From the desire of being approved,

From the desire of being popular,

From the fear of being humiliated,

From the fear of being despised,

From the fear of suffering rebukes,

From the fear of being calumniated,

From the fear of being forgotten,

From the fear of being wronged,

From the fear of being ridiculed,

From the fear of being suspected.

LUCINDA VARDEY, ED.
FROM "MOTHER TERESA: A SIMPLE PATH"

LEAVE IT TO GOD

Can't seem to get where you want to go fast enough?
Leave it to God.

Worried about the kids?
Leave it to God.

Living in a place you'd rather not be?
Leave it to God.

Looks like you won't graduate with honors?
Leave it to God.

No matter how hard you try, your
life's partner simply is not responding?
Leave it to God.

Found a lump and you see the doctor tomorrow?
Leave it to God.

You've said the right words to that friend
who is lost, and you've been all you know to be?
Leave it to God.

Haven't got a date for the prom?
Leave it to God.

A midcareer change seems scary?
Leave it to God.

You did a job, and someone else got the credit?
Leave it to God.

Getting older, alone?
Leave it to God.

CHARLES R. SWINDOLL
FROM "THE FINISHING TOUCH"

13 RULES TO LIVE BY

1.
It ain't as bad as you think; it will look better in the morning.

2.
Get mad, then get over it.

3.
*Avoid having your ego so close to your position that
when your position falls, your ego goes with it.*

4.
It can be done!

5.
Be careful what you choose. You may get it.

6.
Don't let adverse facts stand in the way of a good decision.

7.
Check small things.

8.
Share credit.

9.
You can't make someone else's choices. You shouldn't let someone else make yours.

10.
Remain calm. Be kind.

11.
Have a vision. Be demanding.

12.
Don't take counsel of your fears or naysayers.

13.
*Perpetual optimism is a force multiplier. (In the military, one is always
looking for methods of increasing or multiplying one's forces.)*

GENERAL COLIN POWELL
FROM "PARADE" MAGAZINE

DAY BY DAY

On this day...
I will try to be happy. My happiness is a direct result of my being at peace
with myself; what others do or think will not determine my happiness.

On this day...
I will accept myself and live to the best of my ability.

On this day...
I will make time to pray and meditate on the Scriptures, seeking
God and developing my relationship with Him.

On this day...
I will say what I mean and mean what I say.

On this day...
I will not tackle all my problems at once but
live moment to moment at my very best.

On this day...
I will live my life being assertive, not aggressive; being humble,
not proud; being confident to be exactly who I am.

On this day...
I will take care of my physical health. I will exercise
my mind, my body, and my spirit.

On this day...
I will be kind to those around me. I will be agreeable, finding no
fault with others. Nor will I try to improve or regulate others.

On this day...
I will remind myself that God has a special place in His
heart for me and a special purpose for me to fulfill in this world.

CARL DREIZLER AND MARY E. EHEMANN
FROM "52 WAYS TO LOSE WEIGHT"

HOW ATTITUDE AFFECTS US

*Our attitude at the beginning of a job will affect
the outcome of the job more than anything else.*

Our attitude toward life determines life's attitude toward us.

Our attitude toward others will determine their attitude toward us.

*Before we can achieve the kind of life we want,
we must think, act, walk, talk, and conduct ourselves in
ways characteristic of who we ultimately wish to become.*

*The higher we go in any organization of value,
the better the attitude we'll find.*

*Holding successful, positive thoughts in our minds
will make all the difference in the world.*

*If we always make a person feel needed, important, and
appreciated, he or she will return this attitude to us.*

Part of a good attitude is to look for the best in new ideas.
So look for good ideas everywhere.
We will find them in the most wonderful places:
on the bumpers of cars, on restaurant menus, in books, in travel,
out of the innocent mouths of children.

Don't broadcast personal problems.
It probably won't help you, and it cannot help others.

Don't talk about your health unless it's good.

Radiate the attitude of well-being.
Don't be embarrassed to share visions, desires, and goals.

Treat everyone with whom you come in contact as a fellow member
of the human race—with all the rights, duties, and privileges thereof.
The Golden Rule still applies:
Do unto others as you would have them do unto you.

TED W. ENGSTROM
FROM "MOTIVATION TO LAST A LIFETIME"

HOW TO FORFEIT PEACE

1.

Resent God's ways.

2.

Worry as much as possible.

3.

Pray only about things you can't manage by yourself.

4.

Refuse to accept what God gives.

5.

Look for peace elsewhere than in Him.

6.

Try to rule your own life.

7.

Doubt God's Word.

8.

Carry all your cares.

ELISABETH ELLIOT
FROM "KEEP A QUIET HEART"

HOW TO FIND PEACE

1.
"Great peace have they which love thy law: and nothing shall offend them."
PSALM 119:165 KJV

2.
"Don't worry over anything whatever."
PHILIPPIANS 4:6, PHILLIPS

3.
"In everything make your requests known to God in prayer and petition with thanksgiving. Then the peace of the God...will keep guard over your hearts."
PHILIPPIANS 4:6, 7, NEB

4.
"Take my yoke upon you and learn from me...and you will find rest."
MATTHEW 11:29, NIV

5.
"Peace is my parting gift to you, my own peace, such as the world cannot give."
JOHN 14:27, NEB

6.
"Let the peace of Christ rule in your hearts."
COLOSSIANS 3:15, NIV

7.
"Now the God of hope fill you will all joy and peace in believing."
ROMANS 15:13, KJV

8.
"Cast all your cares on him, for you are his charge."
1 PETER 5:7, NEB

ELISABETH ELLIOT
FROM "KEEP A QUIET HEART"

12 REASONS TO PRAY

1.

It encourages others.

2.

It reminds you of spiritual values.

3.

It gives hope.

4.

It helps you feel better.

5.

It allows you to let go of situations.

6.

It provides comfort.

7.

It relaxes you and reduces anxiety.

8.

It builds faith.

9.

It deepens character.

10.

It broadens your perspective.

11.

It brings you closer to God.

12.

It works.

JOHN VAN DIEST, BOARD OF DIRECTORS
WALK THRU THE BIBLE MINISTRIES

12 THINGS TO PRAY FOR

1.

For a growing relationship with God

2.

For positive relationships
with your family members

3.

For energy and enthusiasm
for your work or career

4.

For wisdom to make
right and wise decisions

5.

For your service to your
church and community

6.

For the special needs of
your family and friends

7.

For the spiritual lives
of your church leaders

8.

For wisdom for our government leaders

9.

For the moral integrity
of today's young people

10.

For the safety of those
serving in our armed forces

11.

For a lasting peace
among peoples and nations

12.

For the opportunity to
be a blessing to someone today

J. CARL LANEY,
PROFESSOR OF BIBLICAL LITERATURE, WESTERN SEMINARY

I'M THANKFUL FOR...

Air and autumn and animals.
Babies and breath and beauty.
Children and compassion and creativity.
Daylight and dew and daffodils.
Emotions and energy and enthusiasm.
Faith and family and friends.
Grandparents and grandchildren and God.
Hands and health and hope.
Ice cream and intelligence and intuition.
Joy and journeys and jokes.
Kindness and kisses and kittens.
Love and laughter and leaves.
Mothers and music and memories.
Night and nature and neighbors.
Order and oranges and oceans.
Peace and patience and prayer.
Quiet and quality and questions.
Rain and rest and romance.
Sunshine and smiles and stars.
Time and teachers and trees.
Unity and understanding and uniqueness.
Vision and values and vacations.
Winter and water and wisdom.
eXcitement and eXpression and eXperience.
Youth and yearning and yesterday.
Zest and zip and zeal.

TAMI STEPHENS
MOTHER OF THREE

WHAT WE CAN CONTROL

WE CANNOT CONTROL

the length of our life, but we can
control its width and depth.

WE CANNOT CONTROL

the contour of our countenance,
but we can control its expression.

WE CANNOT CONTROL

the other person's annoying habits,
but we can do something about our own.

WE CANNOT CONTROL

the distance our head is above the ground,
but we can control the height of the contents we feed into it.

*God help us do something about what we can
control and leave all else in the hands of God!*

JOHN LAWRENCE
FROM "THE SEVEN LAWS OF THE HARVEST"

YOU'RE BLESSED WHEN...

YOU'RE BLESSED

when you're at the end of your rope. With less of you there is more of God and his rule.

YOU'RE BLESSED

when you feel you've lost what is most dear to you. Only then can you be embraced by the One most dear to you.

YOU'RE BLESSED

when you're content with just who you are—no more, no less. That's the moment you find yourselves proud owners of everything that can't be bought.

YOU'RE BLESSED

when you've worked up a good appetite for God. He's food and drink in the best meal you'll ever eat.

YOU'RE BLESSED

when you care. At the moment of being "care-full," you find yourselves cared for.

YOU'RE BLESSED

when you get your inside world—your mind and heart—put right. Then you can see God in the outside world.

YOU'RE BLESSED

when you can show people how to cooperate instead of compete or fight. That's when you discover who you really are, and your place in God's family.

YOU'RE BLESSED

when your commitment to God provokes persecution. The persecution drives you even deeper into God's kingdom.

NO ONLY THAT—

count yourselves blessed every time people put you down or throw you out or speak lies about you to discredit Me. What it means is that the truth is too close for comfort and they are uncomfortable.

JESUS, MATTHEW 5: 3-11
PARAPHRASED BY EUGENE PETERSON IN "THE MESSAGE"

9

Standing Strong

Getting through the struggles of life

CHOOSE TO...

CHOOSE TO LOVE ....rather than hate.

CHOOSE TO SMILE ....rather than frown.

CHOOSE TO BUILD ....rather than destroy.

CHOOSE TO PERSEVERE ....rather than quit.

CHOOSE TO PRAISE ....rather than gossip.

CHOOSE TO HEAL ....rather than wound.

CHOOSE TO GIVE ....rather than grasp.

CHOOSE TO ACT ....rather than delay.

CHOOSE TO FORGIVE ....rather than curse.

CHOOSE TO PRAY ....rather than despair.

AUTHOR UNKNOWN

WINNING OVER WORRY

1.
Don't give up. Hope in God.

2.
Walk by faith, not by sight.

3.
Take time out for a good laugh.

4.
Use the Bible as a window to see your world.

5.
Never trouble trouble until trouble troubles you.

6.
Make choices based on God's Word.

7.
Give thanks to the Lord, for he is good.

8.
Ask for God's strength to get you through.

9.
Stop and enjoy the moment.

10.
Pray as if everything depended upon God—it does.

LINDA SHEPHERD
FROM "LOVE'S LITTLE RECIPES FOR LIFE"

IN THE EYE OF THE STORM

Love God more than you fear hell.

Once a week, let a child take you on a walk.

Make major decisions in a cemetery.

When no one is watching, live as if someone is.

Succeed at home first.

Don't spend tomorrow's money today.

Pray twice as much as you fret.

Listen twice as much as you speak.

Only harbor a grudge when God does.

Never outgrow your love of sunsets.

Treat people like angels; you will meet some and help make some.

'Tis wiser to err on the side of generosity than on the side of scrutiny.

God has forgiven you; you'd be wise to do the same.

When you can't trace God's hand, trust his heart.

Toot your own horn and the notes will be flat.

Don't feel guilty for God's goodness.

The book of life is lived in chapters, so know your page number.

Never let the important be the victim of the trivial.

Live your liturgy.

MAX LUCADO
FROM "IN THE EYE OF THE STORM"

OVERCOMING DEPRESSION
& DISCOURAGEMENT

1.

Visit your physician. Depression might be a symptom of a physical problem
Hypothyroidism, hypoglycemia, an amino imbalance, an endocrine imbalance
or a viral infection can all cause depression.

2.

Eat healthy. Eat plenty of fruits and vegetables. Avoid caffeine, sugar, junk food
and especially alcohol.

3.

Get enough sleep. Exhaustion adds to depression. Sleep refreshes the body and
uplifts the spirit. But too much sleep can be a sign of avoiding important issues
that can get you depressed.

4.

Be active. Physical activity can lift you out of depression. Be active and enjoy the
outdoors, especially when it's sunny. Avoid too much television or too many
passive activities. Activity energizes.

5.

Be social. Surrounding yourself with people, especially positive people, can keep
your mind off your problems and distract you from feeling sorry for yourself
Social interactions help pull you from your depression.

6.

Do fun activities. When you are depressed you don't want to do anything; nothing sounds enjoyable. But getting out and doing what you used to enjoy will
improve your attitude and after a while you will have fun.

7.

Write out your feelings. Emotions trapped inside you increase depression. Getting
them out on paper can release the internal pressure. Write about your anger
grief, confusion, loss, stress, or anything else that's bothering you.

8.

Surround yourself with positives. Fill your life with positive people, positive music, positive books, and positive situations. Stay away from negatives. Positives make you feel better, and as you feel better the depression loses its grip.

9.

Check out your negative self-talk. Listen to what you're saying to yourself. If you are saying negative things about yourself, your world, or the future, it will make you feel worse. Putting a positive spin on life will make you feel better.

10.

Make plans and dreams for the future. Dreaming about the future can be exciting. Make a list of all the things you wish to do in the future and then plan how to make them a reality.

11.

Develop your faith. Faith in God provides hope. It lifts a person above the frustrations and traumas of life. It also gives meaning to our existence. Faith pulls a person above depression and provides perspective to difficulties.

12.

Get help if the depression persists. Meet with a pastor if there are spiritual issues or a counselor if there are emotional problems or your physician for medication. It is a sign of wisdom and courage to seek help if needed.

DR. STEVE STEPHENS
PSYCHOLOGIST AND SEMINAR SPEAKER

A POSITIVE FOCUS

LET YOUR MIND DWELL ON THESE EIGHT THINGS...

Whatever is true

Whatever is noble

Whatever is right

Whatever is pure

Whatever is lovely

Whatever is admirable

Whatever is excellent

Whatever is praiseworthy

PHILIPPIANS 4:8 (NIV)

BE GOOD TO YOU

BE YOURSELF .... truthfully.

ACCEPT YOURSELF .... gratefully.

VALUE YOURSELF .... joyfully.

FORGIVE YOURSELF .... completely.

TREAT YOURSELF .... generously.

BALANCE YOURSELF .... harmoniously.

BLESS YOURSELF .... abundantly.

TRUST YOURSELF .... confidently.

LOVE YOURSELF .... wholeheartedly.

EMPOWER YOURSELF .... prayerfully.

GIVE YOURSELF .... enthusiastically.

EXPRESS YOURSELF .... radiantly.

AUTHOR UNKNOWN

STRESS BUSTERS

1.
DEVELOP ORDER

*Tidy up. Put things away. Toss clutter. You can restore a
sense of calm to a room with a thirty-minute "sort and dump."*

2.
DIVERT YOUR FOCUS

*Diversions give the mind a break from problem solving
and burden bearing. It is impossible to be consumed with
worry when something else is captivating your interest.*

3.
DIFFUSE

*Push the pressures out of your body through
twenty minutes of aerobic exercise.*

4.
DEBRIEF

Talk out your tension with a safe and trusted friend.

5.
DIVERSIFY

*Change channels in your brain.
Problem solving is more effective when the mind frequently rests
from a problem rather than obsessing on it continuously.*

6.
DELIBERATELY REST

*Schedule several five-minute slots during the day to "let down,"
and slow the mind and body. Listen to relaxing music.
Pray and meditate on Scriptures that soothe the soul.*

7.
DEAL WITH UNFINISHED BUSINESS

*Make amends whenever possible.
Grant forgiveness rather than nursing grudges.*

8.
DECIDE TO TRUST

*One of the best prescriptions for fear is to say,
"God, I choose to trust you."*

9.
DEDICATE YOURSELF TO THE BASICS

*To see clearly in the midst of blinding stress:
Sleep eight to nine hours a night;
Eat well-balanced meals;
Exercise twenty to thirty minutes, three times a week.*

10.
DISENGAGE

*When overwhelmed, step back, buy yourself some time,
and stop trying so hard. Everything doesn't have to be "fixed" today.*

11.
DIG IN

*Avoidance heightens anxiety. Evaluate what can be done and do it.
Don't get stuck in the quicksand of an "all or nothing" approach.*

12.
DON'T BE A "TYPE E" PERSON

*No one was designed to be Everything to Everybody.
Only God can fill that job description.*

PAM VREDEVELT
LICENSED PROFESSIONAL COUNSELOR

STANDING STRONG

ARE YOU DOING TOO MUCH?

IF YOU'RE THINKING THAT YOUR LIFESTYLE
NEEDS SIMPLIFYING, TRY ASKING YOURSELF THESE QUESTIONS:

*Have you ever missed an important event in your child's life
because of a conflicting obligation for which you volunteered?*

Do you feel that reading or relaxing is a waste of time?

Does your family have trouble finding time to spend together?

*Are the storage spaces in your home overflowing because you don't
have time to clean out what's been outgrown, broken, or used up?*

Do you spend most of your day feeling tired?

*Are you afraid to say "no" to an opportunity,
fearing it will never come again?*

*Do you give your children material items to make up
for denying them your time and energy?*

*Do you often find you've overscheduled yourself,
underestimating the time needed for each event?*

RAMONA RICHARDS
FROM "HOMELIFE" MAGAZINE

EIGHT QUESTIONS TO
ASK BEFORE SAYING YES

1.
Do I really understand this commitment?

2.
How does this fit into my current goals and priorities?

3.
Do I have the time, energy, and resources?

4.
What impact will this have on me in a year? in five years? in ten years?

5.
How will this impact those I love? Who will it help? Who will it hurt?

6.
What do my friends and family think?

7.
Can someone else do it better?

8.
Do I really want to say yes?

ALICE GRAY AND DR. STEVE STEPHENS
SEMINAR SPEAKERS

NINE GOALS FOR AUTHENTIC GROWTH

1.
Have a passion for excellence.

2.
Ask, listen, and hear—to determine the wants, needs,
and possibilities of all with whom I come in contact.

3.
Provide an example of commitment and integrity.

4.
Follow a path of continual empowerment for myself and others.

5.
Constantly focus on strengths of all with whom I come in contact.

6.
Cultivate optimum physical, mental, and spiritual fitness.

7.
Lead as I would like to be led.

8.
Savor the flavor of each passing moment.

9.
Infuse every thought and relationship
with faith, hope, love, and gratitude.

JOE D. BATTEN
FROM "NEW MAN" MAGAZINE

TEN BELIEFS THAT LEAD TO ANGER

1.
*If I want something, I should have it—no matter
whom it hurts or how I get it.*

2.
It is terrible and unjust to be kept waiting. I can't accept excuses.

3.
I must never be uncomfortable or frustrated. I can avoid distress at all cost.

4.
*I have a right to be angry when others hurt my feelings,
cause me discomfort, or disappoint me.*

5.
*If I don't sleep well or if I've had a bad day,
I have a right to be irritable and others should leave me alone.*

6.
*My parents always helped me.
Others shouldn't expect me to do it by myself.*

7.
*I detest it when others think their way is the only way—
even if they are the bosses.*

8.
I must succeed at everything I choose to do. There is no room for failure.

9.
I deserve immediate gratification. I am entitled to "It."

10.
Other motorists need to get out of my way.

GLENDA HOTTON
MARRIAGE AND FAMILY THERAPIST

DEALING WITH ANGER

1.

ADMIT YOUR ANGER.

If you're angry, be honest with yourself about it.

2.

EVALUATE YOUR ANGER.

Ask yourself, "What triggers my anger?
When am I most likely to feel anger?"

3.

CHOOSE YOUR PERCEPTION.

Slow down and put the problem in perspective.
Frame the situation in as positive a way as you can.

4.

CALM YOURSELF DOWN.

If your anger is getting out of control, lower your voice,
sit down, and breathe deeply. If you still can't calm
down, remove yourself from the situation.

5.

WATCH YOUR WORDS AND ACTIONS.

When you're angry, it is easy to say and do things you will
later regret. Watch carefully what you say; once those words are
out of your mouth, you can never take them back.

6.
WORK YOUR ANGER OUT.

*Anger produces adrenaline and adrenaline seeks release.
You need to work your anger out. Go for a drive, weed
a garden, chop wood, write a letter, or take a walk.*

7.
TALK ABOUT YOUR ANGER.

*Take responsibility for your feelings. Be direct and honest without
blaming or attacking. If you're overreacting, admit it. The better
you can communicate about your anger, the more you can control it.*

8.
DON'T LET THE SUN GO DOWN ON YOUR ANGER.

*Commit yourself to resolving your anger as soon as
possible. Unresolved anger turns into bitterness, revenge,
or both. The sooner you handle your anger, the better.*

9.
SEEK HELP.

*If your anger persists or is out of control, get help
immediately. Talk to a counselor or a pastor or a
physician and develop a more intensive plan.*

DR. STEVE STEPHENS
FROM "MARRIAGE: EXPERIENCE THE BEST"

THE WORLD NEEDS PEOPLE...

Who cannot be bought;

Whose word is their bond;

Who put character above wealth;

Who possess opinions and a will;

Who are larger than their vocations;

Who do not hesitate to take chances;

Who will not lose their individuality in a crowd;

Who will be as honest in small things as in great things;

Who will make no compromise with wrong;

Whose ambitions are not confined to their own selfish desires;

Who will not say they do it "because everybody else does it;"

Who are true to their friends through good report and evil report,
in adversity as well as prosperity;

Who do not believe that shrewdness, cunning, and
hardheadedness are the best qualities for winning success;

Who are not ashamed or afraid to stand for the truth when it is unpopular;

Who can say "no" with emphasis, although all the rest of the world says "yes."

TED W. ENGSTROM
FROM "MOTIVATION TO LAST A LIFETIME"

10
Family Fun

Relax and enjoy

TOP 10 FREE TOYS FOR CHILDREN

1.
Cape made from bath towel

2.
Empty squeeze bottles for tub toys

3.
Arm sling made from dish towel

4.
*Pretend grocery store stocked with empty food packages
(canned goods, cereal boxes, spices, etc.)*

5.
*Binoculars made from empty toilet paper tubes taped together
(add plastic food wrap lenses for professional effect)*

6.
Puppets made from the stray socks piling up in the laundry room

7.
Sewing cards made from styrofoam meat trays and old shoelaces

8.
Pretend post office stocked with junk mail

9.
Tent made from sheets and blankets

10.
Empty cardboard box

Honorary mention: Own library card

CRYSTAL KIRGISS, MOTHER OF THREE BOYS
COLUMMIST FOR THE "DETROIT LAKES TRIBUNE"

FAMILY GUIDELINES FOR TELEVISION

1.
Decide ahead of time what you want to watch.

2.
Include your children when setting up guidelines.

3.
Turn the TV off during meals.

4.
*Set up a limit of how much to watch each day with a goal
to decrease rather than increase your viewing time.*

5.
Watch together as a couple or a family (not alone).

6.
*Always do homework or chores first (a suggested rule for every member
of the family—one hour of reading before one hour of TV).*

7.
Set rules for babysitters.

8.
Acquire a good collection of family videos as alternative choices.

9.
Pay attention to rating guides.

10.
Talk about what you watch.

11.
*Evaluate what you saw in terms of violence, language,
sexual content, morality, respect for individuals, and accuracy.*

12.
Take advantage of viewing time together to snuggle and rub backs.

ALICE GRAY, DR. STEVE STEPHENS, AND JOHN VAN DIEST
SEMINAR SPEAKERS

FAMILY GUIDELINES FOR USING THE INTERNET

YOUR KIDS MAY NOT BE SAFE DRIVING THROUGH THE VIRTUAL VILLAGE ALONE. HERE ARE SOME TIPS TO KEEP THEM FROM SEEING THE SEEDIER SIDE OF CYBERSPACE.

Keep your computer in a commonly visible area of the home.

Encourage your family to telecommute together.

Avoid late-night Internet surfing.

Limit the number of minutes each family member can spend on-line. Periodically review file names of the documents your children download

Don't roam aimlessly. Always have a definite destination in mind.

Decide family standards for what on-line entertainment and communication is acceptable. Explain the rules clearly and stick to them. Be sure to include these three nevers:

1.
Never give out personal information over the computer. This includes full names, addresses, phone numbers, or any financial data (credit card numbers, etc.).

2.
Never respond to anyone who leaves obnoxious, lewd, or threatening e-mail.

3.
Never set up a face-to-face meeting with anyone you meet via bulletin boards or chat forums.

"NEW MAN" MAGAZINE

THE EIGHT BEST SURPRISES
A KID EVER HAD

1.

Pajama Ride—One night, after the kids are in their pajamas and tucked into bed, wait about ten minutes, race into their rooms, flip on the light, and yell, "Pajama ride!" Wrap a blanket around them, toss them in the car, and go to a Dairy Queen for a hot fudge sundae. Your kids will love the memory, they'll get to see Mom and Dad act crazy, and you'll have a wonderful opportunity to talk with them about what's going on in their lives.

2.

Water Fight—When was the last time you asked your kids to help you wash the car, and then got everyone into a big water fight? Is it dumb? You bet—and an absolute riot. (We've got friends who are still talking about a family water fight we had six years ago!) The chance for them to see their parents have fun makes it memorable.

3.

Scavenger Hunt—Wake your kids up one morning and announce they've got an important task. After breakfast, they'll have two hours to find everything on your list (a red button, a yellow rose, a Beanie Baby, two jokers, a picture of a mountain, a penny from the 70s, a mattress advertisement, etc.—the sillier the better!). The fun is in the hunt—and in the chance to let everyone tell their stories at the end of the game.

4.

Build a Fort—Take the time to build something with your kids, be it a tree house, clubhouse, backyard tent, or even a living room fort made of couch cushions. There is something about the memory of working together and building a structure that stays with children.

5.

Kids-in-Charge Night—Put your children in charge some Saturday. Let them choose what you'll do in the afternoon, then ask them to set the table and give them simple recipes to cook for dinner. Use an easy menu (like spaghetti or pancakes) and let them go at it. The lesson will be worth the mess! After dinner, guide them through washing dishes, sorting laundry, emptying the trash, and sewing on buttons. During these activities, talk with your kids about the importance of fulfilling responsibilities.

6.

Notes in Lunch Box—Write an encouraging note to each of your children and stick them in their lunch boxes. If you're really brave, add a cartoon. An unexpected positive word can sometimes make a memory that lasts a lifetime.

7.

Surprise Party—Throw a surprise party. Make a cake, hang decorations, and invite your child's friends (make sure they keep it a secret). If it's for a birthday, that's great...but it doesn't have to be for anything special. Just the thought that you would go to the trouble of creating a surprise will be enough to make it memorable.

8.

Day Off from School—One day, after one of your children has received a good report card, show up at school and say, "Sorry, but I've got to take you out of school today. I need you to do something important with me." Then take him or her fishing. That's right: fishing. Sometimes a day with Mom or Dad is more important than a day with the teacher. (If you can't take the entire day, make it a lunch date!)

JERRY "CHIP" AND PATTI MACGREGOR
CONDENSED FROM "FAMILY TIMES: GROWING TOGETHER IN FUN AND FAITH"

20 FUN ACTIVITIES

1.
Bake cookies.

2.
Help a neighbor.

3.
Enjoy nature (i.e. watch for animals, set up a bird feeder, get an ant farm, collect bugs, find shapes in the clouds, or study the stars).

4.
Visit a zoo or museum or carnival.

5.
Create a painting or a poster.

6.
Put on a play or puppet show.

7.
Find something to collect (shells, coins, rocks, sports cards, anything).

8.
Plant a garden.

9.
Collect cans and bottles and give the money to charity.

10.
Fly a kite.

11.
Take flowers and a card to someone sick or lonely.

12.
Read books aloud.

13.
Make giant pictures on your driveway with sidewalk chalk.

14.
Do a talent show.

15.
Go on a hike or bicycle ride.

16.
Look at family photographs or videos.

17.
Tell stories.

18.
*Make family cards (for Christmas, Valentine's Day,
Thanksgiving, and birthdays).*

19.
Paint each other's faces.

20.
Sing songs and/or make up songs.

TAMI STEPHENS
MOTHER OF THREE

48 GREAT BOOKS TO READ ALOUD

1. *Christie* . . . . .by Catherine Marshall
2. *Paddle to the Sea* . . . . .by Holling Clancy Holling
3. *Where the Red Fern Grows* . . . . .by Wilson Rawls
4. *Caddie Woodlawn* .by Carol Ryrie Brink
5. *Homer Price* . . . . .by Robert McClosky
6. *The Cooper Kids Adventure series* . . . . .by Frank Peretti
7. *The Secret Garden* . . . . .by Frances Hodgson Burnett
8. *The Baker Street Mysteries* . . . . .by Jake and Luke Thoene
9. *Ramona series* . . . . .by Beverly Cleary
10. *Mary Poppins* . . . . .by P. L. Travers
11. *A Wrinkle in Time* .by Madeleine L'Engle
12. *The Mixed-up Files of Mrs. Basil F. Frankweiler*
    . . . . .by E.L. Konigsburg
13. *The Chronicles of Narnia* . . . . .by C.S. Lewis
14. *Little Women* . . . . .by Louisa May Alcott
15. *The Girl of the Limberlost* . . . . .by Gene Stratton Porter
16. *House at Pooh Corner* .by A. A. Milne
17. *Little House on the Prairie* . . . . .by Laura Ingalls Wilder
18. *Charlotte's Web* . . . . .by E. B. White
19. *Anne of Green Gables* . . . . .by L. M. Montgomery
20. *Gentle Ben* . . . . .by Walt Morey
21. *The Boxcar Children* . . . . .by Gertrude Chandler Warner
22. *Stone Fox* . . . . .by John Reynolds Gardiner
23. *Birdie's Lighthouse* . . . . .by Deborah Hopkinson
24. *Heidi* . . . . .by Johanna Spyri

JANICE BYRAM
SCHOOL TEACHER

HOW TO CHOOSE A
VIDEO FOR YOUR FAMILY

1.
CHECK THE RATING.

Unrated means unknown. You have no idea what you are getting.

If the video is rated, you'll find it on the back side of the jacket box. "G" means the movie is suitable for all audiences. "PG" means parental guidance is suggested. "PG13" often contains significant doses of sex, foul language, and violence. "R" means restricted, with no one under seventeen allowed without a parent or adult guardian.

2.
ASK THE RIGHT QUESTIONS.

Even when a rating is displayed on the box, discernment is crucial in choosing a videocassette. The following questions will help you.

What is the premise of the movie? What message does the film communicate? You can often find the premise on the jacket of the videotape. Remember—you have to read between the lines.

Who is the hero and what kind of role model is he or she?
How is religion portrayed?
How is the world portrayed?
How is love portrayed?
How is the family portrayed?

3.
KNOW WHAT YOU WANT TO RENT BEFORE YOU WALK INTO THE STORE.

If you do find yourself browsing,
head for the "classics" or "musicals" sections.
They stand a better chance of being good for family viewing.

4.
TOTALLY AVOID HORROR MOVIES AND TEEN "SEXPLOITATION" FILMS

TED BAEHR
CONDENSED FROM "THE WAR CRY" MAGAZINE

20 GREAT CHILDREN'S MOVIES

(MOST FOR AGE SIX AND OLDER)

1. Adventures of Milo and Otis
2. Anne of Green Gables
3. Babe
4. Beauty and the Beast
5. Benji
6. The Black Stallion
7. Charlie Brown's All Stars
8. Heidi
9. Homeward Bound
10. Lady and the Tramp
11. Mary Poppins
12. Miracle on 34th Street
13. National Velvet
14. Oliver and Company
15. Pinocchio
16. Pollyanna
17. Prince of Egypt
18. Toy Story
19. A Tree Grows in Brooklyn
20. The Velveteen Rabbit

JOHN EVANS, EDITOR "FAMILY VIDEO GUIDE"
(THE ABOVE LIST WAS SELECTED BY THE EDITORS FROM OVER 1000
RECOMMENDED VIDEO MOVIES BASED ON TRADITIONAL FAMILY VALUES.)

20 GREAT FAMILY MOVIES

(FOR AGE 12 AND OLDER)

1. Ben Hur

2. Chariots of Fire

3. Christy

4. Driving Miss Daisy

5. Gone with the Wind

6. The Good Earth

7. Great Expectations (1946)

8. Inn of Sixth Happiness

9. It's a Wonderful Life

10. Little Women (1994)

11. Mr. Smith Goes to Washington

12. North by Northwest

13. The Quiet Man

14. The Preacher's Wife (1996)

15. The Sound of Music

16. Sounder

17. The Yearling

18. To Kill a Mockingbird

19. Twenty Thousand
    Leagues Under the Sea

20. Where the Red Fern Grows

JOHN EVANS, EDITOR "FAMILY VIDEO GUIDE"
(THE ABOVE LIST WAS SELECTED BY THE EDITORS FROM OVER 1000
RECOMMENDED VIDEO MOVIES BASED ON TRADITIONAL FAMILY VALUES.)

20 GREAT TABLE GAMES

1. Candyland
2. Chutes and Ladders
3. Sorry
4. Pictionary
5. Concentration
6. Checkers
7. Chess
8. Dominoes
9. Chinese Checkers
10. Scrabble

11. Scattergories
12. Boggle
13. Payday
14. Life
15. Yatzee
16. Cribbage
17. Jenga
18. Uno
19. Old Maid
20. Monopoly

TAMI STEPHENS
MOTHER OF THREE

11
Family Life

Growing together

THE JOB OF PARENTS

Parents can and must:

TRAIN,

SHAPE,

MOLD,

CORRECT,

GUIDE,

PUNISH,

REWARD,

INSTRUCT,

WARN,

TEACH,

AND LOVE

their kids during the formative years.

DR. JAMES C. DOBSON
FROM "PARENTING ISN'T FOR COWARDS"

10 FAMILY COMMITMENTS

1.

I will not hit.

2.

I will not keep secrets.

3.

I will not lie.

4.

I will not use bad language.

5.

*I will not use drugs, and if I know somebody
who is using drugs, I'll try to help them.*

6.

I will treat others with respect.

7.

If I make a mess, I'll clean it up.

8.

I'll pick up my clothes and keep my room neat.

9.

I'll talk to Mom and Dad about my problems.

10.

I'll do my homework before I go out to play.

GREG CYNAUMON, PH.D.
FROM "HOW TO AVOID ALIENATING YOUR KIDS IN 10 EASY STEPS"

SIX STEPS TO SUCCESSFUL COMMUNICATION

Thinking of the word "ladder" will help you remember these steps.

L ook at the person speaking to you.

A sk questions.

D on't interrupt.

D on't change the subject.

E mpathize.

R espond verbally and nonverbally.

AUTHOR UNKNOWN
AS CITED IN "MORE OF...THE BEST OF BITS & PIECES," ROB GILBERT, PH.D., ED.

20 CONVERSATION STARTERS

*Here are twenty questions you can use to
strike up a conversation with your kids:*

What was the neatest birthday present you ever received?

What makes you laugh?

What is your favorite food?

Where would you like to go for a vacation if you could go anyplace
in the whole world?

If you had to move and could take only three things with you, what
would you take?

How would you describe the "ideal" father or mother?

What is something you can do pretty well?

What is your favorite song?

What is your best friend like?

How would you describe yourself to someone who does not know you?

Has there been a time when you felt proud of yourself?

What kind of store would you like to own and operate?

If you received $5,000 as a gift—how would you spend it?

What is your favorite room in our house? Why?

What kind of a job do you want to have in twenty years?

What talent do you wish you had?

If someone could give you anything in the world for

　　your birthday—what would you like it to be?

What would you like to invent to make life better?

What is something that bugs you?

What kind of trophy would you like to win?

JERRY "CHIP" AND PATTI MACGREGOR
FROM "FAMILY TIMES: GROWING TOGETHER IN FUN AND FAITH"

WHY DIVORCE HURTS
CHILDREN

1.

It signals the collapse of the family structure—the child feels alone and frightened. This loneliness can be acute and long remembered.

2.

A couple's capacity to be parents is diminished. They are preoccupied with their own emotional survival during the critical months (or years) of the divorce.

3.

Divorce creates conflicts of loyalty in the children. Whose side do they take? They feel pulled by love and loyalty in both directions.

4.

Uncertainty about the future often causes deep-seated insecurity in children. Being dependent mainly on one parent can create a great deal of anxiety.

5.

Anger and resentment between parents, which is prevalent in most divorces, creates intense fear in the child. The younger he or she is, the more damaging the climate of anger can be.

6.

Children take upon themselves anxiety concerning their parents. They worry intensely about their mother in particular, with the departure of the father being a terrifying event.

7.

If the family moves, a child may lose an "at-home" parent, a home, a school, a church, and friends. Divorce represents the loss of so many things that a deep depression is almost inevitable. Yet most parents fail to recognize this depression in their children.

A prominent child psychologist, Dr. Lee Salk, has said, "The trauma of divorce is second only to death. Children sense a deep loss and feel they are suddenly vulnerable to forces beyond their control."

ARCHIBALD HART
CONDENSED FROM "MOODY" MAGAZINE

10 WAYS TO BE A GREAT DAD

1.
RESPECT YOUR CHILDREN'S MOTHER.

One of the best things a father can do for his children is to respect their mother. If you are married, keep your marriage strong and vital. If you're not married, it is still important to respect and support the mother of your children.

2.
SPEND TIME WITH YOUR CHILDREN.

How a father spends his time tells his children what's important to him. If you always seem too busy for your children, they will feel neglected no matter what you say.

3.
EARN THE RIGHT TO BE HEARD.

All too often the only time a father speaks to his children is when they have done something wrong. Begin talking with your kids when they are very young so that difficult subjects will be easier to handle as they get older. Take time and listen to their ideas and problems.

4.
DISCIPLINE WITH LOVE.

All children need guidance and discipline, not as punishment, but to set reasonable limits. Remind your children of the consequences of their actions and provide meaningful rewards for desirable behavior.

5.
BE A ROLE MODEL.

Fathers are role models to their kids, whether they realize it or not. A girl who spends time with a loving father grows up knowing she deserves to be treated with respect by boys, and what to look for in a husband. Fathers can teach sons what is important in life by demonstrating honesty, humility, and responsibility.

6.
BE A TEACHER.

Too many fathers think teaching is something others do. But a father who teaches his children about right and wrong, and encourages them to do their best, will see his children make good choices.

7.
EAT TOGETHER AS A FAMILY.

Sharing a meal together (breakfast, lunch, or dinner) can be an important part of healthy family life. In addition to providing some structure in a busy day, it gives kids the chance to talk about what they are doing and want to do.

8.
READ TO YOUR CHILDREN.

Begin reading to your children when they are very young. When they are older, encourage them to read on their own. Instilling your children with a love for reading is one of the best ways to ensure they will have a lifetime of personal and career growth.

9.
SHOW AFFECTION.

Children need security that comes from knowing they are wanted, accepted, and loved by their family. Parents, especially fathers, need to feel both comfortable and willing to hug their children. Showing affection every day is the best way to let your children know that you love them.

10.
REALIZE THAT A FATHER'S JOB IS NEVER DONE.

Even after children are grown and ready to leave home, they will still look to their fathers for wisdom and advice. Whether it's continued schooling, a new job, or a wedding, fathers continue to play an essential part in the lives of their children as they grow and, perhaps, marry and build their own families.

THE NATIONAL FATHERHOOD INITIATIVE

FAMILY LIFE

HELP FOR DISCOURAGED PARENTS

1.

You are not to blame for the temperament with which your child was born. He is simply a tough kid to handle and your task is to rise to the challenge.

2.

He is in greater danger because of his inclination to test the limits and scale the walls. Your utmost diligence and wisdom will be required to deal with him.

3.

If you fail to understand his lust for power and independence, you can exhaust your resources and bog down in guilt. It will benefit no one.

4.

If it is not already too late, by all means, take charge of your babies. Hold tightly to the reins of authority in the early days, and build an attitude of respect during your brief window of opportunity. You will need every ounce of "awe" you can get during the years to come. Once you have established your right to lead, begin to let go systematically, year by year.

5.

Don't panic, even during the storms of adolescence. Better times are ahead. A radical turnaround usually occurs in the early twenties.

6.

Stay on your child's team, even when it appears to be a *losing* team. You'll have the rest of your life to enjoy mutual fellowship if you don't overreact to frustration now.

7.

Give him time to find himself, even if he appears not to be searching.

8.

Most importantly, I urge you to hold your children before the Lord in fervent prayer throughout their years at home. I am convinced that there is no other source of confidence and wisdom in parenting.

DR. JAMES C. DOBSON
FROM "PARENTING ISN'T FOR COWARDS"

FAMILY TEAM BUILDING

1.
GREAT GOALS

Promote activities in which siblings
must work together to reach a goal.

2.
GAMES

During family time, join the children as a team.

3.
WORKING TOGETHER

Assign chores that must be completed with cooperation.

4.
CHARITY WORK

Unite your children to reach out to the less fortunate.

5.
FUN PROJECTS

Promote sibling activities such as large puzzles, birdhouses, or
craft kits to develop a sense of teamwork. Use limited supplies
such as glue and markers, so children will have to share.

6.
AN OFFERING FOR EVERY OCCASION

Unite forces to create gifts, such as cookies,
for neighbors or presents for grandparents.

7.
BOOK TIME

*Have children read to each other, or have an older child read
to a younger sibling. Also, make up your own "sibling" stories for
your children. Have Super Brother save little sister from the
scary bear, or add your children as characters to Bible stories.*

8.
KING OR QUEEN FOR THE DAY

*Have one day a week be "Royal Kid Day."
One child is the king or queen and will receive special treatment.
The other "servant" children will also enjoy themselves as they
prepare food and games for the queen or king of the day.*

9.
SPECIAL PARENT DAY

*Siblings will have tons of fun working together to fulfill
the needs of the chosen adult. (This is great for the adults, too!)*

10.
FAMILY TALENT NIGHT

*Encourage each child to shine like a star in front of the family.
Tumbling acts, singing specials, or the presentation of school
projects will bring claps and support from other siblings.*

TRICIA GOYER AND CINDY MCCORMICK MARTINUSEN
CONDENSED FROM "HOMELIFE" MAGAZINE

BE A PARENT TEACHERS LIKE TO SEE

1.
ESTABLISH A POSITIVE RELATIONSHIP

Try to work together. If you become acquainted with your child's teacher before problems occur, you will have a greater impact when a need arises.

2.
GIVE HELP, NOT ADVICE

Most teachers need help, not more information. When helping, try to do what the teacher wants, not necessarily what you want.

3.
SHOW APPRECIATION

Even in the most positive schools, an amazingly small number of parents (and students!) ever show appreciation. We all work harder for those who say thanks.

4.
BE POSITIVE

If your child struggles, make the teacher aware of the problem and ask for suggestions. Don't be afraid to tell the teacher your plans and how she can help. Focus on changing your child, not the teacher, the school, or the child in the next seat.

5.
PICK YOUR BATTLES

Don't overlook important issues, but choose your battles carefully. Realize that if you fight, people get hurt. Is it worth it? Many battles aren't.

6.
RESPECT THE TEACHER

For a good idea of how you might be perceived by a teacher, ask yourself this question: What would the teacher's life be like if every parent did what I do?

7.
PRAY FOR THE TEACHER

If you multiply your needs as a parent times the teacher's twenty-five students, you will feel the need to pray for her.

JOE NEFF, DIRECTOR OF GUIDANCE AT WHEATON ACADEMY
CONDENSED FROM "FOCUS ON THE FAMILY" MAGAZINE

FIVE MUSTS FOR EVERY FAMILY

1.
AN ATTITUDE OF SERVICE.

When family members help each other the whole family benefits.

2.
INTIMACY BETWEEN A HUSBAND AND WIFE.

When a couple connects, it satisfies their inner longings and gives the children a loving model of what family is all about.

3.
PARENTS WHO TEACH AND TRAIN.

Guiding your children is a team effort.

4.
HUSBANDS WHO ARE LOVING LEADERS.

A man needs to lead his wife and children in a loving way and live his spiritual and moral values. It inspires his family to do the same.

5.
CHILDREN WHO OBEY AND HONOR THEIR PARENTS.

Kids need to learn that living by rules is good for them and everyone around them.

GARY CHAPMAN
FROM "FIVE SIGNS OF A FUNCTIONAL FAMILY"

12
Family Values
Learning together

QUALITIES TO PASS ON
TO YOUR CHILDREN

DETERMINATION ...."Stick with it, regardless."

HONESTY ...."Speak and live the truth—always."

RESPONSIBILITY ...."Be dependable, be trustworthy."

THOUGHTFULNESS ...."Think of others before yourself."

CONFIDENTIALITY ...."Don't tell secrets. Seal your lips."

PUNCTUALITY ...."Be on time."

SELF-CONTROL ...."When under stress, stay calm."

PATIENCE ...."Fight irritability. Be willing to wait."

PURITY ...."Reject anything that lowers your standards."

COMPASSION ...."When another hurts, feel it with him."

DILIGENCE ...."Work hard. Tough it out."

CHARLES R. SWINDOLL
FROM "GROWING STRONG IN THE SEASONS OF LIFE"

FAMILY VALUES

12 SURE-FIRE WAYS TO RAISE DELINQUENT CHILDREN

1.

Begin from infancy to give the child everything he wants. In this way he will grow up to believe the world owes him a living.

2.

When he picks up bad words, laugh at him. This will make him think he's cute. It will also encourage him to pick up "cuter" phrases that will blow off the top of your head later.

3.

Never give him any spiritual training. Wait till he is twenty-one and then let him "decide for himself."

4.

Avoid use of the word "wrong." It may develop a guilt complex. This will condition him to believe that society is against him, and he is being persecuted.

5.

Pick up everything he leaves lying around (books, shoes, and clothing). Do everything for him so he will be experienced in throwing all responsibility onto others.

6.

Let him read any printed matter he can get his hands on. Be careful that the silverware and drinking glasses are sterilized, but let his mind feast on garbage.

7.

Quarrel frequently in the presence of your child. In this way he will not be too shocked when the home is broken up later.

8.

Give a child all the spending money he wants. Never let him earn his own. Why should he have things as tough as you had them?

9.

Satisfy his every craving for food, drink, and comfort. See that every sensual desire is gratified. Denial of his desires may lead to harmful frustration.

10.

Take his part against neighbors, teachers, and policemen. They are all prejudiced against your child.

11.

When he gets into real trouble, apologize for yourself by saying, "I never could do anything with him."

12.

Prepare for a life of grief.

AUTHOR UNKNOWN

THE 10 COMMANDMENTS
OF DISCIPLINE

1.
EXAMINE THE EVIDENCE

Examine all the evidence and interview all witnesses before bringing charges.

2.
JUSTICE SHOULD BE SWIFT

Don't make your kids sit on "death row" for hours waiting for a pardon from the governor.

3.
DON'T DISCIPLINE OUT OF ANGER

Try not to discipline in the heat of the moment, when emotions are peaking. Before you lose control, call a parenting time-out.

4.
KEEP YOUR WORD

Don't make threats you don't intend to keep. If you warn your child that he will be disciplined the next time he breaks a certain household rule, be sure to follow through.

5.
DON'T EXHUME THE BODIES OF THE PAST

Stay current. Discipline your children for today's "mess-up," not the one that occurred last week, last month, or even last year.

6.
NEVER ARGUE WITH YOUR KIDS

Some kids use arguing as a stalling tactic to avoid discipline. They figure if they plead their case vehemently enough, they might get you to reverse your decision.

7.
PUNISHMENT SHOULD FIT THE CRIME

Don't give your kids the death penalty for a misdemeanor—for instance, if your teenager misses curfew by a few minutes. Any discipline should reflect the severity of the problem.

8.
HELP YOUR KIDS SEE THEIR ROLE BEFORE YOU DISCIPLINE

Help your kids understand their mistakes and the possible motivation behind the misdeed or misconduct. If an apology is in order be sure they know why and to whom it should be directed. This ends the case by bringing "closure" to their act.

9.
DON'T WITHHOLD FORGIVENESS—IT BECOMES MANIPULATIVE

Some parents stay mad as a way to remain in a one-up power position over their children. Letting go of your anger and communicating forgiveness helps a child do the right thing next time.

10.
NEVER DISCIPLINE YOUR CHILDREN FOR AN ACCIDENT

GREG CYNAUMON, PH.D.
CONDENSED FROM "HOW TO AVOID ALIENATING YOUR KIDS IN 10 EASY STEPS"

FAMILY VALUES

THE SIX A'S OF PARENTING

1.
BE AWARE

Study your children. They're wonderful creations. Listen to them, watch them, ask them questions. Talk with them, not to them. Discover their likes and dislikes, their dreams and fears, their strengths and weaknesses. Recognize how special they are.

2.
BE ASSERTIVE

There are lessons you've learned from life, so pass them on. Teach truth. Provide reasonable rules and consistent consequences when those rules are broken. Be strong and give your children security without being rigid, insensitive, abusive, angry, or exasperating.

3.
BE ACCEPTING

Focus on the positives and assist children with their negatives. Don't expect perfection from them, lest they turn and expect it from you. Remember that children are often immature and teenagers are frequently impulsive. Be patient with them.

4.
BE APPROACHABLE

One of the biggest problems is emotional distance from your children. Be close to your children. Spend quality time with them. Laugh with them; play with them; enjoy them. Take them on walks and outings and vacations. Truly connect with them.

5.
BE AFFECTIONATE

Hug them often and tell them you love them every day. Give them compliments and encourage them versus discouraging them. Don't yell, hit, name call, or belittle them. Treat them gently and with respect. Treasure them.

6.
BE ALERT

The world is full of dangers and temptations. As parents we are protectors. Watch over your children and warn them. Protect them without being paranoid. Most importantly of all, pray for them daily.

DR. STEVE STEPHENS
PSYCHOLOGIST AND FATHER OF THREE

PARENTING 101

1.
PAY MORE ATTENTION TO YOUR MARRIAGE—OR YOURSELF, IF YOU'RE A SINGLE PARENT—THAN YOU DO TO THE CHILDREN.

Your marriage, if it is strong and satisfying, will give your children more security than any amount of attention. If you are single, your sense of self-respect and fulfillment as a person can act as the same sort of anchor for children.

2.
EXPECT YOUR CHILDREN TO OBEY.

Don't apologize for decisions you make in their lives. Children need powerful parents upon whom they can count to be authoritative, decisive, and trustworthy. *You* are in charge of the family.

3.
NURTURE YOUR CHILDREN'S RESPONSIBILITY WITHIN THIS STRUCTURE.

Allow them to make choices, and let them know that they must accept the outcomes. From an early age, expect them to make regular, tangible contributions to the family. That means chores they don't get paid for. And it means letting your children take responsibility for their own actions.

4.
SAY NO AND SAY IT OFTEN.

If the response is a tantrum, so be it. Exposure to frustration prepares children for the realities of adulthood and gives them a tolerance of frustration that eventually develops perseverance—a key ingredient to every success story. Your obligation is not to make your children happy, but to give them the skills to pursue happiness on their own.

5.
WHERE TOYS ARE CONCERNED, LESS IS MORE.

Having too many toys destroys a young child's ability to make creative decisions. If a youngster has too many options, he becomes overwhelmed and can't decide what to play with.

6.
TURN OFF THE TUBE.

Preschool children need to play so they can develop basic competency skills, learned by touching and exploring their environment. Nothing happens when a child sits passively in front of a television screen.

7.
DON'T BE INTIMIDATED BY THE EXPERTS.

Use suggestions and ideas that make sense to you, but remember that all parents make mistakes now and then...and children aren't permanently scarred by it. Raise your children your way and enjoy it.

JOHN ROSEMOND
CONDENSED FROM "BOTTOM LINE PERSONAL"

10 THINGS TO DO WHEN CHILDREN ARE AFRAID

1.
BE CLOSE

Just the presence of someone safe is calming.

2.
TOUCH THEM

Holding hands, hugs, rubbing their back and any form of reassuring affection helps.

3.
SPEAK GENTLY AND CONFIDENTLY

Your voice is a point of familiarity and safety, so watch your tone.

4.
LISTEN

Let them tell you about their fears no matter how irrational. Be attentive and patient. Remember, what they say is very important to them.

5.
GIVE THEM SOMETHING SPECIFIC TO DO

Taking action helps children feel like they have some power when overwhelmed.

6.
GIVE THEM A POSITIVE FOCUS

When they think of something good or safe or reassuring, fears don't seem so big.

7.
PRAY WITH THEM

Seeking God's protection or comfort is something we all need.
Remind them God is always close and he always cares.

8.
GIVE THEM SOMETHING FAMILIAR

Familiar objects (such as a blanket, photograph, necklace,
ring, or stuffed animal) help children relax.

9.
REASSURE THEM THAT THERE IS ALWAYS A WAY OUT

Teach them how to problem solve and figure out what to do. Come up
with as many solutions as possible. Reassure them that things which
seem very frightening now often don't seem so bad in a year or two.

10.
REMIND THEM THAT WE ALL HAVE FEARS

Tell them about what frightened you at their age
and how you handled it.

DR. STEVE STEPHENS
PSYCHOLOGIST AND FATHER OF THREE

JOBS KIDS CAN DO

FOUR TO SIX-YEAR-OLDS CAN:

Sort laundry

Dust

Make bed

Set table

Pick up toys

Feed pets

Wipe floors

SIX TO TEN-YEAR-OLDS CAN:

Fold clothes

Vacuum

Change bed linens

Clean bathroom

Empty dishwasher

Prepare lunch

Groom pets

Plan & plant garden

Water plants

Pull weeds

TEN TO THIRTEEN-YEAR-OLDS CAN:	THIRTEEN TO HIGH SCHOOL CAN:
Wash, dry, & fold clothes	Wash windows
Mow lawn	Paint
Rake	Clean oven
Wash & dry dishes	Wash walls
Wash & vacuum car	Trim hedges
Plan & prepare meals	Tutor younger siblings
Clean refrigerator	Defrost freezer
Shovel snow	Wash & wax floors
	Run errands

DOREEN BUTTON
MOM TO THREE BUSY HOME-SCHOOL KIDS

WINNING OVER THE PICKY EATER

1.
SCALE DOWN YOUR EXPECTATIONS

If your child eats small portions, don't worry.

2.
LIMIT AFTERNOON SNACKS

*Don't deprive children of an afternoon snack, but make it small
and nutritious if you expect them to eat a full dinner.
Offer fresh fruit, cheese, or graham crackers.*

3.
LIMIT DRINKS

Parents often underestimate how filling fruit juice and milk can be.

4.
SERVE SMALL PORTIONS

*Put less on their plate than you think they will eat.
You can always serve seconds.*

5.
MAKE MEALTIME PLEASANT

*Include children in conversation, and don't make the dinner hour
a time for criticism or arguments.
Don't force your child to remain at the table with a plate of food
after the rest of the family is finished.*

6.
EXPECT GOOD MANNERS

*Let your child know he or she is to be at the table on time and
to refrain from making faces and rude comments about the food.*

7.
DON'T BECOME A SHORT-ORDER COOK

*Serve a well-balanced meal, and let your child make choices
from what is prepared.*

8.
AVOID THE DESSERT DOWNFALL

Denying a picky eater dessert is another no-win situation.

9.
LOOK AT THE BIG PICTURE

*Keep in mind your child's diet over the long haul and not just
at a particular meal. Your responsibility is to provide healthful food
in a happy setting. Children are most likely to develop new tastes when
they are free to discover food on their own without bribery or praise.*

ELLYN SATTER
FROM "HOW TO GET YOUR KID TO EAT...BUT NOT TOO MUCH"

TABLE MANNERS

REMEMBER—THERE IS A REASON FOR EVERY RULE.

PLACE   no elbows on the table unless all the dishes are removed following the meal.

CHEW   with your mouth closed.

HOLD   the silverware correctly.

CUT   one bit of meat at a time.

PASS   food to the right.

PASS   both the salt and pepper shakers.

SIT   up straight in your chair.

MODIFY   your voice so that only your tablemates can hear you.

EXCUSE   yourself to individuals on each side of you if you must leave the table.

REFUSE   food only if you must by saying kindly, "No, thank you."

SAY,   "Please pass the…"

WATCH to see that all condiments near you are passed around the table.

UNFOLD a large restaurant napkin halfway. Place the fold toward your knees. Leave it in your lap until you leave the table, except when you use the napkin.

EAT at a moderate speed. Don't make others wait for you to finish.

PLACE used silverware on a plate, not on the tablecloth (even during a course).

EAT quietly, making no noise with your mouth or silverware.

REMOVE seeds, pits, gristle, etc. from your mouth with the utensil you used to put it into your mouth. Do not use a cloth napkin. Small bones may be removed with one's thumb and forefinger for safety.

REFUSE beverage by simply saying, "No, thank you." Do not invert the cup or glass. (The wait staff may turn it over.)

WHEN TO TEACH
YOUR CHILD MANNERS

AGE THREE TO FOUR:

Saying "Hello" and "Goodbye"
Saying "Please" and "Thank you"
Shaking hands

AGE FOUR TO SIX:

Saying "Excuse me"
Using a fork and spoon properly
Asking for food to be passed
Using a napkin
Talking without a mouth full of food
Not making a scene in public

AGE SIX TO TWELVE:

Not interrupting others
Saying "Excuse me" when interrupting becomes necessary
Offering help when it is needed
Showing respect for elders
Refraining from making hurtful comments
Responding when spoken to
Respecting property at home and away

Answering the telephone properly

Keeping his or her room clean and picked up

Doing assigned chores cheerfully, punctually, and efficiently

Playing music at a reasonably low decibel level

Respecting the privacy of others

Waiting one's proper turn in line

Saying "Excuse me" when bumping into someone

Attending to one's guest

Writing thank-you notes for gifts, overnight visits, and special treats
of any kind

Being punctual

Depositing trash in proper receptacle

Observing rules of safety such as walking, biking, skating

JUNE HINES MOORE
FROM "YOU CAN RAISE A WELL-MANNERED CHILD"

THE 10 MOST IMPORTANT MANNERS
TO TEACH YOUR CHILDREN

1.
Meeting and greeting people properly.

2.
Being a gracious host and a welcome guest.

3.
*Good mouth manners: "Yes" and "No" (or "Yes, ma'am"and
"No, ma'am," not "Yeah" or a grunt), "hello, goodbye,
thank you, please, excuse me, I'm sorry, may I?"*

4.
Proper conduct for church and other public places.

5.
Writing, coloring, or drawing thank-you notes.

6.
Properly responding to invitations and following through on the response.

7.
Good (not perfect) table manners.

8.
Proper telephone talk.

9.
Showing deference to elders and authority figures.

10.
Opening doors for others.

JUNE HINES MOORE
FROM "YOU CAN RAISE A WELL-MANNERED CHILD"

13
Family Love
Bonding together

LOVING YOUR KIDS

Take time with your children.

Set your children a good example.

Give your children ideals for living.

Have a lot of activities planned.

Discipline your children.

Teach them about God.

BILLY GRAHAM
FROM "GOD'S LITTLE INSTRUCTION BOOK FOR DAD"

TODAY'S KIDS DESPERATELY NEED HEROES WHO...

...play catch, enjoy tea parties, or wrestle because the heart of a child is there and they set out to capture it.

...laugh till their belly hurts and tears fall from their eyes while secretly creating deep friendships and memories that last a lifetime.

...make mistakes but consider them to be wonderful opportunities to learn.

...place an out-of-tune preschool concert or a ten-year-old's baseball game on life's agenda because they are of infinite worth to those playing.

...love at all times, because love is a gift freely given and not a reward for service well done.

...listen eye to eye and with both ears even if it means getting on one knee.

...admit when they are wrong and work to make things right.

...hear about those in need and say, "Let's do something to help right now!" and set off an uncontrollable wildfire of generosity and kindness.

...give the credit to others and empower those they touch to succeed in all that they do.

...model love as action, commitment, and truth even when it hurts because they believe God can work miracles in even the hardest heart.

...love the Lord with all their heart, soul, and mind and know that the rest is just details.

MARTY WILKINS
DAD OF THREE, HIGH SCHOOL TEACHER AND COACH

FAMILY LOVE

BLESSED ARE PARENTS WHO...

1.
Blessed are parents who listen to their children, for they in turn will be heard.

2.
Blessed are they who do not expect more of their children than is appropriate for their level of maturity, for they shall not be disappointed.

3.
Blessed are parents who do not attempt to tackle the new math, for they shall not fail.

4.
Blessed are parents who can laugh at themselves, for their children will laugh with them and not at them.

5.
Blessed are the parents who may be called "old-fashioned." They can be assured they are on the right track, for so have children persecuted parents for generations, and their opinions will change by the time they are old enough to pay taxes.

6.

Blessed are they who teach their children to understand and love each other, for they shall not get caught in the crossfire of a sibling war.

7.

Blessed are the parents who let their children do for themselves what they are capable of doing, for they shall not be merely unpaid servants.

8.

Blessed are the parents who take their children with them often, for they shall see the world with fresh eyes.

9.

Blessed are the parents who have found success-outlets for their energies, for they will not need their children as status symbols or as justifications.

10.

Blessed are the parents who do not pretend to be perfect, for their children will not be disillusioned.

ASSOCIATION FOR CHILDREN AND ADULTS WITH LEARNING DISABILITIES (ACLD)
PITTSBURGH, PENNSYLVANIA

FAMILY LOVE

A CHILD'S 10 COMMANDMENTS
TO PARENTS

COMMANDMENT 1:

My hands are small; please don't expect perfection whenever I make a bed, draw a picture, or throw a ball. My legs are short; please slow down so that I can keep up with you.

COMMANDMENT 2:

My eyes have not seen the world as yours have; please let me explore safely. Don't restrict me unnecessarily.

COMMANDMENT 3:

Housework will always be there. I'm only little for such a short time—please take time to explain things to me about this wonderful world, and do so willingly.

COMMANDMENT 4:

My feelings are tender; please be sensitive to my needs. Don't nag me all day long. (You wouldn't want to be nagged for your inquisitiveness.) Treat me as you would like to be treated.

COMMANDMENT 5:

I am a special gift from God; please treasure me as God intended you to do, holding me accountable for my actions, giving me guidelines to live by, and disciplining me in a loving manner.

COMMANDMENT 6:

I need your encouragement to grow. Please go easy on the criticism; remember, you can criticize the things I do without criticizing me.

COMMANDMENT 7:

Please give me the freedom to make decisions concerning myself. Permit me to fail, so that I can learn from my mistakes. Then someday I'll be prepared to make the kinds of decisions life requires of me.

COMMANDMENT 8:

Please don't do things over for me. Somehow that makes me feel that my efforts didn't quite measure up to your expectations. I know it's hard, but please don't try to compare me with my brother or my sister.

COMMANDMENT 9:

Please don't be afraid to leave for a weekend together. Kids need vacations from parents, just as parents need vacations from kids. Besides, it's a great way to show us kids that your marriage is very special.

COMMANDMENT 10:

Please take me to Sunday school and church regularly, setting a good example for me to follow. I enjoy learning more about God.

DR. KEVIN LEMAN
FROM "GETTING THE BEST OUT OF YOUR KIDS"

FAMILY LOVE

MEANINGFUL TOUCH

Hold hands during mealtime prayers.

Walk, one-on-one, with each child. Swing hands and talk.
Tell jokes. Sing.

Bad day? Sigh dramatically and say,
"I sure could use a great big hug from someone special."

Wonderful day? Shout, "Hey, everybody!
Come hug me! I had the best day!"

Make "Hug Sandwiches."
With your spouse, gently surprise unsuspecting children.

Declare "100 Hugs Day." Count.

Do Four-Direction Kisses: north (foreheads),
south (chins), east/west (cheeks).

Wrap your arm around your children during church,
while waiting together, or watching TV.

Apply The Pat Principle: "When in doubt, pat."
God made lots of patting places—heads, cheeks, knees,
hands, shoulders, backs.

LORRI CARDWELL-CASEY
FROM "HOMELIFE" MAGAZINE

50 WAYS TO LOVE YOUR CHILDREN

1. Hug every morning. 2. Go to zoos, parades, and amusement parks. 3. Hang their art and awards on the refrigerator. 4. Create family traditions. 5. Be patient. 6. Apologize when grumpy. 7. Go camping. 8. Play tic-tac-toe and hide-and-seek. 9. Always carry Band-Aids and gumdrops. 10. Know their strengths. 11. Compliment them. 12. Encourage them. 13. Appreciate them. 14. Eat meals together. 15. Slow down. 16. Respect their privacy. 17. Listen. 18. Don't discipline in anger. 19. Be consistent. 20. Say "I love you" frequently. 21. Let them be silly. 22. Accept imperfections. 23. Reward good behavior. 24. Explain the rules clearly. 25. Laugh often. 26. Go to their favorite restaurant. 27. Invite their friends over. 28. Buy ice cream cones. 29. Go on vacations. 30. Know when to be gentle and when to be firm. 31. Make birthdays unforgettable. 32. Teach responsibility and respect. 33. Choose your battles. 34. Don't embarrass them. 35. Help with schoolwork. 36. Protect them. 37. Build memories. 38. Keep promises. 39. Say "no" when needed. 40. Don't yell. 41. Give gifts. 42. Model virtues. 43. Pray with them. 44. Pray for them. 45. Talk with their teachers. 46. Tell them you're proud of them. 47. Reach out. 48. Count stars together. 49. Talk every bedtime. 50. Let go with a blessing.

DR. STEVE STEPHENS
FROM "STORIES FOR THE FAMILY'S HEART"

WORDS FOR YOUR FAMILY

I'm proud of you.

Way to go!

Bingo! You did it.

Magnificent.

I knew you could do it.

What a good helper.

You're very special to me.

I trust you.

What a treasure.

Hooray for you!

Beautiful work.

You're a real trooper.

Well done.

That's so creative.

You make my day.

You're a joy.

Give me a big hug.

You're such a good listener.

You figured it out.

I love you.

You're so responsible.

You remembered.

You're the best.

You sure tried hard.

I've got to hand it to you.

I couldn't be prouder of you.

You light up my day.

My buttons are popping off.

I'm praying for you.

You're wonderful.

I'm behind you.

GARY SMALLEY AND JOHN TRENT
FROM "LEAVING THE LIGHT ON"

18 MEMOS FROM YOUR CHILD

1.
Don't spoil me. I know quite well that I ought not to have all I ask for. I'm testing you.

2.
Don't be afraid to be firm with me. I prefer it; it makes me feel more secure.

3.
Don't let me form bad habits. I have to rely on you to detect them in the early stages.

4.
Don't make me feel smaller than I am. It only makes me behave stupidly big.

5.
Don't correct me in front of people if you can help it. I'll take much more notice if you talk quietly with me in private.

6.
Don't protect me from consequences. I need to learn the painful way sometimes.

7.
Don't be too upset when I say "I hate you." It isn't you I hate, but your power to thwart me.

8.
Don't take too much notice of my small ailments. Sometimes they get me the attention I need.

9.
Don't nag. If you do, I shall have to protect myself by appearing deaf.

10.
Don't make rash promises. Remember that I feel badly let down when promises are broken.

11.
Don't forget that I cannot explain myself as well as I should like. That is why I'm not always very accurate.

12.
Don't be inconsistent. That completely confuses me and makes me lose faith in you.

13.
Don't tell me my fears are silly. They are terribly real and you can do much to reassure me if you try to understand.

14.
Don't put me off when I ask questions. If you do you will find that I stop asking and seek my information elsewhere.

15.
Don't ever suggest that you are perfect or infallible. It gives me too great a shock when I discover you are neither.

16.
Don't ever think it is beneath your dignity to apologize to me. An honest apology makes me feel surprisingly warm toward you.

17.
Don't forget how quickly I am growing up. It must be very difficult for you to keep pace with me, but please try.

18.
Don't forget I need lots of understanding and love.

AUTHOR UNKNOWN

10 IDEAS FOR MAKING A
MEMORABLE MOTHER'S DAY

1.
*Have a florist deliver a corsage and
on the card tell her you're taking her to dinner.*

2.
*Create a May-to-May calendar using family pictures.
Place a star on a day each month for a special date you will have with her.*

3.
Gather scrapbook supplies and spend the day working on it together.

4.
Plant some colorful summer flowers in her yard and/or patio pots.

5.
*Have each family member write a special memory they have of her.
Tuck each note in a separate Mother's Day card
selected or created by each individual.*

6.
Prepare a picnic lunch and let her pick the place it will be enjoyed.

7.
*Have the family gather around her and ask her to share
favorite memories of her childhood.
Be sure to have a video or tape recorder going.*

8.

Give her a basket full of things that help her relax.
Include a long, narrow tablet and ask her to list things
she's been wishing help with. Recruit family members
to get the jobs done in the next few weeks.

9.

Give the gift of your time by helping her sort through pictures
and bring her photo album up-to-date.

10.

Remember to tell her how much you love her
and what you love about her.

MARILYN MCAULEY
MOTHER OF THREE, GRANDMOTHER OF SIX

10 IDEAS FOR A FABULOUS, UNFORGETTABLE FATHER'S DAY

1.

If you can't be together, mark your calendar so you will be sure to call your father. Include comments about what he means to you as a father, mentor, and friend.

2.

Pick a photo of you and your father together and write a note to him about why the picture is meaningful to you. Send it in time to arrive a day before Father's Day.

3.

Buy tickets to a game of his favorite sport and go together.

4.

Offer to join him at his church for the Father's Day services.

5.

Write him a letter thanking him for two or more traits he taught you that really make you a more successful adult.

6.

Record a cassette for him that shares a special memory of childhood that you both cherish so he can enjoy it in the car or at home.

7.

Order a beef stick and cheese box, or some other favorite snack gift package, and have it delivered a day early. Enclose a card that says you will join him to watch a game or movie of his choice.

8.

Make a video for him of your childhood home and include a commentary on memories and lessons you really value from your childhood.

9.

Take him to a dinner place of his choice and surprise him with two or three of his friends that he may not see often. Plan this for the day before or after Father's Day so they will be available.

10.

Ask your brothers and sisters to join you in writing notes sharing how your father's influence and availability over the years has benefited your family life. Include them in a memory book with a nice masculine cover.

WHAT KIDS APPRECIATE

1.
We were often spontaneously getting hugged even apart from completing a task or chore.

2.
They would let me explain my side of the story.

3.
They would take each of us out individually for a special breakfast with Mom and Dad.

4.
My mother always carried pictures of each of us in her purse.

5.
They would watch their tone of voice when they argued.

6.
My parents made sure that each one of us kids appeared in the family photos.

7.
They were willing to admit when they were wrong and say "I'm sorry."

8.
I saw my parents praying for me even when I didn't feel I deserved it.

9.
My folks wrote up a special "story of my birth" that they read to me every year.

10.
They attended all of my open houses at school.

11.
My mother and father would ask us children our opinions on important family decisions.

12.
My mom had a great sense of humor, but she never made us kids the brunt of her jokes.

13.
My parents wouldn't change things in my bedroom without asking me if it was okay with me.

14.
When I wrecked my parents' car, my father's first reaction was to hug me and let me cry instead of yelling at me.

15.

My parents were patient with me when I went through my long-hair stage in high school.

16.

My mother would pray with me about important decisions I was facing, or even that I would have a good day at school.

17.

We would have "family meetings" every two weeks where everyone would share their goals and problems.

18.

Even though I didn't like it at the time, the chores my parents made me do helped me learn responsibility.

19.

When I was down about my boyfriend breaking up with me, my father took extra time just to listen to me and cry with me.

20.

My parents never acted like they were perfect, and they never expected us to be perfect either.

21.

My mother would let me explain my point of view on issues—even when she disagreed with me. She always made me feel that my opinion was important.

22.

My parents didn't compare my abilities with those of my older brother or the other kids at school, but helped me see my own unique value.

GARY SMALLEY AND JOHN TRENT
SELECTED FROM A LIST OF ONE HUNDRED, FROM "THE BLESSING"

LONG-DISTANCE GRANDPARENTING

Call your grandchild regularly.
Keep up with your grandchild's interests and
activities and talk about them when you phone.

If you have access to a video recorder,
your grandchildren will love
a videotape of you reading a bedtime story.
Mail the tape and the book.

Cut out newspaper comic strips.
White out the words and write in your own.
Mail them to your grandchild.
Children love to receive mail addressed to them.

Send inexpensive gifts—a bookmark or stickers
on a day other than a birthday or holiday;
a little something that says "I love you."

As your grandchild learns to read, write an
original story of three or four paragraphs,
glue it to colored paper and mail it.

Take your grandchild's address with you
when you travel and send postcards.

Write letters about even simple things that happen at
your house: squirrels stashing their food under the
tree stump or birds singing in the feeder.
Ask simple questions and enclose self-addressed
stamped envelopes for the answers.

Send audio tapes telling your grandchild
what is happening at your house. Listening to the
tape makes the child feel part of your everyday
life. Tapes laced with expressions of love for the
child will reinforce feelings for you.

Know what interests your grandchild who's
in high school. If it's sports, be up on his or her
favorite team when they play.

Weave your faith in God into letters
and phone calls in a loving, honest way.

IRENE ENDICOTT
FROM "GRANDPARENTING BY GRACE"

TAKE THE TIME

1.
For parents of more than one child, choose one activity in each child's school that you will be involved in.

2.
Help your child choose at least one sport or group activity outside of school to be involved in.

3.
Choose one way in which your family can help the community, and talk about why community service is important.

4.
Read to or with your child every day, even if it's only for ten minutes.

5.
Include your children in some decisions about family activities, and work together to create a family calendar to record what you decide.

6.
Choose one fun activity that the whole family can do together— play music or softball, or plant a garden, bike, or cook together.

7.
Start a family scrapbook and ask everyone to add something to it each month.

8.
Ask your children to think of three ways to make your neighborhood safer, and then work on it together.

THE SEARCH INSTITUTE

14

Wisdom

Learning from the experience of others

WISE THINGS YOUR GRANDMA TOLD YOU

You are special.

Manners matter.

Treat others the way you want to be treated.

Your life can be what you want it to be.

Take the days one day at a time.

Always play fair.

Count your blessings, not your troubles.

Don't put limits on yourself.

It's never too late.

Put things back where you found them.

Decisions are too important to leave to chance.

Reach for the stars.

Clean up after yourself.

Nothing wastes more energy than worrying.

The longer you carry a problem, the heavier it gets.

Say "I'm sorry" when you've hurt someone.

A little love goes a long way.

Friendship is always a good investment.

Don't take things too seriously.

PATTI MACGREGOR
FROM "FAMILY TIMES: GROWING TOGETHER IN FUN AND FAITH"

TRUE UNDERSTANDING

WE DO NOT UNDERSTAND:

Joy...until we face sorrow.

Faith...until it is tested.

Peace...until faced with conflict.

Trust...until we are betrayed.

Love...until it is lost.

Hope...until confronted with doubts.

AUTHOR UNKNOWN

A SHORT COURSE
IN HUMAN RELATIONS

The six most important words: "I admit I made a mistake."

The five most important words: "You did a good job."

The four most important words: "What is your opinion?"

The three most important words: "If you please."

The two most important words: "Thank you."

The one most important word: "We."

The least important word: "I"

AUTHOR UNKNOWN
AS CITED IN "MORE OF... THE BEST OF BITS & PIECES," ROB GILBERT, PH.D. ED.

RULES FOR LIVING

If you open it, close it.

If you turn it on, turn it off.

If you unlock it, lock it up.

If you break it, admit it.

If you can't fix it, call in someone who can.

If you borrow it, return it.

If you value it, take care of it.

If you make a mess, clean it up.

If you move it, put it back.

If it belongs to someone else and you want to use it, get permission.

If you don't know how to operate it, leave it alone.

If it's none of your business, don't ask questions.

If it ain't broke, don't fix it.

If it will brighten someone's day, say it.

If it will tarnish someone's reputation, keep it to yourself.

AUTHOR UNKNOWN

PLANTING

If you plant for days
—plant flowers

If you plant for years
—plant trees

If you plant for eternity
—plant people

AUTHOR UNKNOWN

THINK WITH DISCERNMENT

He who knows not,
and knows not that he knows not,
is a fool;
shun him.

He who knows not,
and knows that he knows not,
is a child;
teach him.

He who knows,
and knows not that he knows,
is asleep;
wake him.

He who knows,
and knows that he knows,
is wise;
follow him.

PERSIAN PROVERB

RESPONSIBILITY

1.
Never put off till tomorrow what you can do today.

2.
Never trouble another for what you can do yourself.

3.
Never spend your money before you have it.

4.
Never buy what you do not want because it is cheap.

5.
Pride costs us more than hunger, thirst, and cold.

6.
We never repent of having eaten too little.

7.
Nothing is troublesome that we do willingly.

8.
How much pain have cost us the evils which have never happened.

9.
Take things always by their smooth handle.

10.
When angry, count to ten before you speak; if very angry, a hundred.

THOMAS JEFFERSON
THIRD PRESIDENT OF THE UNITED STATES

WISE SAYINGS FROM THE
BOOK OF PROVERBS

1.
Wise men store up knowledge.
But with the mouth of the foolish, ruin is at hand (10:14).

2.
When there are many words, transgression is unavoidable.
But he who restrains his lips is wise (10:19).

3.
He who goes about as a talebearer reveals secrets.
But he who is trustworthy conceals a matter (11:13).

4.
The one who guards his mouth preserves his life.
The one who opens wide his lips comes to ruin (13:3).

5.

He who goes about as a slanderer reveals secrets,
Therefore do not associate with a gossip (20:19).

6.

Like a bad tooth and an unsteady foot.
Is confidence in a faithless man in time of trouble (25:19).

7.

Like a city that is broken into and without walls.
Is a man who has no control over his spirit (25:28).

CHARLES R. SWINDOLL
FROM "COME BEFORE WINTER"

WISDOM

WISE SAYINGS FROM
POOR RICHARD'S ALMANAC

1.

To lengthen thy life, lessen thy meals.

2.

He that lies down with dogs shall rise up with fleas.

3.

Better slip with foot than tongue.

4.

Teach your child to hold his tongue; he'll learn fast enough to speak.

5.

Humility makes great men twice honorable.

6.

Tis easy to see, hard to foresee.

7.

Creditors have better memories than debtors.

8.

God heals, and the doctor takes the fees.

9.

No better relation than a prudent and faithful friend.

10.

Sell not virtue to purchase wealth, nor liberty to purchase power.

11.

Keep your eyes wide open before marriage, half shut afterward.

12.

Wish not so much to live long as to live well.

13.

He that sows thorns should not go barefoot.

14.

There are three things extremely hard: steel,
a diamond, and to know one's self.

15.

Success has ruin'd many a man.

BENJAMIN FRANKLIN
STATESMAN, INVENTOR, AND SCIENTIST

WHEN SOMETHING RIGHT
CAN GO WRONG

1.

When in our determination to be bold we become brazen

2.

When in our desire to be frank we become rude

3.

When in our effort to be watchful we become suspicious

4.

When we seek to be serious and become somber

5.

When we mean to be conscientious and become overscrupulous

A. W. TOZER
FROM "THE QUOTABLE TOZER"

SEVEN THINGS GOD HATES

1.
Haughty eyes

2.
A lying tongue

3.
Hands that shed innocent blood

4.
A heart that devises wicked schemes

5.
Feet that are quick to rush into evil

6.
A false witness who pours out lies

7.
A man who stirs up dissension among brothers

KING SOLOMON
FROM PROVERBS 6:16–19 (NIV)

KNOWING YOURSELF

1.

What we want most.

2.

What we think about most.

3.

How we use our money.

4.

What we do with our leisure time.

5.

The company we enjoy.

6.

Whom and what we admire.

7.

What we laugh at.

A. W. TOZER
FROM "THE QUOTABLE TOZER"

SIX DESTRUCTIVE MISTAKES

1.

The delusion that personal gain is made by crushing others

2.

*The tendency to worry about things
that cannot be changed or corrected*

3.

Insisting that a thing is impossible because we cannot accomplish it

4.

Refusing to set aside trivial preferences

5.

*Neglecting development and refinement of the mind, and
not acquiring the habit of reading and studying*

6.

Attempting to compel others to believe and live as we do

MARCUS TULLIUS CICERO
STATESMAN, PHILOSOPHER, AND ORATOR

LOVE...

Is very patient

Is kind

Is never jealous

Is never envious

Is never boastful

Is never proud

Is never haughty

Is never selfish

Is never rude

Does not demand its own way

Is not irritable or touchy

Does not hold grudges

Will hardly even notice when others do it wrong

Is never glad about injustice

Rejoices whenever truth wins out

Is loyal no matter what the cost

Will always believe

Will always expect the best

Will always defend

Goes on forever

ST. PAUL THE APOSTLE
CONDENSED FROM 1 CORINTHIANS 13:4-8

HOPE...

HOPE looks for the good in people instead of harping
on the worst in them.

HOPE opens doors where despair closes them.

HOPE discovers what can be done instead of
grumbling about what cannot be done.

HOPE draws its power from a deep trust in God
and the basic goodness of mankind.

HOPE "lights a candle" instead of "cursing the darkness."

HOPE regards problems, small or large, as opportunities.

HOPE cherishes no illusions, nor does it yield to cynicism.

AUTHOR UNKNOWN

*Delight yourself in the LORD and He will give you
the desires of your heart.*
PSALM 37:4, NIV

ACKNOWLEDGMENTS

More than a thousand books and magazines were researched and dozens of professionals interviewed for this collection. A diligent effort has been made to attribute original ownership of each list, and when necessary, obtain permission to reprint. If we have overlooked giving proper credit to anyone, please accept our apologies. If you will contact Multnomah Publishers, Inc., 601 N. LARCH ST., Sisters, Oregon 97759, with written documentation, corrections will be made prior to additional printings.

Notes and acknowledgments are shown in the order the lists appear in each section of the book. For permission to reprint a list, please request permission from the original source shown in the following bibliography. The editors gratefully acknowledge authors, publishers, and agents who granted permission for reprinting these lists.

SUCCESS

"Three Secrets to Success" by Sally Ride, astronaut. Source unknown.

"Five Reasons It's Easier to Succeed" by Cathy S. Truett from *It's Easier to Succeed Than to Fail* by Cathy S. Truett. Used by permission of Thomas Nelson, Inc., Nashville, TN, ©1989.

"Six Ways to Bury a Good Idea" as cited in *More of…The Best of Bits & Pieces,* Rob Gilbert, Ph.D., editor. © 1997 by The Economics Press, Inc., 12 Daniel Road, Fairfield, NJ 07004-2565; Phone: 800-526-2554 (US/Canada) or (+1 973) 227-1224 (worldwide). FAX: 973-227-9742 (US/Canada) or (+1 973) 227-9742 (worldwide). E-mail: *info@epinc.com.* Web site: *www.epinc.com.* Please contact The Economics Press, Inc., directly to purchase this book or for subscription information.

"Taking Control of Your Time" by Louise A. Ferrebee, Associate Editor, taken from "Squeezed for Time," *Marriage Partnership* magazine, Summer 1998.

"25 Traits of Entrepreneurs" by Earl Nightingale, co-founder Nightingale Conant, today the largest publisher of audio self-improvement programs in the world. For a catalog, call 1-800-525-9000.

"How to Give Constructive Criticism" by Glenda Hotton, MA DCD LMFT, family counselor in private practice, Valencia, California, specializing in chemical dependency, crisis, and trauma.

"Why We Procrastinate" taken from *The 15-Minute Money Manager* by Bob and Emilie Barnes. © 1993 by Harvest House Publishers, Eugene, Oregon 97402. Used by permission.

"Eight Things You Need to Know about Failure" by Dale Galloway from *How to Feel Like a Somebody Again!* © 1978 by Harvest House Publishers, Eugene, Oregon 97402. Used by permission of the author.

"Commonly Asked Interview Questions" excerpted from *About…Getting Your First Job,* one of the *Life Advice®* pamphlets produced by MetLife's Consumer Education Center (© 1996 by the Metropolitan Life Insurance Company, New York, NY). Used by permission. All rights reserved. To order a free copy of this booklet or any of the over eighty *Life Advice®* pamphlets, call 1-800-METLIFE or visit their web site at *www.metlife.com.*

"What to Include on a Resume" excerpted from *About…Getting Your First Job,* a *Life Advice®* pamphlet produced by MetLife's Consumer Education Center. See above for detailed information.

"Top 10 List for Interviewees" by Lani Williams, Director of Advancement, Western Seminary,

Portland, OR.

"10 Qualities of Successful Bosses" by June Hines Moore, author of *You Can Raise a Well-Mannered Child* and *The Etiquette Advantage*, published by Broadman & Holman, 127 Ninth Ave. N., Nashville, TN 37234. E-mail: *manners@artistotle.net*. Used by permission of Broadman & Holman and the author.

"12 Qualities of Successful Employees" by June Hines Moore. Used by permission of Broadman & Holman and the author.

"14 Ways to Shock Your Boss" by David Sanford, freelance writer. David Sanford is a lay pastor and senior director of publishing for the Luis Palau Evangelistic Association in Portland, Oregon. Used by permission.

"12 Steps to Creative Thinking" by James Lund, Marketing Copy Editor. Used by permission of author.

"How to Become a Lifelong Learner" by Bill Mowry from "Lifelong Learning," *Discipleship Journal*, May/June 1998. Bill Mowry provides leadership to Creation Resources, a Navigator ministry committed to helping people become ministry innovators and lifelong learners.

"Your Future Depends On..." taken from *The 15-Minute Money Manager* by Bob and Emilie Barnes. © 1993 by Harvest House Publishers, Eugene, Oregon 97402. Used by permission.

"What Is Success?" by Ralph Waldo Emerson (1803-1882).

FRIENDSHIP

"Hints for a Happy Friendship" by Bruce and Cheryl Bickel and Stan and Karin Jantz from *Life's Little Handbook of Wisdom*, published by Barbour Publishing, P.O. Box 719, Uhlrichsville, Ohio, 44683, ©1992. Used by permission.

"How to Get Along with People" by Norman Vincent Peale from *Help Yourself With God's Help* booklet. Used by permission of the Peale Center, Pawling, NY.

"Celebrate Your Differences" by Dr. Steve Stephens from *Marriage: Experience the Best*, published by Vision House Publishing, Gresham, OR, ©1996. Used by permission of the author.

"Rating Yourself as a Friend" from *In the Company of Friends* by Brenda Hunter and Holly Larson, Multnomah Publishers, Inc., Sisters, OR, © 1996. Used by permission.

"To Be a Good Friend" taken from *Friends Through Thick and Thin* by Gloria Gaither, Sue Buchanan, Peggy Benson, and Joy MacKenzie. © 1998 by The Zondervan Corporation. Used by permission of Zondervan Publishing House.

"Watch What You Say" from *God Came Near* by Max Lucado, Multnomah Publishers, Inc., Sisters, OR, © 1987. Used by permission.

"How to Forgive and Forget" excerpted from *Forgive And Forget* by Lewis B. Smedes. © 1984 by Lewis B. Smedes. Reprinted by permission of HarperCollins Publishers, Inc.

"12 Times to Say 'I'm Sorry'" by Dr. Steve Stephens, Clackamas, Oregon. Used by permission of the author.

"Mending a Friendship" by Alan Loy McGinnis. Reprinted from *The Friendship Factor* by Alan Loy McGinnis, © 1979 Augsburg Publishing House, Minneapolis, MN. Used by permission of Augsburg Fortress.

"If You're Going to Fight..." from *Somehow Inside Eternity: Thoughts to Last an Eternity* by Dr. Richard

C. Halverson, Multnomah Publishers, Inc., Sisters, OR, ©1980. Used by permission.

"How to Build a Friendship with Someone You're Dating" by Dick Purnell. This article was taken from *Decision* magazine, February, 1998; © 1998 Billy Graham Evangelistic Association, used by permission, all rights reserved.

"Finding a Listening Ear" by Janis Long Harris from *Marriage Partnership* magazine, Winter 1997. Used by permission of the author.

"Keeping a Confidence" by Joanna Wallace and Deanna Wallace from *Especially for a Woman* by Joanna Wallace and Deanna Wallace. Used by permission of Thomas Nelson, Inc., Nashville, TN, © 1994.

"10 Ways to Welcome a New Neighbor" by Barbara Baumgardner, freelance writer, Bend, Oregon. Used by permission of the author.

"Nurturing Long-Distance Friendships" by Renée Sanford. Renée Sanford is a freelance writer living in Portland, Oregon. Married with four children; her best friend lives in Europe.

"What Is Love?" by Father James Keller, founder, The Christophers, as cited in *More of...The Best of Bits & Pieces,* Rob Gilbert, Ph.D., editor. © 1997 by The Economics Press, Inc.

VIRTUE

"Destiny" by Frank Outlaw, as cited in *More of...The Best of Bits & Pieces,* Rob Gilbert, Ph.D., editor. © 1997 by The Economics Press, Inc.

"20 Gifts to Give" by Charles R. Swindoll from *The Finishing Touch,* Charles R. Swindoll, © 1994, Word Publishing, Nashville, Tennessee. All rights reserved.

"Actions That Take Courage" by Dr. Steve Stephens, Clackamas, Oregon. Used by permission of the author.

"Benjamin Franklin's 13 Virtues" from *The Autobiography and Other Writings by Benjamin Franklin,* Peter Shaw, editor, Bantam Books, NY ©1982.

"What I Believe In and Value" from *Getting the Right Things Right* by Charlie Hedges, Multnomah Publishers, Inc., Sisters, OR, ©1996. Used by permission of the author.

"People with Character" from *A Diamond in the Rough* compiled by Andrew Stanley. Used by permission of Thomas Nelson, Inc., Nashville, TN, ©1997.

"10 Reasons for Going to Church" by Theodore Roosevelt, condensed from the Ladies' Home Journal, 1917.

"Extreme Virtues" by Ashley Cooper, American columnist, quoted from *More of...The Best of Bits & Pieces.*

"The Adventure of Giving" by Becky Brodin, Minneapolis, MN. Condensed from *Discipleship Journal,* Issue 88, 1995. Used by permission of the author.

"Kindness" by Mother Teresa.

"Rules for Christian Living" by John Wesley.

"Moral Guidance for Your Family" by Mary Ann Kuharski, Minneapolis, MN. Condensed from *HomeLife* magazine, April 1997. Used by permission of the author.

"The 10 Commandments" from *The Holy Bible,* New Living Translation (NLT) © 1996. Used by permission of Tyndale House Publishers, Inc. All rights reserved.

LIFE'S TRANSITIONS

"Things to Feel Nostalgic About" taken from *Growing Strong in the Seasons of Life* by Charles R. Swindoll. ©1983, The Zondervan Corporation. Used by permission of Zondervan Publishing House.

"Don't Let Your New Baby Drive You Apart" by Rob Parsons from *The 60-Minute Marriage Builder* published by Broadman & Holman, Nashville, TN, ©1998. Used by permission.

"Countdown to College" by Kathy Chapman Sharp and Rebekah D. Sharp from *HomeLife* magazine, July 1997. Used by permission of the authors.

"When Your Adult Children Want to Move Back Home" by Florence Littauer, adapted from *Wake Up, Women!* (Word Publishing). Florence is an author of twenty-seven books and is best known for her book, *Personality Plus,* which has sold a million copies and is translated into eighteen languages. Used by permission of the author.

"Preparing for Retirement" by Alice Gray, Dr. Steve Stephens, and John Van Diest. Used by permission of the authors.

"Four Ways to Grow Old Gracefully" by Abigail Van Buren from *The Oregonian*, July 4, 1998.

"Stay Young While Growing Old" by Tress Van Diest. Used by permission of the author.

"Tough Questions to Ask Elderly Parents" by The Financial Literacy Center, from *New Man* magazine, March/April 1998. Used by permission.

"How Adult Children Can Help Their Parents" by David O. Moberg. Taken from *Decision* magazine, May, 1998; © 1998 Billy Graham Evangelistic Association, used by permission, all rights reserved.

"Questions Parents Should Ask before Moving in with Their Children" by The Mayo Foundation from Mayo Clinic Health Letter, Vol. 9, Dec. 1991 and *A Better Tomorrow* magazine, Nov./Dec. 1994. Used by permission.

"Nursing Home Checklist" by Dan Grady, Chaplain for Nursing Home Ministries. Used by permission of the author.

"A Road Map through Grief" excerpted from *Harsh Grief, Gentle Hope* by Mary White. Used by permission of NavPress, Colorado Springs, CO, ©1995. All rights reserved.

"Recovery from Grief" by Sister Teresa McIntier from *Hospice of Bend Grief Manual*. Used by permission.

"Heaven Is a Place..." by Jay Carty from *Playing the Odds*, published by Vision House Publishing, Gresham, OR, ©1995. Used by permission of the author.

MARRIAGE

"18 Attributes to Look for in a Marriage Partner" by Al and Alice Gray, Redmond, Oregon. Used by permission of the authors.

"What Keeps a Marriage Strong?" by Dr. Steve Stephens, Clackamas, Oregon. Used by permission of the author.

"His Needs, Her Needs" by Willard Harley from *His Needs, Her Needs: Basic Needs in Marriage*. Used by permission of Baker Book House, Grand Rapids, Michigan, ©1986.

"Springboards to Deeper Conversation" by Carole Mayhall from *Lord, Teach Me Wisdom*. Used by permission of NavPress, Colorado Springs, CO, ©1979.

"Things *Not* to Say to Your Spouse" by Dr. Steve Stephens from *Marriage: Experience the Best*, published by Vision House Publishers, Gresham, OR, ©1996. Used by permission of the author.

"Things to Say to Your Spouse" by Dr. Steve Stephens from *Marriage: Experience the Best*, published by Vision House Publishers, Gresham, OR, ©1996. Used by permission of the author.

"How to Make Your Marriage Healthy" by Jeff Herring. Reprinted with permission of Knight-Ridder/Tribune Information Services. Condensed from *The Oregonian* newspaper, April 13, 1998.

"20 Ways to Make Your Wife Feel Special" by Al Gray, Redmond, Oregon. Used by permission of the author.

"20 Ways to Make Your Husband Feel Special" by Alice Gray, Redmond, Oregon. Used by permission of the author.

"Togetherness" by Dr. Steve Stephens, Clackamas, Oregon. Used by permission of the author.

"50 Gifts for Marriage" taken from *Understanding the One You Love* by Dr. Steve Stephens, © 1998, published by Harvest House Publishers, Eugene, Oregon 97402. Used by permission.

"Being a Real Man" by Dr. Robert Lewis. Dr. Robert Lewis, teaching pastor at Fellowship Bible Church in Little Rock, Arkansas, also gives leadership to Men's Fraternity, which reaches and teaches men throughout the church and community in the biblical principles of authentic manhood. This exciting ministry is catching on across the country and around the world, where countless small groups are undertaking this study together in churches, neighborhoods, cell blocks, corporate offices, and college campuses. Used by permission.

"Bonds of Intimacy" by Ed Wheat, M.D., condensed from *Love Life for Every Married Couple* by Ed Wheat with Gloria Oakes Perkins. © 1980, 1987 by Ed Wheat, M.D. Used by permission of Zondervan Publishing House.

"Reigniting Romance after Age 50" by Claudia and David Arp from *New Man* magazine, May 1998. Used by permission of Strang Communications.

"20 Creative, Romantic Ideas That Cost under $20" by Gary Smalley with John Trent from *Love is a Decision*, Gary Smalley with John Trent, ©1989, Word Publishing, Nashville, Tennessee. All rights reserved.

"10 Suggestions for Touching" by Ed Wheat, M.D., condensed from a list of twenty-five suggestions from *Love Life for Every Married Couple* by Ed Wheat with Gloria Oakes Perkins. © 1980, 1987 by Ed Wheat, M.D. Used by permission of Zondervan Publishing House.

"Wedding Anniversary Gifts," selected.

HOME

"Overcoming Clutter" by Allison Allison, an interior designer and homeschooler who resides in Milwaukie, Oregon, with her husband and two children.

"Hints for Kitchen Organization" by Emilie Barnes. Taken from *More Hours in My Day* by Emilie Barnes. © 1982, 1989, 1994 by Harvest House Publishers, Eugene, Oregon 97402. Used by permission.

"How Long to Keep It" excerpted from *Your Financial Organizer*, © 1997 TIAA-CREF. Used by permission.

"Time Makers" by Allison Allison, an interior designer and homeschooler who resides in Milwaukie, Oregon, with her husband and two children.

"Babysitter Checklist" compiled by Alice Gray, Redmond, Oregon. Used by permission of the author.

"Four Axioms of Spending" by Howard L. Dayton, Jr., © 1979 from *Getting Out of Debt*. Used by permission of Tyndale House, Publishers, Inc., Wheaton, IL. All rights reserved. Adapted from *Money, Frustration or Freedom*.

"Simple Ways to Cut Expenses" from *Say Goodbye to Regret* by Robert Jeffress. Published by Multnomah Publishers, Inc., Sisters, OR, © 1998. Used by permission.

"Planning Ahead for Holiday Shopping" by Becky McClure, Milwaukie, Oregon. Used by permission of the author.

"Holiday Entertaining With Less Stress" by Becky McClure, Milwaukie, Oregon. Used by permission of the author.

"Make Your Old Home Feel Like New" by Nancy Larson, Gresham, Oregon. Used by permission of the author.

"Home Safety Tips" by Tom Philbin, Centerport, New York, from *Parade* magazine, February 15, 1998. Used by permission of the author.

"Crime Stoppers' Checklist" excerpted from *About...Keeping Your Home Safe,* a *Life Advice*® pamphlet produced by MetLife's Consumer Education Center (© 1996 by the Metropolitan Life Insurance Company, New York, NY). Used by permission. All rights reserved. To order a free copy of this booklet or any of the over eighty *Life Advice*® pamphlets, call 1-800-METLIFE or visit their web site at *www.metlife.com*.

"Fire Safety Checklist" excerpted from *About...Keeping Your Home Safe,* a *Life Advice*® pamphlet produced by MetLife's Consumer Education Center (© 1996 by the Metropolitan Life Insurance Company, New York, NY). See above details.

"Prepare for Disasters" provided by The American Red Cross, Oregon Trail Chapter. Used by permission.

HEALTH

"Danger Signals of Stress" by Carol Clifton, Ph.D., Licensed Psychologist. Used by permission of the author.

"21 Factors for a Long, Healthy Life" from *The Prevention Index* (Emmaus, PA, Rodale Press). Used by permission.

"Do You Need More Sleep?" by Patricia Anstett. Reprinted with permission of Knight-Ridder/Tribune Information Services.

"Keys to a Lifetime of Fitness" excerpted from *About...Fitness and Exercise,* a *Life Advice*® pamphlet produced by MetLife's Consumer Education Center (© 1996 by the Metropolitan Life Insurance Company, New York, NY). Used by permission. All rights reserved. To order a free copy of this booklet or any of the over eighty *Life Advice*® pamphlets, call 1-800-METLIFE or visit their web site at *www.metlife.com*.

"Benefits of Exercise" excerpted from *About...Fitness and Exercise,* a *Life Advice*® pamphlet produced by MetLife's Consumer Education Center (© 1996 by the Metropolitan Life Insurance Company, New York, NY). Used by permission. All rights reserved. See above details.

"10 Simple Ways to Build Exercise into Your Day" by Carl Dreizler and Mary E. Ehemann from *52 Ways to Lose Weight*. Used by permission of Thomas Nelson, Inc., Nashville, TN, ©1992.

"Back Savers" from *The Back Almanac*. Used by permission of Lanier Publishing International, Ltd., Petaluma, California.

"12 Reasons to Keep Your Child Home from School" by Pat Van Diest, R.N. Used by permission of the author.

"10 Ways to Help Prevent Heart Disease" by Terry Shintani and Janice M. T. Miller from *52 Ways to Prevent Heart Disease*. Used by permission of Thomas Nelson, Inc., Nashville, TN, ©1993.

"Recognize a Heart Attack!" is taken from the American Heart Association booklet titled *Heart Attack and Stroke: Signals and Action*. Used by permission.

"Recognize a Stroke!" is taken from the American Heart Association booklet titled *Heart Attack and Stroke: Signals and Action*. Used by permission.

"Fourteen Warning Signs for Cancer" from the American Cancer Society, Bend, Oregon office. Used by permission. For more information, call 1-800-227-2345.

CONTENTMENT

"A Better Life" from *Taking the Lead* by Ron Jenson. Published by Multnomah Publishers, Inc., Sisters, OR, © 1998. Used by permission.

"Choices" from *The Seven Laws of the Harvest* by John Lawrence. ©1975 published by Kregel Publications, Grand Rapids, MI. Used by permission.

"Nine Essentials for Contented Living" by Goethe.

"A Prayer of Mother Teresa" from *Mother Teresa: A Simple Path*, compiled by Lucinda Vardey. © 1995 by Mother Teresa. Reprinted by permission of Ballantine Books, a Division of Random House, Inc.

"Leave It to God" from *The Finishing Touch*, Charles R. Swindoll, ©1994, Word Publishing, Nashville, Tennessee. All rights reserved.

"13 Rules to Live By" by General Colin Powell from *Parade* magazine, an August 13, 1989 article by David Wallechinsky. Used by permission.

"Day by Day" by Carl Dreizler and Mary E. Ehemann from *52 Ways to Lose Weight*. Used by permission of Thomas Nelson, Inc., Nashville, TN, ©1992.

"How Attitude Affects Us" taken from *Motivation to Last a Lifetime* by Ted W. Engstrom with Robert C. Larson. © 1984 by The Zondervan Corporation. Used by permission of Zondervan Publishing House.

"How to Forfeit Peace" by Elisabeth Elliot from *Keep a Quiet Heart*. Published by Servant Publications, Ann Arbor, MI, ©1995. Published in the United Kingdom, 1997 edition, by Paternoster Press, P.O.Box 300, Carisle, Cumbria, CA3 OQS. Used by permission of the author.

"How to Find Peace" by Elisabeth Elliott from *Keep a Quiet Heart*. Published by Servant Publications, Ann Arbor, MI, ©1995. Published in the United Kingdom, 1997 edition, by Paternoster Press, P.O.Box 300, Carisle, Cumbria, CA3 OQS. Used by permission of the author.

"12 Reasons to Pray" by John Van Diest. Used by permission of the author.

"12 Things to Pray For" by J. Carl Laney, Professor of Biblical Literature, Western Seminary. Used by permission of the author.

"I'm Thankful For…" by Tami Stephens, Clackamas, Oregon. Used by permission of the author.

"What We Can Control" by John Lawrence from *The Seven Laws of the Harvest*. ©1975. Published by Kregel Publications, Grand Rapids, MI. Used by permission.

"You're Blessed When…" by Eugene H. Peterson from *The Message*. © 1993, 1994, 1995. Used by permission of NavPress Publishing Group, Colorado Springs, CO.

STANDING STRONG

"Winning Over Worry" by Linda Shepherd from *Love's Little Recipes for Life*. Published by Multnomah Publishers, Inc., Sisters, OR, ©1997. Used by permission.

"In the Eye of the Storm" by Max Lucado from *In the Eye of the Storm*, Max Lucado, © 1991, Word Publishing, Nashville, Tennessee. All rights reserved.

"Overcoming Depression & Discouragement" by Dr. Steve Stephens, Clackamas, Oregon. Used by permission of the author.

"A Positive Focus," Philippians 4:8, *The Holy Bible,* New International Version (NIV), ©1973, 1978, 1984 by International Bible Society, used by permission of Zondervan Publishing House. All rights reserved.

"Stress Busters" by Pam Vredevelt, Licensed Professional Counselor. ©1999. Used by permission of the author.

"Are You Doing Too Much?" by Ramona Richards from *HomeLife* magazine, April 1998. Ramona is a singer, writer, and speaker. Her specialty topics include prayer, single parents, the Internet, and women in the Bible. Contact her ministry at *Psalm98Min@aol.com* or P.O. Box 716, Goodlettsville, TN 37070 for more information. Used by permission.

"Eight Questions to Ask before Saying Yes" by Alice Gray and Dr. Steve Stephens. Used by permission of the authors.

"Nine Goals for Authentic Growth" by Joe D. Batten from *New Man* magazine, March/April 1998. Used by permission of Strang Communications.

"10 Beliefs that Lead to Anger" by Glenda Hotton, MA, COC, LMFT, family counselor in private practice in Valencia, California, specializing in chemical dependency, crisis, and trauma. ©1998. Used by permission.

"Dealing With Anger" by Dr. Steve Stephens from *Marriage: Experience the Best*, published by Vision House Publishing, Gresham, OR, ©1996. Used by permission of the author.

"The World Needs People…" taken from *Motivation to Last a Lifetime* by Ted W. Engstrom with Robert C. Larson. © 1984 by The Zondervan Corporation. Used by permission of Zondervan Publishing House.

FAMILY FUN

"Top 10 Free Toys for Children" by Crystal Kirgiss, mother of three boys and columnist for the *Detroit Lake Tribune*. ©1996. Used by permission of the author.

"Family Guidelines for Television" by Alice Gray, Dr. Steve Stephens, and John Van Diest. Used by permission of the authors.

"Family Guidelines for Using the Internet," from *New Man* magazine, September/October 1995. Used by permission of Strang Communications.

"The Eight Best Surprises a Kid Ever Had" condensed from a list of ten from *Family Times: Growing Together in Fun and Faith* by Jerry and Patti MacGregor. © 1999 by Harvest House Publishers, Eugene, Oregon 97402. Used by permission.

"20 Fun Activities" by Tami Stephens, Clackamas, Oregon. Used by permission of the author.

"48 Great Books to Read Aloud" by Janice E. Byram, teacher. Used by permission of the author.

"How to Choose a Video for Your Family" by Ted Baehr condensed from *The War Cry*, The Salvation Army magazine, September 10, 1994. Used by permission.

"20 Great Children's Movies" selected from *Family Video Guide to Recommended Movies* edited by John H. Evans. Published by Movie Morality Ministries, Inc., Richardson, TX, © 1996. To order the video guide or to subscribe to a semi-monthly guide called *Preview Family Movie and TV Review*, call 1-800-807-8071 or visit their web site at *www.previewonline.org*.

"20 Great Family Movies" selected from *Family Video Guide to Recommended Movies* edited by John H. Evans. Published by Movie Morality Ministries, Inc., Richardson, TX, © 1996. See above for additional information.

"20 Great Table Games" by Tami Stephens, Clackamas, Oregon. Used by permission of the author.

FAMILY LIFE

"The Job of Parents" from *Parenting Isn't for Cowards*, James C. Dobson, © 1987, Word Publishing, Nashville, Tennessee. All rights reserved.

"10 Family Commitments" by Dr. Greg Cynaumon from *How to Avoid Alienating Your Kids in 10 Easy Steps*, published by Mood Press, Chicago, IL, © 1993. Used by permission of the author.

"Six Steps to Successful Communication" as cited in *More of... The Best of Bits & Pieces*, Rob Gilbert, Ph.D., editor. © 1997 by The Economics Press, Inc.

"20 Conversation Starters" from *Family Times: Growing Together in Fun and Faith* by Jerry and Patti MacGregor. © 1999 by Harvest House Publishers, Eugene, Oregon 97402. Used by permission.

"Why Divorce Hurts Children" by Archibald Hart from *Moody* magazine, May 1985. Used by permission of the author.

"10 Ways to Be a Great Dad" condensed from the pamphlet *10 Ways to Be A Better Date*, published by The National Fatherhood Initiative. Used by permission.

"Help for Discouraged Parents" from *Parenting Isn't for Cowards*, Dr. James C. Dobson, © 1987, Word Publishing, Nashville, Tennessee. All rights reserved.

"Family Team Building" by Tricia Goyer and Cindy McCormick Martinusen from *HomeLife* magazine, July 1998. Used by permission of Cindy McCormick Martinusen.

"Be a Parent Teachers Like to See" by Joe Neff condensed from *Focus on the Family* magazine, September 1998. Used by permission of the author.

"Five Musts for Every Family" by Gary Chapman from *Five Signs of a Functional Family*, © 1997 by Northfield Publishing, Chicago, Illinois. Used by permission.

FAMILY VALUES

"Qualities to Pass on to Your Children" taken from *Growing Strong in the Seasons of Life* by Charles R. Swindoll. © 1983 by Charles R. Swindoll, Inc. Used by permission of Zondervan Publishing House.

"The 10 Commandments of Discipline" by Dr. Greg Cynaumon from *How to Avoid Alienating Your Kids in 10 Easy Steps*, © 1993. Used by permission of the author.

"The Six A's of Parenting" by Dr. Steve Stephens, Clackamas, Oregon. Used by permission of the author.

"Parenting 101" by John Rosemond from *Bottom Line Personal*, Vol. 13, No. 3. Family psychologist John Rosemond is the author of eight bestselling parenting books and is one of America's most popular public speakers. For more information, see his web site at *www.rosemond.com*. Used by permission.

"10 Things to Do When Children Are Afraid" by Dr. Steve Stephens, Clackamas, Oregon. Used by permission of the author.

"Jobs Kids Can Do" by Doreen Button, mom to three busy home-school kids. Used by permission of the author.

"Winning Over the Picky Eater" excerpted with permission from *How to Get Your Kid to Eat...But Not Too Much*, Bull Publishing, Palo Alto, CA. For more information about Ellyn Satter's books and teaching materials, see *www.ellynsatter.com* or call 1-800-808-7976.

"Table Manners" by June Hines Moore, etiquette consultant with fifteen years' experience. Author of *You Can Raise a Well-Mannered Child* and *The Etiquette Advantage*.

"When to Teach Your Child Manners" from *You Can Raise a Well-Mannered Child* by June Hines Moore. Used by permission of the author and Broadman & Holman Publishers, 127 Ninth Avenue, North, Nashville, TN 37234, ©1996.

"The 10 Most Important Manners to Teach Your Children" from *You Can Raise a Well-Mannered Child* by June Hines Moore.

FAMILY LOVE

"Loving Your Kids" by Billy Graham from *God's Little Instruction Book for Dad*, Published by Honor Books, Tulsa, OK, ©1995.

"Today's Kids Desperately Need Heroes Who..." by Marty Wilkins, Milwaukie, Oregon. Used by permission of the author.

"Blessed Are Parents Who..." from The Association for Children and Adults with Learning Disabilities, Pittsburgh, PA. Used by permission.

"A Child's 10 Commandments to Parents" taken from *Getting the Best Out of Your Kids* (a revised and updated edition of the book formerly titled *Parenthood Without Hassles*) by Dr. Kevin Leman. © 1992 by Harvest House Publishers, Eugene, Oregon 97402. Used by permission.

"Meaningful Touch" by Lorri Cardwell-Casey from *HomeLife* magazine. Used by permission of the author. Lorri Cardwell-Casey has over 350 magazine credits. She lives in Bella Vista, AK and can be reached at *lorricasey@aol.com*. Her telephone number is 501-855-0590.

"50 Ways to Love Your Children" by Dr. Steve Stephens from *Stories for the Family's Heart* by Alice Gray. Published by Multnomah Publishers, Inc., Sisters, OR, ©1998. Used by permission of Dr. Steve

Stephens.

"Words for Your Family" from *Leaving the Light On* by Gary Smalley and John Trent. Published by Multnomah Publishers, Inc., Sisters, OR, © 1991. Used by permission.

"10 Ideas for Making a Memorable Mother's Day" by Marilyn McAuley, Milwaukie, Oregon. Used by permission of the author.

"10 Ideas for a Fabulous, Unforgettable Father's Day" by Daniel L. McAuley, Milwaukie, Oregon. Used by permission of the author.

"What Kids Appreciate" by Gary Smalley and John Trent condensed from a list of one hundred from *The Blessing* by Gary Smalley and John Trent. Used by permission of Thomas Nelson, Inc., Nashville, TN, ©1986.

"Long-Distance Grandparenting" by Irene Endicott condensed from *Grandparenting by Grace*. © 1994, Broadman & Holman, 127 Ninth Avenue, North, Nashville, TN 37234. Used by permission.

"Take the Time" reprinted with permission from *Take the Time*, Search Institute, Minneapolis, MN. All rights reserved by Search Institute, 1-800-888-7828. © 1998.

WISDOM

"Wise Things Your Grandma Told You" by Patti MacGregor from *Family Times: Growing Together in Fun and Faith* by Jerry and Patti MacGregor. © 1999 by Harvest House Publishers, Eugene, Oregon 97402. Used by permission.

"A Short Course in Human Relations" as cited in *More of…The Best of Bits & Pieces,* Rob Gilbert, Ph.D., editor. © 1997 by The Economics Press, Inc.

"Responsibility" by Thomas Jefferson.

"Wise Sayings From the Book of Proverbs" taken from *Come Before Winter* by Charles R. Swindoll. © 1985, by The Zondervan Corporation. Used by permission of Zondervan Publishing House.

"Wise Sayings From Poor Richard's Almanac" by Benjamin Franklin selected from *Poor Richard's Almanac.*

"When Something Right Can Go Wrong" by A. W. Tozer from *The Quotable Tozer*, compiled by Harry Verploegh, Christian Publications, Camp Hill, PA, ©1994. Page 158.

"Seven Things God Hates" from the *NIV Study Bible, New International Version,* ©1985 by the Zondervan Corporation, Grand Rapids, MI.

"Knowing Yourself" by A. W. Tozer from *The Quotable Tozer*, compiled by Harry Verploegh, Christian Publications, Camp Hill, PA, ©1994. Page 165.

"Six Destructive Mistakes" Marcus Tullius Cicero (106-43 B.C.).

"Love…" by St. Paul the Apostle, adapted from 1 Corinthians 13:4–8.

LISTS TO LIVE BY

"*Lists to Live By* is sometimes humorous, often thought-provoking, and always practical and inspiring. At a time when most of us live by our daily 'to-do' lists, this book reminds us how 'to-be.'"

—NANCY STAFFORD
Actress / author

"Every home will be blessed to have a copy of this extraordinary book, *Lists to Live By*, in its library. Any question you might have about living in our fast-paced world can be answered thanks to an easy-reference style and wise, practical advice and counsel.

"You will find each list in this marvelous book a key to living a successful, happy life. Here is the invaluable advice that we need for ourselves as well as a resource to guide our children. This book will change your life if you apply these insightful lists…they will bring order, peace, and love!

"Read it, use it, share it, live by it…you'll live a better life."

—KEN WALES
Executive producer,
CBS television series "Christy"; author / speaker

2

Lists
to live by

FOR EVERYTHING
THAT REALLY MATTERS

COMPILED BY

ALICE GRAY

STEVE STEPHENS

JOHN VAN DIEST

Multnomah® Publishers *Sisters, Oregon*

CONTENTS

PEOPLE LOVE LISTS!

LISTS ARE...

- *short*
- *to the point*
- *neat and tidy*
- *easy to read*
- *hard to forget*
- *and you can live your life by them!*

Throughout history, people have had lists. From Moses to Mother Teresa to Colin Powell, lists have helped people to prioritize life and bring into focus what is of greatest value.

Reading a single list is like having the best parts of a whole book gathered into a few words. Huge truths wrapped in small packages. In this second collection of Lists to Live By, you have a virtual library of information at your fingertips.

One wise sage said, "The book of life is lived in chapters, so know your page number." But as life gets more cluttered with too many things, too many activities, and even too many words…perhaps instead of page numbers, we should know our lists—lists about wisdom, contentment, success, health, marriage, family, friends, and virtue. These are the things that really matter…and they are all here in this book, just waiting for you to discover them.

ALICE GRAY   DR. STEVE STEPHENS   JOHN VAN DIEST

1
Success

Growing through learning and creativity

SEVEN FAVORITE QUOTATIONS
OF ZIG ZIGLAR

1.

Happiness is not a when or a where, but a here and a now!

2.

When you associate with winners, your chances of winning go up!

3.

You don't have to be great to start, but you have to start to be great.

4.

If you aren't on fire, then your wood is wet.

5.

I'm not going to ease up, slow up, or give up until I'm taken up.

6.

You don't drown by falling into water. You only drown if you stay there.

7.

You can have everything you want
if you help enough other people get what they want.

ZIG ZIGLAR
AUTHOR OF "I'LL SEE YOU AT THE TOP"
FROM "CHRISTIAN READER" MAGAZINE

PERSISTENCE

Realize that failure does not mean you should quit.

A test is not a signal to give up.

In every failure, God plants a seed of success.

Never blame others for your lack of success.

CHARLES STANLEY
FROM "IN TOUCH" MAGAZINE

THREE GREAT ESSENTIALS

THREE ESSENTIALS FOR ACHIEVING
ANYTHING WORTHWHILE:

1.
Hard work

2.
Stick-to-itiveness

3.
Common sense

THOMAS EDISON
INVENTOR

20 POWER THOUGHTS

1.
Curiosity leads to creativity.

2.
Trust your positive instincts.

3.
When it's dark, look for the stars.

4.
Faith is always stronger than failure.

5.
Build a dream and the dream builds you.

6.
Obstacles are opportunities in disguise.

7.
When the going gets tough—laugh.

8.
Don't miss the best things in life.

9.
Itemize your assets.

10.
Fix the problem, not the blame.

11.
Share the credit.

12.

Never make an irreversible decision in a down time.

13.

Treasure time like gold.

14.

Never judge reality by your limited experiences.

15.

You will never win if you never begin.

16.

Success without conflict is unrealistic.

17.

Make sure your dreams are big enough for God to fit in.

18.

Never let a problem become an excuse.

19.

*When it looks like you've exhausted all possibilities,
remember this: you haven't.*

20.

Always look at what you have left. Never look at what you have lost.

ROBERT H. SCHULLER
FROM "POWER THOUGHTS"

THE TRUE MEASURE OF SUCCESS

To be able to carry money without spending it;

To be able to bear an injustice without retaliating;

To be able to do one's duty when critical eyes watch;

To be able to keep at a job until it is finished;

To be able to do the work and let others receive the recognition;

To be able to accept criticism without letting it whip you;

To like those who push you down;

To love when hate is all about you;

To follow God when others put detour signs in your path;

To have a peace of heart and mind because you have given God your best;

This is the true measure of success.

AUTHOR UNKNOWN

LADDER OF SUCCESS

Plan purposefully.

Prepare prayerfully.

Proceed positively.

Pursue persistently.

AFRICAN-AMERICAN PROVERB

PEOPLE WHO MAKE A
DIFFERENCE HAVE...

INITIATIVE *being a self-starter with*
contagious energy.

VISION *seeing beyond the obvious,*
claiming new objectives.

UNSELFISHNESS *releasing the controls and the glory.*

TEAMWORK *involving, encouraging,*
and supporting others.

FAITHFULNESS *hanging in there in season and out.*

ENTHUSIASM *providing affirmation,*
excitement to the task.

DISCIPLINE *modeling great character*
regardless of the odds.

CONFIDENCE *representing security, faith,*
and determination.

CHARLES R. SWINDOLL
FROM "THE FINISHING TOUCH"

THOUGHTS THAT HOLD US BACK

I can't

That's a problem

That's not fair

I won't

It's been tried before

Never

Stupid

It won't work

It's too hard

Impossible

It's hopeless

I'm not good enough

Hate

I'll get even

JOHN VAN DIEST
ASSOCIATE PUBLISHER

EFFECTIVE LEADERS

1.
EFFECTIVE LEADERS LISTEN

If we do not hear what is said to us, our leadership will be impertinent.

2.
EFFECTIVE LEADERS HAVE VISION

*A leader charts a course, navigates difficult places,
and sets an example.*

3:
EFFECTIVE LEADERS ARE PASSIONATE

They have a passion for their role, their task, and their partners.

4.
EFFECTIVE LEADERS ARE FACILITATORS

*Leaders do not shelter those they care for from the harsh realities of life.
They facilitate the ability of others to live passionate lives.*

5.
EFFECTIVE LEADERS EMPOWER

*This will occur as you talk with them [those who follow], share your
struggles with them, convey your convictions, declare your doubts,
and tell them about the difficulties you are experiencing.*

PRESTON GILLHAM
CONDENSED FROM "THINGS ONLY MEN KNOW"

DON'TS FOR DECISION MAKING

❧

Don't focus on doing *more* tasks, but on doing *fewer* tasks well.

❧

Don't accept impossible deadlines—factor in extra "pad" time.

❧

Don't leave decisions hanging—decide immediately on a course of action each time you can.

❧

Don't let the desires of others dictate how you spend your time.

❧

Don't assume that the "emergencies" of others are your emergencies.

❧

Don't say *yes* when you should say *no*.

JUNE HUNT
FROM "HEALING THE HURTING HEART"

ARE YOU A GOOD TIME MANAGER?

DO YOU
have a clear picture of what you want to accomplish each day?

DO YOU
list tasks and appointments on your calendar?

DO YOU
have a few clear goals for each activity and project you're involved in?

DO YOU
group similar tasks together to do at the same time?

DO YOU
feel free not to read everything that crosses your desk?

DO YOU
*balance your time on projects so you don't require
frenzied hours of overtime to finish?*

DO YOU
prioritize your tasks in order and stick to top-priority items?

DO YOU
*keep important references and supplies within
arm's reach of your work area?*

DO YOU
*give clear instructions to coworkers so they can take care of
minor jobs without interrupting you?*

DO YOU
work on highly involved tasks when you feel the most alert?

DO YOU
stop working when you feel fatigued?

DO YOU
*break large projects down into manageable
pieces to finish one at a time?*

DO YOU
survey your long-term goals regularly?

CONDENSED FROM "TYME MANAGEMENT"

SMART GOALS ARE...

❧

SPECIFIC

❧

MEASURABLE

❧

ACHIEVABLE

❧

REALISTIC

❧

TIMED

⌐∼◦

ALICE GRAY, DR. STEVE STEPHENS, AND JOHN VAN DIEST

CRITICISM KILLS...

❧

MOTIVATION

❧

ENTHUSIASM

❧

CONFIDENCE

❧

JOY

❧

DREAMS

❧

HOPE

❧

SPIRIT

⁓

DR. STEVE STEPHENS
PSYCHOLOGIST AND SEMINAR SPEAKER

SIX-STEP RECIPE FOR SUCCESS

1.
BE PASSIONATE.
Love what you do.

2.
THE GREATEST WEALTH IS FAMILY AND FRIENDS.
Enjoy their love.

3.
EVERY DAY IS SPECIAL.
Make it the best it can be.

4.
"NO" IS UNACCEPTABLE.
Don't stop there. Go for "yes."

5.
CELEBRATE EXCELLENCE.
Make people feel important.

6.
THE GREATEST FAILURE IS NOT TO TRY.
When you dream, wake up and do.

JEFFREY GITOMER
FROM "WOMEN AS MANAGERS"

FIVE KEYS TO CONVERSATION

1.
STAND UP STRAIGHT, LOOK THEM IN THE EYE, AND SMILE

A warm, confident greeting communicates acceptance and responsibility.

2.
RESPOND WITH CONFIDENCE—DON'T MUTTER

When we meet a person who has the confidence to speak to us clearly with sparkling eyes and a warm grin, we immediately connect with them.

3.
LEARN PEOPLE'S NAMES AND USE THEIR NAMES PROPERLY

Learning to use people's names with respect and courtesy is fundamental to basic conversation.

4.
DEVELOP A GENERAL KNOWLEDGE BASE

Versatility in conversation is invaluable. With a general understanding of politics, entertainment, sports, and religion you'll be amazed at the depth of conversation and friendships that will emerge.

5.
FOCUS ON THE OTHER PERSON

Many people fail at conversation simply because they are too interested in fronting their own point of view. They don't want to talk to someone—they want to talk at someone.

TED HAGGARD AND JOHN BOLIN
CONDENSED FROM "CONFIDENT PARENTS, EXCEPTIONAL TEENS"

THE TEN COMMANDMENTS
OF GIVING A SPEECH

1.
THOU SHALT NOT BE UNPREPARED.

Be so familiar with your material that you are not dependent on your notes or your manuscript.

2.
THOU SHALT NOT HAVE ONE METHOD OF GIVING A SPEECH.

Be careful to fit your methodology to your audience.

3.
THOU SHALT NOT CONCENTRATE ON THYSELF.

If you are totally concentrated on yourself, you will miss the whole reason for your speech: communicating something important to an audience.

4.
THOU SHALT NOT MAKE LONG SPEECHES.

The longer the speech, the greater chance of failure.

5.
THOU SHALT NOT LISTEN TO EVERYONE'S CRITICISM.

Find someone you trust and ask that person to give you honest criticism. It will be worth the comments of a thousand others.

6.
THOU SHALT NOT MUMBLE.

Speaking clearly is prerequisite to an audience hearing clearly.

7.
THOU SHALT BE THYSELF.

Be the best you can within your own style and gifts.

8.
THOU SHALT SPEAK GENTLY.

Wise communicators turn down the volume.
They should communicate "Can we talk?" rather than
"This is the law and you will obey."

9.
THOU SHALT WATCH BODY LANGUAGE.

In communication, body language is almost as important as the
words you speak.

10.
THOU SHALT DEVIATE.

Variety is the spice of life and the stuff of a good speech.

STEVE BROWN, PRESIDENT OF KEY LIFE NETWORK, INC.
CONDENSED FROM "HOW TO TALK SO PEOPLE WILL LISTEN"

2
Stepping
Forward

Changing through the seasons of life

THREE PILLARS OF LEARNING

1.

Seeing much.

2.

Suffering much.

3.

Studying much.

BENJAMIN DISRAELI
FORMER PRIME MINISTER OF ISRAEL

ONE STEP FURTHER

Do more than exist LIVE

Do more than touch FEEL

Do more than look OBSERVE

Do more than read ABSORB

Do more than hear LISTEN

Do more than listen UNDERSTAND

Do more than think REFLECT

Do more than just talk SAY SOMETHING

AUTHOR UNKNOWN

WANTED!

More to *improve*
>and fewer to *disapprove.*

More *doers*
>and fewer *talkers.*

More to say *It can be done*
>and fewer to say *It's impossible.*

More to *inspire* others
>and fewer to *throw cold water* on them.

More to *get into the thick of things*
>and fewer to *sit on the sidelines.*

More to point out *what's right*
>and fewer to *show what's wrong.*

More to *light a candle*
>and fewer to *curse the darkness.*

AUTHOR UNKNOWN

SEVEN LESSONS TO LEARN

1. LEARN TO
   respect and esteem others.

2. LEARN TO
   maximize your strengths and minimize your weaknesses.

3. LEARN TO
   be an encourager.

4. LEARN TO
   be friendly.

5. LEARN TO
   approach life with joy and hope.

6. LEARN TO
   forgive.

7. LEARN TO
   treat children special.

JOHN VAN DIEST
ASSOCIATE PUBLISHER

SEVEN IMPORTANT CHOICES

1. CHOOSE
     a goal.

2. CHOOSE
     to use wisdom.

3. CHOOSE
     how you will
     spend your time.

4. CHOOSE
     your battles.

5. CHOOSE
     your words.

6. CHOOSE
     your friends.

7. CHOOSE
     your attitude.

SHERI ROSE SHEPHERD
FROM "7 WAYS TO A BETTER YOU"

LIVING LIKE THERE'S NO TOMORROW

IF TODAY WERE THE LAST OF ALL DAYS, WOULD YOU:

- Start the business you have always wanted to?
- Take that special trip you had always planned?
- Heal an old hurt?
- Forgive an old offense?
- Visit someone who would love to see you?
- Reconnect and catch up with an old friend?
- See a sight you have always dreamed of seeing?
- Learn how to do something new?
- Go on an adventure?
- Ask someone to forgive you?
- Learn how to communicate with your spouse?
- Learn how to communicate with your kids?
- Learn how to communicate with your parents?
- Make love with your spouse like you mean it?
- Tell someone how much you love him or her?
- See a movie or read a book?
- Quit sweating the small stuff?
- Finally get it that it's almost all small stuff?

§ Tell someone how much you appreciate what he or she has contributed to your life?

§ Thank someone for believing in you?

§ Gather your family members around you and just hold them?

§ Get your priorities in order?

§ Finish that project you left hanging?

§ Consider what the meaning of your life has been?

§ Focus on what's important?

§ Balance your family and work life?

§ Get to know your kids?

§ Get to know your spouse?

§ Get to know yourself?

§ Let someone in front of you in traffic?

§ Find out the names of the people who live next door, across the street, behind you?

§ Slow down and enjoy what you have worked so hard for?

JEFF HERRING
FROM THE "OREGONIAN"

SEVEN WAYS TO MAKE
YOURSELF MISERABLE

1. Count your troubles, name them one by one—at the breakfast table, if anybody will listen, or as soon as possible thereafter.

2. Worry every day about something. Don't let yourself get out of practice.

3. Pity yourself. If you do enough of this, nobody else will have to do it for you.

4. Make it your business to find out what the Joneses are buying this year and where they're going. Try to do them at least one better even if you have to take out another loan.

5. Stay away from absolutes. It's what's right for *you* that matters. Be your own person and don't allow yourself to get hung up on what others expect of you.

6. Make sure you get your rights. Never mind other people's. You have your life to live, they have theirs.

7. Don't fall into any compassion traps—the sort of situation where people can walk all over you. If you get too involved in other people's troubles, you may neglect your own.

ELISABETH ELLIOT
CONDENSED FROM "KEEP A QUIET HEART"

RULES FOR A PERFECT DAY

JUST FOR TODAY I will try to strengthen my mind by reading something that requires effort, thought, and concentration.

JUST FOR TODAY I will do somebody a good turn and not get found out.

JUST FOR TODAY I will do a task that needs to be done but which I have been putting off. I will do it as an exercise in willpower.

JUST FOR TODAY I will dress as becomingly as possible, talk low, act courteously, be liberal with praise, and criticize not one bit nor find fault with anything.

JUST FOR TODAY I will have a quiet half hour all by myself and relax. In this half hour sometime I will think of God so as to get more perspective in my life.

JUST FOR TODAY I will be unafraid. Especially, I will not be afraid to be happy, to enjoy what is beautiful, to love, and to believe that those I love, love me.

AUTHOR UNKNOWN

LIFE 101

I'M LEARNING...

    §   that a good sense of humor is money in the bank. In life. On the job. In a marriage.

    §   that a good attitude can control situations you can't. That any bad experience can be a good one. It all depends on me.

    §   to slow down more often and enjoy the trip. To eat more ice cream and less bran.

    §   that you can do something in an instant that will give you heartache for life.

    §   that bitterness and gossip accomplish nothing, but forgiveness and love accomplish everything.

    §   that it takes years to build trust and seconds to destroy it.

    §   to always leave loved ones with loving words. It may be the last time I see them.

    §   that if I'm standing on the edge of a cliff, the best way forward is to back up. That you don't fail when you lose, you fail when you quit.

    §   that too many people spend a lifetime stealing time from those who love them most, trying to please the ones who care about them the least.

    §   that money is a lousy way of keeping score. That true success is not measured in cars, or homes, or bank accounts, but in relationships.

🎵 that having enough money isn't nearly as much fun as I thought it would be when I didn't have any. That money buys less than you think.

🎵 that helping another is far more rewarding than helping myself. That those who laugh more worry less.

🎵 that you cannot make anyone love you. But you can work on being lovable.

🎵 that degrees, credentials, and awards mean far less than I thought they would.

🎵 that I will never regret a moment spent reading the Bible or praying. Or a kind word. Or a day at the beach.

🎵 that laughter and tears are nothing to be ashamed of. To celebrate the good things. And pray about the bad.

🎵 And I'm learning that the most important thing in the world is loving God. That everything good comes from that.

PHIL CALLAWAY
CONDENSED FROM "WHO PUT THE SKUNK IN THE TRUNK?"

GOALS FOR AUTHENTIC GROWTH

I WILL   *have a passion for excellence.*

I WILL   *ask, listen, and hear—to determine the wants,
          needs, and possibilities of all with whom I come
          in contact.*

I WILL   *provide an example of commitment and integrity.*

I WILL   *follow a path of continual empowerment for
          myself and others.*

I WILL   *constantly focus on the strengths of all with
          whom I come in contact.*

I WILL   *cultivate optimum physical, mental, and spiritual
          fitness.*

I WILL   *lead as I would like to be led.*

I WILL   *savor the flavor of each passing moment.*

I WILL   *infuse every thought and relationship with
          faith, hope, love, and gratitude.*

JOE D. BATTEN
FROM "NEW MAN" MAGAZINE

FIVE WAYS TO START
THE NEW YEAR RIGHT

1.
DON'T MAKE RESOLUTIONS.
*Make plans. Resolutions are pie-in-the-sky, down-the-road goals.
Plans are doable, step-by-step.*

2.
TURN THE TV OFF.
*Think how much time you could have to accomplish dreams if
you used even the daily half hour you normally watch TV.*

3.
LEARN TO SAY NO.
*Prioritize instead of becoming overwhelmed with all your to-dos and
opportunities. Include time for rest/recreation and time for meditation.*

4.
WRITE THANK-YOU NOTES FOR SIMPLE REASONS.
Gratitude is a priceless gift, so give it freely!

5.
PRAY ABOUT EVERYTHING.
*Talk to God about everyday details, as well as big-picture items.
Nothing is too small—or too big—for Him to care about.*

LIITA FORSYTH
FROM "VIRTUE" MAGAZINE

FOUR TRAITS OF THOSE
WHO IMPACT OUR LIVES

1. CONSISTENCY.

Those who impact lives stay at the task with reliable regularity. They seem unaffected by the fickle winds of change.

2. AUTHENTICITY.

People who impact others are real to the core; no alloy covered over with a brittle layer of chrome, but solid, genuine stuff right down to the nubbies.

3. UNSELFISHNESS.

Those who impact us the most watch out for themselves the least. They notice our needs and reach out to help, honestly concerned about our welfare. Their least-used words are "I," "me," "my," and "mine."

4. TIRELESSNESS.

With relentless determination they spend themselves. They refuse to quit. Possessing an enormous amount of enthusiasm for their labor, they press on regardless of the odds.

CHARLES R. SWINDOLL
CONDENSED FROM "GROWING STRONG IN THE SEASONS OF LIFE"

WHAT IS MATURITY?

1. Facing the truth honestly.

2. Looking beyond personal comfort and gratification, to the greater good.

3. Dealing with change without falling apart.

4. Working hard and completing a job, whether supervised or not.

5. Keeping the stresses and worries of life from taking control.

6. Doing the right thing regardless of what others say and do.

7. Finding more joy in giving than receiving.

8. Bearing an injustice without having to get even.

9. Relating to others in a consistently positive and helpful manner.

10. Being a person of your word.

11. Demonstrating respect.

12. Showing love in both word and deed.

13. Learning to be content based upon internal attitudes rather than external circumstances.

DR. STEVE STEPHENS
PSYCHOLOGIST AND SEMINAR SPEAKER

VITAL QUESTIONS

Ask yourself:

What are the options?

What are my priorities?

How can I grow?

Ask others:

Will you forgive me?

Will you help me?

What can I do for you?

Ask God:

Who am I?

What is Your will?

What is eternal?

DAVID SANFORD
DIRECTOR OF PRINT MEDIA, LUIS PALAU EVANGELISTIC ASSOCIATION

HOW TO PUT A WOW
IN EVERY TOMORROW

DEVELOP AN ATTITUDE OF GRATITUDE.
*Even when you are experiencing tough times, remember the blessings in your life.
It's like sprinkling sunshine on a cloudy day.*

ENCOURAGE OTHERS.
*When someone has a goal, most people point out the obstacles.
You be the one to point out the possibilities.*

GIVE SINCERE COMPLIMENTS.
We all like to be remembered for our best moments.

KEEP GROWING.
Walk a different path. Take a class. Read something inspiring.

GIVE THE GIFT OF FORGIVENESS.
*Forgiveness is a blessing for the one who forgives
as well as for the one who is forgiven.*

TAKE CARE OF YOURSELF.
Exercise, eat a healthy diet, sing, and dance a little bit every day.

DO RANDOM ACTS OF KINDNESS.
The most fun is when the other person doesn't know who did it.

TREASURE RELATIONSHIPS.
Eat meals together, take walks, listen. Share laughter and tears. Make memories.

SHARE YOUR FAITH.
*You can wish someone joy and peace and happy things,
but when you share your faith—you've wished them everything.*

ALICE GRAY
INSPIRATIONAL CONFERENCE SPEAKER
FROM HER SEMINAR, "TREASURES OF THE HEART"

WE ARE SHAPED BY...

Friends.

Literature.

Music.

Pleasures.

Ambitions.

Thoughts.

A. W. TOZER
FROM "THE QUOTABLE TOZER"

HOW TO LIGHTEN UP

Don't take yourself so seriously.

Thank God for the little things.

Look for an opportunity to help other people.

Choose joy.

Look for the silver lining in every grey cloud.

Add humor to conflicts and difficulties.

Don't base happiness on outward circumstances.

Don't try to be perfect.

Don't be easily offended.

Laugh every chance you get.

KEN DAVIS, COMEDIAN
ADAPTED FROM "LIGHTEN UP"

THE OPTIMIST CREED

COMMIT YOURSELF:

To be so strong that nothing can disturb your peace of mind.

To talk health, happiness, and prosperity to every person you meet.

To make all your friends feel that there is something special in them.

To look at the sunny side of everything and make your optimism come true.

To think only of the best, to work only for the best, and to expect only the best.

To be just as enthusiastic about the success of others as you are about your own.

To forget the mistakes of the past and press on to the greater achievements of the future.

To wear a cheerful countenance at all times and give every living creature you meet a smile.

To give so much time to the improvement of yourself that you have no time to criticize others.

To be too large for worry, too noble for anger, too strong for fear, and too happy to permit the presence of trouble.

3

Virtue

Marks of character and quality

GREAT SAYINGS ON VIRTUE

I am nothing, but truth is everything.

ABRAHAM LINCOLN

We are shaped and fashioned by what we love.

GOETHE

Integrity without knowledge is weak and useless,
and knowledge without integrity is dangerous and dreadful.

SAMUEL JOHNSON

Always do right—this will gratify some and astonish the rest.

MARK TWAIN

How sweet it is when the strong are also gentle.

LIGGIE FUDIM

Resolved: never to do anything which I should be
afraid to do if it were the last hour of my life.

JONATHAN EDWARDS

A BALANCED LIFE

SELF-RELIANT but not Self-sufficient

STEADFAST but not Stubborn

TACTFUL but not Timid

SERIOUS but not Sullen

UNMOVABLE but not Stationary

GENTLE but not Hypersensitive

TENDERHEARTED but not Touchy

CONSCIENTIOUS but not Perfectionistic

DISCIPLINED but not Demanding

GENEROUS but not Gullible

MEEK but not Weak

HUMOROUS but not Hilarious

FRIENDLY but not Familiar

HOLY but not Holier-than-thou

DISCERNING but not Critical

PROGRESSIVE but not Pretentious

AUTHORITATIVE but not Autocratic

~~~

CHARACTER AND CONDUCT

Conduct is what we do;   *character* is what we are.

Conduct is the outward life;   *character* is the life unseen, hidden within, yet evidenced by that which is seen.

Conduct is external, seen from without;   *character* is internal—operating within.

Character is the state of the heart;   **conduct** is its outward expression.

Character is the root of the tree;   **conduct,** the fruit it bears.

E. M. BOUNDS
THEOLOGIAN

GOOD CHARACTER IS...

§ Showing LOVE when those around are not lovable.

§ Having JOY when those around are discouraged and discontent.

§ Exuding PEACE when those around are anxious.

§ Practicing PATIENCE when those around are hurried and frantic.

§ Reaching out in KINDNESS when those around are difficult.

§ Shining with GOODNESS when those around do evil.

§ Standing in FAITHFULNESS when those around have no commitment.

§ Flowing with GENTLENESS when those around are harsh and cruel.

§ Demonstrating SELF-CONTROL when those around have none.

BASED ON THE TEACHINGS OF ST. PAUL, THE APOSTLE

100 POSITIVE VIRTUES

1. Accepting 2. Agreeable 3. Ambitious 4. Appreciative 5. Attentive 6. Available 7. Brave 8. Calm 9. Caring 10. Cheerful 11. Clean 12. Clever 13. Committed 14. Compassionate 15. Concerned 16. Conscientious 17. Considerate 18. Consistent 19. Content 20. Cooperative 21. Courteous 22. Curious 23. Dependable 24. Determined 25. Diligent 26. Discerning 27. Disciplined 28. Encouraging 29. Enthusiastic 30. Fair 31. Faithful 32. Flexible 33. Forgiving 34. Friendly 35. Generous 36. Gentle 37. Giving 38. Godly 39. Graceful 40. Grateful 41. Happy 42. Helpful 43. Honest 44. Hospitable 45. Humble 46. Industrious 47. Ingenious 48. Insightful 49. Joyful 50. Kind 51. Loving 52. Loyal 53. Mature 54. Meek 55. Merciful 56. Modest 57. Moral 58. Neat 59. Observant 60. Optimistic 61. Organized 62. Patient 63. Peaceful 64. Persistent 65. Playful 66. Polite 67. Positive 68. Principled 69. Punctual 70. Reassuring 71. Relaxed 72. Reliable 73. Reflective 74. Respectful 75. Responsible 76. Reverent 77. Satisfied 78. Secure 79. Self-Controlled 80. Sensible 81. Sensitive 82. Sincere 83. Sociable 84. Steadfast 85. Straightforward 86. Supportive 87. Sympathetic 88. Tactful 89. Teachable 90. Tender 91. Thorough 92. Thoughtful 93. Trustworthy 94. Truthful 95. Understanding 96. Unselfish 97. Virtuous 98. Well-Mannered 99. Willing 100. Wise

ALICE GRAY, DR. STEVE STEPHENS, AND JOHN VAN DIEST

YOU CAN DO IT

You've got a telephone.
MAKE A CALL.

You've got paper.
WRITE A LETTER.

You've got a kitchen.
MAKE A MEAL.

You've got a billfold.
GIVE SOME MONEY.

You've got two hands.
PUT THEM TO WORK FOR OTHERS.

You've got two feet.
GO SEE A FRIEND IN PAIN.

You've got two ears.
LISTEN TO THE CRIES OF THE WOUNDED.

You've got two eyes.
LIFT THEM UP TO SEE THE WORLD AS GOD SEES IT.

You've got two lips.
PREACH THE GOSPEL OF PEACE.

RAY PRITCHARD
FROM "THE ABCS OF WISDOM"

TIMELESS GIFTS

TO YOUR NEIGHBORS—give thoughtful consideration. Be slow to gossip, quick to sympathize, ready to help—praying all the while that God will give them the necessary patience to live next to you.

TO EVERYONE YOU MEET—remember that each person carries burdens known only to himself or herself, and some have burdens too big to cope with—say the kind things you want (but hesitate) to say.

TO YOUR PARENTS—give loving appreciation for the years of time and effort—and money—that they invested in you. Do for them the little things that give them pleasure.

TO YOUR SPOUSE—remember how much he or she has had to put up with and for how long—give a frank, honest reappraisal of yourself. Ask yourself, "If I were my spouse, am I the sort of person I would want to come home to?"

TO YOUR CHILDREN—be more articulate about your appreciation of them as persons. You are not a perfect parent, but at least give them more of the one they do have—and make that one more loving. Be available, knowing that a parent needs to be, as God is, "a very present help in trouble." Take time to listen, time to play, time to counsel, time to encourage.

RUTH BELL GRAHAM
FROM "DECISION" MAGAZINE

CHOOSING HUMILITY IN AN ARROGANT WORLD

The humble can wait patiently,
while the arrogant wants it now!

The humble demonstrates kindness,
while the arrogant doesn't even notice the need.

The humble are content, not jealous or envious,
while the arrogant feel they deserve more.

The humble honors and esteems the other,
while the arrogant brags on himself.

The humble does not act unbecomingly,
while the arrogant's manners are rude.

The humble shows a servant spirit,
while the arrogant demands to be served.

The humble are not easily provoked,
while the arrogant are quick to take offense.

The humble quickly forgive a wrong suffered,
while the arrogant can't rest until they even the score.

H. DALE BURKE AND JAC LA TOUR
FROM "A LOVE THAT NEVER FAILS"

BASIC MANNERS THAT TEACH RESPECT

DO *make eye contact with people.*

DO *shake hands when you are introduced to new acquaintances.*

DON'T *interrupt when others are speaking.*

DO *open doors for others, particularly for women, elders, and superiors.*

DON'T *sit when others are standing.*

DO *address people as "Mr." "Mrs." or "Miss" until they give you permission to use a more familiar form of address.*

DON'T *call people by their last names only.*

DO *express an interest in other people.*

DON'T *refer to a person by derogatory names or ethnic terms.*

DO *ask others for their opinions.*

DON'T *confuse attacks on a person's character or intelligence with respectful disagreement.*

DO *praise publicly and reprimand privately.*

BOB HOSTETLER
FROM "HOMELIFE" MAGAZINE

WHY I WRITE THANK-YOU NOTES

1.

To acknowledge receipt of a gift

2.

To be courteous

3.

To express appreciation

4.

To reflect on the giver's thoughtfulness

5.

To absorb the blessing of being remembered

6.

To value their time and expense

7.

To seal it to my memory

8.

To encourage the giver

MARILYN MCAULEY
A WOMAN KNOWN FOR GRACIOUSNESS

THE SECRET LIST OF
SOCIAL FAUX PAS

- ⚉ Pointing

- ⚉ Chewing gum in public

- ⚉ Drinking loudly with a straw

- ⚉ Breaking in line

- ⚉ Loud music

- ⚉ Talking during a church service

- ⚉ Gossip

- ⚉ Racial or ethnic jokes

- ⚉ Poor hygiene

- ⚉ Arguing in public

- ⚉ Telling people off

- ⚉ Leaving a party too soon

- ⚉ Leaving a party too late

- Being disrespectful

- Interrupting others

- Being negative

- Reaching for food

- Leaning back in your chair

- Putting on airs

- Staring

- Shouting

- Not holding the door open for the next person

- Not giving up your seat to an older person

- Asking too many personal questions

- Confronting people to tell them it's your turn

ANN PLATZ AND SUSAN WALES
FROM "SOCIAL GRACES: MANNERS, CONVERSATION, AND CHARM FOR TODAY"

A VIRTUOUS PERSON...

Is clean both inside and outside.

Neither looks up to the rich or down on the poor.

Loses, if need be, without squealing.

Wins without bragging.

Is always considerate of women, children, and old people.

Is too brave to lie.

Is too generous to cheat.

Takes his share of the world and lets other people have theirs.

GEORGE WASHINGTON CARVER
SCIENTIST AND INVENTOR

THREE BASIC INGREDIENTS
OF INTEGRITY

1.

Telling the truth.

2.

Keeping one's promises.

3.

Taking responsibility for one's behavior.

DR. ROSS CAMPBELL
FROM "RELATIONAL PARENTING"

GEORGE WASHINGTON'S
RULES OF CIVILITY

1. Every action done in company ought to be with some sign of respect to those that are present.

2. Show nothing to your friend that may frighten him.

3. In the presence of others sing not to yourself with a humming noise, nor drum with your fingers or feet.

4. Sleep not when others speak, sit not when others stand, speak not when you should hold your peace, walk not on when others stop.

5. Let your countenance be pleasant but in serious matters somewhat grave.

6. Show not yourself glad at the misfortune of another though he were your enemy.

7. Use no reproachful language against anyone, neither curse nor revile.

8. Associate yourself with men of good quality if you esteem your own reputation; for 'tis better to be alone than in bad company.

9. Speak not injurious words neither in jest nor earnest at none although they give occasion.

10. Think before you speak, pronounce not imperfectly nor bring out your words too hastily but orderly and distinctly.

11. Undertake not what you cannot perform but be careful to keep your promise.

12. Speak not evil of the absent for it is unjust.

13. When you speak of God or his attributes, let it be seriously and with reverence.

14. Labor to keep alive in your breast that little spark of celestial fire called conscience.

34 THINGS WE MUST RESPECT

1. God
2. Truth and wisdom
3. Life
4. Nature and all of creation
5. Our country
6. Our laws
7. Those older
8. Those younger
9. Our parents and grandparents
10. Our children
11. Our spouse
12. Our friends and neighbors
13. Those who teach us
14. Those who love us
15. Those who protect us
16. Those in charge of us
17. Those who look up to us
18. What does not belong to us
19. Compassion
20. Courage
21. Character
22. Humility
23. Peace
24. Patience and perseverance
25. Purity
26. Faith
27. Generosity
28. A task well done
29. A course well run
30. A life well lived
31. Our bodies
32. Our talents and abilities
33. Our mortality
34. All that is good and right and worthy of praise

DR. STEVE STEPHENS
PSYCHOLOGIST AND SEMINAR SPEAKER

SEVEN SACRED VIRTUES

Having HUMILITY instead of Pride
The humility to know that we are not alone in the world.

Having GENEROSITY instead of Covetousness
The generosity to allow others to have what they deserve.

Having RESTRAINT instead of Lust
The restraint to control our most passionate impulses.

Having KINDNESS instead of Anger
The kindness to tolerate the mistakes of our fellow man.

Having MODERATION instead of Gluttony
The moderation to satisfy ourselves with the necessities.

Having CHARITY instead of Envy
The charity to help those who are unable to help themselves.

Having DILIGENCE instead of Sloth
The diligence to make ourselves useful in the modern world.

~~~

MARILYN VOS SAVANT
FROM "PARADE" MAGAZINE

VIRTUE

SCOUT'S LAW

A SCOUT IS...

TRUSTWORTHY.
A Scout tells the truth. He is honest,
and he keeps his promises. People can depend on him.

LOYAL.
A Scout is true to his family, friends, school, and nation.

HELPFUL.
A Scout cares about other people. He willingly volunteers
to help others without expecting payment or reward.

FRIENDLY.
A Scout is a friend to all.

COURTEOUS.
A Scout is polite to everyone regardless of age or
position. He knows that using good manners
makes it easier for people to get along.

KIND.
A Scout knows there is strength in being gentle.
He treats others as he wants to be treated.

OBEDIENT.
A Scout follows the rules of his family and school and
obeys the laws of his community and country.

CHEERFUL.
A Scout looks for the bright side of life. He cheerfully
does tasks that come his way. He tries to make others happy.

THRIFTY.
A Scout works to pay his way and to help others.
He saves for the future.

BRAVE.
A Scout can face danger although he is afraid.
He has the courage to stand for what he thinks is
right even if others laugh at him or threaten him.

CLEAN.
A Scout keeps his body and mind fit. He chooses the
company of those who live by high standards.
He helps keep his home and community clean.

BOY SCOUTS OF AMERICA
NATIONAL COUNCIL

4
Friendship
A heart for others

WHY FRIENDS ARE IMPORTANT

1.

They laugh with us.

2.

They cry with us.

3.

They build memories with us.

4.

They stand beside us.

5.

They confront us.

6.

They believe the best in us.

7.

They help us grow.

8.

They keep us from temptation.

9.

They enrich our lives.

DR. STEVE STEPHENS
PSYCHOLOGIST AND SEMINAR SPEAKER

10 RULES FOR GETTING
ALONG WITH PEOPLE

1.

Remember their names.

2.

Be comfortable to be with.
Don't cause strain in others.

3.

Try not to let things bother you.
Be easygoing.

4.

Don't be egotistical or know-it-all.

5.

Learn to be interesting so that people will
get something stimulating from being with you.

6.

Eliminate the "scratchy" elements in your personality,
traits that can irritate others.

7.

Never miss a chance to offer support
or say "Congratulations."

8.

Work at liking people.
Eventually you'll like them naturally.

9.

Honestly try to heal any misunderstandings
and drain off grievances.

10.

Develop spiritual depth in yourself
and share this strength with others.

NORMAN VINCENT PEALE
FROM "TIME TALK"

FRIENDSHIP

A FRIEND IS ONE WHO...

…follows through with what he or she says.

…understands and inspires.

…sacrifices for the other.

…invests in another.

…joyfully gives and serves.

…respects and honors.

…is courteous.

…builds character.

…loves at all times.

…challenges growth and maturity.

…tells the truth and restores dignity.

…keeps a promise.

…shares dreams.

…keeps in touch forever.

…is forgiving.

GLENDA HOTTON, M.A.
COUNSELOR

FRIENDSHIP WORDS

Concern

Courtesy

Contact

Caring

Comfort

Celebration

Cultivation

Connection

Continuity

Cherish

Companionship

Communication

Closeness

Consistency

EMILIE BARNES AND DONNA OTTO
FROM "FRIENDS OF THE HEART"

THE FOUR PROMISES
OF FORGIVENESS

1.

"I will no longer dwell on this incident."

2.

"I will not bring up this incident
again and use it against you."

3.

"I will not talk to others about this incident."

4.

"I will not allow this incident to stand
between us or hinder our relationship."

KEN SANDE
FROM "THE PEACEMAKER"

THE FINE ART OF FRIENDSHIP

1.
Develop friendships in which you demand nothing in return.

2.
Nurture an authentic interest in others.

3.
Always take time—often a long time—
to understand one another.

4.
Commit yourself to learning how to listen.

5.
Simply be there to care, whether you
know exactly what to do or not.

6.
Always treat others as equals.

7.
Be generous with legitimate praise and encouragement.

8.
Make your friends Number One,
preferring them above yourself.

9.
Emphasize the strengths and virtues of others,
not their sins and weaknesses.

DR. TED ENGSTROM
EXCERPTS FROM "CHRISTIAN LEADERSHIP LETTER"

20 QUESTIONS
TO ASK A FRIEND

These questions provide a fun forum for getting to know your new friends and for getting to know your old friends better. Use them for party games, for conversation starters. With an old and treasured friend, see how many you can guess about him or her.

1. Where did your family live when you were six? When you were twelve?

2. What was your favorite subject in school?

3. Have you ever played a musical instrument? What was it?

4. What is your favorite sport? Did you ever play it—or did you prefer to watch?

5. What was your least favorite food as a child?

6. Name your first boyfriend/girlfriend. How old were you when you met?

7. If you were beginning life again and could choose any career, what would you choose?

8. What is the most valuable thing you've learned in the past ten years?

9. What lost person or thing in your life do you miss the most?

10. What is the most encouraging word anyone can say to you?

11. Describe the most wonderful vacation you've ever taken. Why was it so great?

12. In what areas of your life do you feel most successful? Least successful?

13. What was the loneliest moment of your life? Why?

14. What single accomplishment in your life have you been proudest of?

15. What is your favorite season of the year and why?

16. Name an older person (not your parents) who influenced you as a younger person. What did you learn from that person?

17. If you had an unlimited budget to remodel just one room in your house, what would you do? In which room?

18. What was your favorite song when you were sixteen?

19. If you had to spend a year alone on a desert island and could take just three things with you, what would you take?

20. What's your idea of a truly perfect morning? What would you do?

EMILIE BARNES AND DONNA OTTO
FROM "FRIENDS OF THE HEART"

GOOD FRIENDS ARE HARD TO FIND

⁓

When things go sour and you really feel lousy,
do you have a friend you can tell?

⁓

Do you have a friend you can express any honest
thought to without fear of appearing foolish?

⁓

Do you have a friend who will let you
talk through a problem without giving you advice?
Who will just be a "sounding board"?

⁓

Will your friend risk your disapproval to suggest
you may be getting off track in your priorities?

⁓

Do you have a friend who will take the risk to
tell you that you are sinning? Or using poor judgment?

*If you had a moral failure, do you know
that your friend would stand with you?*

*Is there a friend with whom you feel
you are facing life together?*

*Do you have a friend you believe you can trust, so if you
share confidential thoughts they will stay confidential?*

*When you are vulnerable and transparent with your friend,
are you convinced he or she will not think less of you?*

*Do you meet with a friend weekly or biweekly for
fellowship and prayer, and possibly for accountability?*

PATRICK M. MORLEY
CONDENSED FROM "THE MAN IN THE MIRROR"

FRIENDSHIP

HEALTHY EXPECTATIONS
OF FRIENDS

Be honest.

Keep promises made.

Share ideas and dreams.

Have respect for my faith.

Never knowingly hurt me.

Purpose to resolve conflict.

Show respect for our differences.

Encourage my growth and maturity.

Demonstrate congruent values and beliefs.

GLENDA HOTTON, M.A.
COUNSELOR

UNHEALTHY EXPECTATIONS
OF FRIENDS

Never disagree with my ideas.

Have no other friends but me.

Love my family and friends.

Call or see me every day.

Do whatever I request.

Like everything I like.

Be perfect.

GLENDA HOTTON, M.A.
COUNSELOR

ANTIGOSSIP PACT

In 1752, a group of Methodist men, including John Wesley, signed a covenant that each man agreed to hang on the wall of his study. The six articles of this solemn agreement were as follows:

1. That we will not listen or willingly inquire after ill concerning one another;

2. That, if we do hear any ill of each other, we will not be forward to believe it;

3. That as soon as possible we will communicate what we hear by speaking or writing to the person concerned;

4. That until we have done this, we will not write or speak a syllable of it to any other person;

5. That neither will we mention it, after we have done this, to any other person;

6. That we will not make any exception to any of these rules unless we think ourselves absolutely obliged in conference.

JOHN WESLEY AND FRIENDS
FROM "GOD'S LITTLE DEVOTIONAL BOOK"

PROVERBS ON FRIENDSHIP

꒕

A true friend is always loyal, and
a brother is born to help in time of need.
PROVERBS 17:17

꒕

Wounds from a friend are better than kisses from an enemy!
PROVERBS 27:6

꒕

There are "friends" who pretend to be friends,
but there is a friend who sticks closer than a brother.
PROVERBS 18:24

꒕

Love forgets mistakes; nagging about
them parts the best of friends.
PROVERBS 17:9

꒕

Never abandon a friend—either yours or your father's.
Then you won't need to go to a distant
relative for help in your time of need.
PROVERBS 27:10

KING SOLOMON
THE BOOK OF PROVERBS

GREAT SAYINGS ON FRIENDSHIP

A friend is a present you give yourself.
ROBERT LOUIS STEVENSON

A friend is one who makes me do my best.
OSWALD CHAMBERS

The only way to have a friend is to be one.
RALPH WALDO EMERSON

Give and take makes good friends.
SCOTTISH SAYING

Loyalty is what we seek in friendship.
CICERO

To have a good friend is one of the highest delights of life;
to be a good friend is one of the noblest
and most difficult undertakings.
AUTHOR UNKNOWN

The real friend is he or she who can share all
our sorrow and double our joys.
B. C. FORBES

A cheerful friend is like a sunny day,
which sheds its brightness on all around.
JOHN LUBBOCK

One who knows how to show and to accept kindness
will be a friend better than any possession.
SOPHOCLES

In prosperity our friends know us;
in adversity we know our friends.
JOHN CHURTON COLLINS

Friendship begins with gratitude.
GERTRUDE ELIOT

If you want an accounting of your worth,
count your friends.
MERRY BROWNE

10 IDEAS FOR STAYING CLOSE WHEN YOU'RE FAR AWAY

1. ORGANIZE A REUNION.
How often you do this will depend on time, distance,
finances, and many other factors. But if at all possible,
try to get together in person at least once a year.

2. INVEST IN MA BELL.
The telephone can be a lifeline between long-distance friends.
Think of the bills as investments in your friendship.

3. DON'T FORGET TO WRITE.
There's just something special about receiving a card
or letter in the mailbox. A letter, unlike a phone call,
can be reread and treasured for years.

4. GO HIGH TECH.
If you have a computer or fax, explore the advantages
of using these high-tech tools to keep in touch.
E-mail is an especially handy, immediate, and inexpensive
way to keep current with long-distance friends.

5. SEND PICTURES.
This is a great way to keep current with each other's lives.
Do you have duplicate shots of the same pose?
Send one to your friend with a note on the back.

6. VACATION TOGETHER.
Meet somewhere between your homes for a week of
fun and renewing your friendship. Check out
hotels, resorts, spas, or retreat centers.

7. WORK TOGETHER ON A LONG-DISTANCE PROJECT.
Planning a college reunion or cosponsoring a child from another
country gives you an excuse and a reminder to stay in touch.

8. AT LEAST SAY HI.
During very busy times when you barely have time to breathe,
much less write or even phone, a simple postcard or a five-minute
phone call can still keep the lines of communication open.

9. PRAY FOR EACH OTHER
—always and faithfully.

10. SEND YOUR FRIEND A SUBSCRIPTION OR ENROLL
HIM OR HER IN AN "OF THE MONTH" CLUB.
Whether it's magazines, books, flowers, fruits, or even steaks,
the monthly arrival will bring thoughts of you. Just be sure the
subscription doesn't require your friend to do or pay something!

EMILIE BARNES AND DONNA OTTO
CONDENSED FROM "FRIENDS OF THE HEART"

10 COMMANDMENTS OF FRIENDSHIP

1. SPEAK TO PEOPLE.

There is nothing as nice as a cheerful word of greeting.

2. SMILE AT PEOPLE.

It takes 72 muscles to frown, but only 14 to smile!

3. CALL PEOPLE BY NAME.

The sweetest music to anyone's ear

is the sound of his or her own name.

4. BE FRIENDLY AND HELPFUL.

If you would have friends, be friendly.

5. BE CORDIAL.

Speak and act as if everything you do were a real pleasure.

6. BE GENUINELY INTERESTED IN PEOPLE.

You can like everyone IF YOU TRY.

7. BE GENEROUS WITH PRAISE, CAUTIOUS WITH CRITICISM.

Try for a ratio of seven praises to each criticism.

8. BE CONSIDERATE OF THE FEELINGS OF OTHERS.

It will be appreciated.

9. BE THOUGHTFUL OF THE OPINIONS OF OTHERS.

People love their opinions as they do their own children;

calling them ugly won't get you anything but anger.

10. BE ALERT TO GIVE SERVICE.

What counts most in life is what we do for others!

AUTHOR UNKNOWN
FROM "THE POWER OF ENCOURAGEMENT"

FUN ACTIVITIES FOR COUPLE FRIENDS

Take a trip to the mountains.

Plan a picnic in the park.

Cook dinner together.

Visit a museum.

Go hiking.

Start a book club.

Share prayer requests.

Learn a new card game together.

Rent old movies.

Fly kites.

Attend a play or sporting event.

Explore an arts and crafts fair.

Rest and relax at a recreation area such as a lake, river, or park.

TRICIA GOYER
CONDENSED FROM "HOMELIFE" MAGAZINE

BEING A GOOD NEIGHBOR

Share your time and your possessions.

Be friendly, but respect their space.

Watch what you say over the fence.

Be a good listener.

Respect sleeping hours (between 10 P.M. and 8 A.M.).

Be positive and cheerful.

Provide meals when there is an illness, birth, death, or crisis.

Watch their property when they aren't home.

Volunteer to pick up mail, water plants, or feed pets when they are away.

Help out when they are working on a big project.

Remember them at Christmas.

Treat them as you'd like to be treated.

TAMI STEPHENS
MOTHER OF THREE

5
Health
A long and satisfying life

STRESS BUSTERS

GUIDELINES FOR GOOD SLEEP

HOW TO KEEP YOUR IMMUNE SYSTEM STRONG

20 WAYS TO RELAX

WHY LAUGHTER IS HEALTHY

FIVE TIPS FOR STAYING YOUNG

WARNING SIGNS OF EMOTIONAL PAIN

DON'TS FOR EMOTIONAL FITNESS

RESULTS OF ANXIETY

AVOID GETTING AND DOING TOO MUCH

WHAT GUYS NEED TO KNOW ABOUT PMS

DEFUSING ANGER

TOP 10 HABITS FOR HEALTH AND VITALITY

EATING HEALTHY

GUIDELINES FOR CHOOSING HEALTHY FOODS

TRAVEL FIRST-AID KIT

STAY ACTIVE

HOW TO STOP SMOKING

STRESS BUSTERS

Take a break.

Take a bath.

Take a walk.

Take a breath.

Take a nap.

ALICE GRAY, DR. STEVE STEPHENS, AND JOHN VAN DIEST

GUIDELINES FOR GOOD SLEEP

ꝺ Get up about the same time every day.

ꝺ Go to bed only when you are sleepy.

ꝺ Establish relaxing presleep rituals such as a warm bath, a light bedtime snack, or ten minutes of reading.

ꝺ Exercise regularly. If you exercise vigorously, do this at least six hours before bedtime. Mild exercise—such as simple stretching or walking—should not be done within four hours of bedtime.

ꝺ Maintain a regular schedule. Regular times for meals, taking medications, doing chores, and other activities help keep your "inner clock" running smoothly.

ꝺ Don't eat or drink anything containing caffeine within six hours of bedtime. Don't drink alcohol within several hours of bedtime, or when you are sleepy. Tiredness can intensify the effects of alcohol.

ꝺ Avoid smoking close to bedtime.

ꝺ If you take naps, try to do so at the same time every day. For most people, a midafternoon nap is most helpful.

ꝺ Avoid sleeping pills, or use them conservatively. Most doctors avoid prescribing sleeping pills for a duration of longer than three weeks. Never drink alcohol while taking sleeping pills.

AMERICAN ACADEMY OF SLEEP MEDICINE

HOW TO KEEP YOUR IMMUNE SYSTEM STRONG

Practice good nutrition.

Stop smoking.

Get regular exercise.

Avoid physical stress.

Avoid emotional stress.

Watch your weight.

Stop environmental pollution.

Keep a positive attitude.

Pray as often as possible.

TERRY T. SHINTANI, M.D., M.P.H
DIRECTOR OF INTEGRATIVE MEDICINE, WAIMAE COAST HEALTH CENTER

20 WAYS TO RELAX

1.
Watch a sunrise.

2.
Learn to play a musical instrument.

3.
Sing in the shower.

4.
Never refuse homemade brownies.

5.
Whistle.

6.
Take someone bowling.

7.
Sing in a choir.

8.
Be romantic.

9.
Buy a bird feeder and place it where
it can be seen from your kitchen window.

10.
Wave at children on school buses.

11.
Lie on your back and look at the stars.

12.

Rekindle old friendships.

13.

Reread your favorite book.

14.

Try everything offered by
supermarket food demonstrators.

15.

Never waste an opportunity to
tell someone you love them.

16.

Save one evening a week
for just you and your spouse.

17.

Begin each day with your favorite music.

18.

Laugh a lot.

19.

Give thanks for every meal.

20.

Count your blessings.

H. JACKSON BROWN, JR.
CONDENSED FROM "LIFE'S LITTLE INSTRUCTION BOOK"

WHY LAUGHTER IS HEALTHY

It is contagious.

> *When you laugh, so do others.*

It kills depression.

> *It is hard to laugh and be depressed simultaneously.*

It reduces stress.

> *By distracting you from the worries and seriousness of life.*

It attracts others.

> *People are drawn to a warm smile and a hearty laugh.*

It makes difficult situations tolerable.

> *A laugh lightens even the heaviest load.*

DR. STEVE STEPHENS
PSYCHOLOGIST AND SEMINAR SPEAKER

FIVE TIPS FOR STAYING YOUNG

1.

Your mind is not old; keep developing it.

2.

Your humor is not over; keep enjoying it.

3.

Your strength is not gone; keep using it.

4.

Your opportunities have not vanished; keep pursuing them.

5.

God is not dead; keep seeking Him.

WARNING SIGNS OF
EMOTIONAL PAIN

- ð Do you live in your past and worry about your future?

- ð Are you depressed and feeling empty inside?

- ð Do you feel defeated because of a poor self-image?

- ð Are you in bondage to other people's opinions of you?

- ð Do you take everyone's stress personally or fall apart when someone looks at you the wrong way?

- ð Do you keep yourself excessively busy to the point that your life feels out of control?

- ð Do you have compulsive behavior patterns?

- ð Do you feel guilty for saying no, even if you've said it for the right reasons?

- ð Are you paralyzed by fear?

- ð Do you have a short fuse? How do you react to disappointment?

- ð Do you have a history of destructive relationships?

- ð Are you an approval addict?

SHERI ROSE SHEPHERD
FROM "FIT FOR EXCELLENCE"

DON'TS FOR EMOTIONAL FITNESS

🕉 DON'T IGNORE IT!

Ignoring the warning signs will not make them go away any more than ignoring a gas tank that says "empty" will allow the car to continue to run.

🕉 DON'T EXCUSE IT!

Many of us make excuses for our emotional pain rather then looking at the problem that's causing it.

🕉 DON'T DECORATE IT!

Many times we decorate our pain with a pretty house, pretty clothes, and prestigious positions.

🕉 DON'T COVER IT UP!

Many of us cover up with accomplishments and excessive busyness.

🕉 DON'T PRETEND IT'S NOT THERE!

Many of us have no idea why we're feeling pain because we pretend that everything is okay.

🕉 DON'T POSTPONE DEALING WITH IT!

Don't postpone dealing with your warning signs, or they will deal with you.

SHERI ROSE SHEPHERD
FROM "FIT FOR EXCELLENCE"

RESULTS OF ANXIETY

DIVIDES OUR MINDS

Instead of focusing on goals, the stress-filled person allows anxiety to steal many of his thoughts.

DRAINS OUR ENERGY

Naturally, when we are consumed with a situation, the psychological and emotional calisthenics sap strength. Anxiety slows productivity. Reduced energy means poor production and poor judgment.

AFFECTS RELATIONSHIPS

Friends and family also suffer when we allow the drone of worry's whispers to keep us in the dumps.

CAUSES US TO MAKE UNWISE DECISIONS

Mistakes come when we try in our own strength and timing to remedy a situation that God will handle if we only wait in faith.

STEALS OUR PEACE AND JOY

This is evidence that stress and worry are tools of the enemy. Peace and joy are gifts from God, regardless of the storm.

HARMS OUR PHYSICAL BODIES

Our bodies deteriorate under the weight we try to carry on our shoulders.

CHARLES STANLEY
FROM IN "IN TOUCH" MAGAZINE

AVOID GETTING AND
DOING TOO MUCH

---

    §   *Is this really important to me?*

    §   *Do I truly enjoy this?*

    §   *Do I really need this?*

    §   *Does this cause stress and drain my energy?*

    §   *Does this cause me to hurry too much?*

    §   *What are healthier alternatives?*

    §   *How did I manage without this?*

ROBERT AND DEBRA BRUCE AND ELLEN OLDACRE
FROM "STANDING UP AGAINST THE ODDS"

WHAT GUYS NEED TO KNOW ABOUT PMS

1.
It's Real.

2.
Respect Her Feelings.

3.
Don't Take It Personally.

4.
Get Educated.

5.
Help Her Understand Her Options.

6.
Don't Try to Fix Her.

7.
Pray for Her and with Her.

8.
Learn to Communicate.

J. RON EAKER, M.D.
CONDENSED FROM "NEW MAN" MAGAZINE

DEFUSING ANGER

1.
KEEP SHORT ACCOUNTS.
This serves to minimize the pent-up
emotions that lead to anger.

2.
THINK BEFORE YOU SPEAK.
If you dump the whole emotional load first,
without thinking, you'll spend more time
than you care to imagine cleaning up the mess.

3.
DESCRIBE HOW YOU FEEL.
Preferably in a controlled tone of voice;
you're likely to create a cooler atmosphere.

4.
SEEK RESOLUTION QUICKLY.
Anger left to fester becomes a deep emotional
infection that only gets worse as time passes.

H. DALE BURKE AND JAC LA TOUR
CONDENSED FROM "A LOVE THAT NEVER FAILS"

TOP 10 HABITS FOR
HEALTH AND VITALITY

1. GO TO SLEEP.

Most of us need at least eight hours of slumber and we're not getting it. If you rearrange your night and morning routines to provide the sleep you need, you (and your coworkers) will notice a positive difference!

2. GIVE YOURSELF A BREAK.

Midmorning and midafternoon, retreat from your work station for ten minutes and shift your mind into neutral. Do some deep breathing and stretch to loosen neck, shoulder, and back muscles. Take a brief walk or climb and descend a stairwell. After just a few minutes you will feel calm and refreshed.

3. ENJOY THESE HEALTHY FOODS AS OFTEN AS YOU CAN.

These foods are especially effective in supplying your body and brain with the nutrients they need for strength and efficiency—while helping prevent problems such as cancer, heart attack, diabetes, and stroke: fresh, brightly colored fruits and vegetables, whole grains, olive oil, nuts (especially walnuts), salmon and tuna, and green and black tea.

4. SAY GOOD-BYE TO AN UNHEALTHY HABIT.

Do you smoke? Over-imbibe alcohol, coffee, soft drinks, high-fat foods or snacks? Pick one unhealthy habit you'd like to stop—just one for now—and dedicate yourself to expunging it from your life. Then, one at a time, knock off your other unhealthy habits.

5. LAUGH!

Laughter releases powerful endorphins that soothe your nerves and strengthen mind, body, and spirit against the stresses of life. Look for the lighter side (it's there!) and let 'er rip.

6. SUPPLEMENT YOUR NUTRITION

As we grow older we should pay special attention to our intake of calcium for bone density and to selenium and vitamins C, E, and beta carotene for their antioxidant benefits.

7. GET AWAY FROM IT ALL—SOON AND OFTEN.

Spread out your vacations and long weekends to provide frequent getaways from your everyday labors. There's a huge, wonderful world outside your window—take full advantage of it.

8. GET MOVING.

A brisk thirty-minute walk, jog, bike ride, or aerobic workout at least three days a week for the cardiovascular system. A moderate resistance workout three days each week for muscle tone and strength. Aerobic and resistance training are not only essential for health and vitality, but they also work wonders for morale!

9. MAKE WATER YOUR BEVERAGE OF CHOICE.

Water flushes toxins from your system and supplies your cells with the life-giving elements they need. Drink at least *eight* glasses each day. More before, during, and after exercise.

10. COVER UP.

With skin cancers on the rise, there is no such thing as a healthy suntan. If you spend time outside during the day, do yourself and your loved ones a big favor: Cover as much skin as possible. What you can't cover, use a sunscreen.

DAN BENSON
FROM "THE NEW RETIREMENT:
HOW TO SECURE FINANCIAL FREEDOM AND LIVE OUT YOUR DREAMS"

EATING HEALTHY

- Maintain a desirable weight.

- Restrict fat.

- Get enough fiber

  whole-grain cereals, breads, and pasta; vegetables; fruit.

- Eat foods rich in vitamin A

  yellow/orange fruits and yellow/orange or dark green vegetables.

- Eat foods rich in vitamin C

  citrus fruits, strawberries, tomatoes, raw or lightly-cooked green vegetables.

- Eat more cabbage-family vegetables

  cabbage, broccoli, brussels sprouts, cauliflower. Restrict salt-cured, smoked, and nitrite-cured foods.

- Avoid/restrict alcoholic beverages.

THE HOPE HEART INSTITUTE
CONDENSED FROM "LIFEWISE" NEWSLETTER

GUIDELINES FOR CHOOSING HEALTHY FOODS

1. CHOOSE A WIDE VARIETY OF FOODS.
No one food or small selection of foods will
meet all your nutritional needs.

2. SELECT A MAJORITY OF YOUR FOODS
FROM FRUITS, VEGETABLES, AND WHOLE GRAINS.
Eat at least five servings of fruits and vegetables and six to
eleven servings of whole grain foods each day.

3. CHOOSE LOW-FAT FOODS.
Keep your fat intake to 30 percent or less of your
daily total calorie intake.

4. EAT SMALLER PORTIONS OF MEATS.
Six to eight ounces per day is enough to
support your need for protein.

5. EAT CALCIUM-RICH FOODS EACH DAY.

6. EAT WHEN YOU ARE HUNGRY.
Stop when you are satisfied.

7. DRINK AT LEAST 64 OUNCES OF WATER EACH DAY.

BRANDA POLK
FROM "HOMELIFE" MAGAZINE

TRAVEL FIRST-AID KIT

- A thermometer

- An assortment of bandages, including gauze and tape

- Pain medication

- An antiseptic

- Cotton swabs and cotton balls

- A large clean handkerchief in case you need to make a temporary sling

- Insect repellent

- Sunscreen

- Cold medication

- Diarrhea medication

- Antacids

KATE REDD
FROM "52 WAYS TO MAKE FAMILY TRAVEL MORE ENJOYABLE"

STAY ACTIVE

Go for a ten-minute walk after each meal.

Walk or use your bike to run small errands.

Park your car in the space farthest from where you're going.

Get off the bus a stop or two early and walk the rest of the way.

Take the stairs instead of the elevator.

AMY GIVLER
FROM "HOMELIFE" MAGAZINE

HOW TO STOP SMOKING

THINK ABOUT WHY YOU SMOKE.

Are you trying to look more mature? Do you think smoking makes you less anxious? Do stressful situations trigger your smoking? Have you tried to quit but couldn't (and now you realize you're addicted)?

THINK ABOUT HOW SMOKING HURTS YOU.

It makes you smell bad and have bad breath. It's expensive. It interferes with your stamina and makes you more anxious, not less. Also, you're more likely to get sick or have allergies.

SET A QUIT DATE WITHIN THE NEXT TWO WEEKS.

Tell everyone you know. Throw away cigarettes and ashtrays. Plan to avoid situations that always lead to smoking (such as reading the newspaper with a cup of coffee after breakfast).

QUIT.

You may feel some withdrawal symptoms (crankiness, trouble sleeping, fuzzy-headedness), but they will pass. Chew sugar-free gum. Drink lots of water to flush the tobacco toxins from your system.

REWARD YOURSELF (BUT NOT WITH FOOD).

You've done it! You've become a nonsmoker.

AMY GIVLER
FROM "HOMELIFE" MAGAZINE

6
Contentment
Finding peace and fulfillment

SEVEN WONDERS OF THE WORLD

1.

Seeing

2.

Hearing

3.

Tasting

4.

Touching

5.

Running

6.

Laughing

7.

Loving

～⌒

A LITTLE GIRL
(WRITTEN WHEN HER TEACHER ASKED THE CLASS TO MAKE
A LIST OF THE SEVEN NATURAL WONDERS OF THE WORLD)

WHAT MONEY CAN
AND CANNOT BUY

A bed but not sleep.

Books but not brains.

Food but not appetite.

Finery but not beauty.

A house but not a home.

Medicine but not health.

Luxuries but not culture.

Amusements but not happiness.

Companions but not friends.

Flattery but not respect.

~~~

ONE IS POOR IF HE...

Cannot enjoy what he has.

Is not content.

Is short on good works.

Has no self-respect.

Has no real friends.

Has lost the zest for living.

Has little joy.

Has lost his health.

Has no eternal hope.

LEROY BROWNLOW
CONDENSED FROM "A PSALM IN MY HEART"

I AM THANKFUL FOR...

...the mess to clean after a party because it means I have been surrounded by friends.

...the taxes I pay because it means that I'm employed.

...the clothes that fit a little too snug because it means I have enough to eat.

...my shadow who watches me work because it means that I am out in the sunshine.

...a lawn that needs mowing, windows that need cleaning and gutters that need fixing because it means I have a home.

...the spot I find at the far end of the parking lot because it means I am capable of walking.

…all the complaining I hear about our government because it means we have freedom of speech.

…my huge heating bill because it means I am warm.

…the lady behind me in church who sings off key because it means that I can hear.

…the alarm that goes off in the early morning hours because it means that I'm alive.

…the piles of laundry and ironing because it means my loved ones are nearby.

…weariness and aching muscles at the end of the day because it means I have been productive.

⁓

NANCIE J. CARMODY
FROM "FAMILY CIRCLE" MAGAZINE

CONTENTMENT

JOY FOR TODAY

❦

I would like to read a noble poem.

❦

I would like to see a beautiful picture.

❦

I would like to hear a bit of inspiring music.

❦

I would like to meet a great soul.

❦

I would like to say a few sensible words.

GOETHE
PHILOSOPHER AND PLAYWRIGHT

IF I HAD IT TO DO OVER AGAIN

   ♪   I would love my wife more in front of my children.

   ♪   I would laugh with my children more—at our mistakes and joys.

   ♪   I would listen more—even to the youngest child.

   ♪   I would be more honest about my own weaknesses and stop pretending perfection.

   ♪   I would do more things with my children.

   ♪   I would be more encouraging and bestow more praise.

   ♪   I would pay more attention to little things, deeds, and words of love and kindness.

JOHN MACARTHUR
FROM "THE FAMILY"

RANDOM ACTS OF KINDNESS

1. Let someone cut in front of you. 2. Send a thank-you note. 3. Take a bag of groceries to someone in need. 4. Volunteer. 5. Give a larger tip than normal. 6. Open a door for someone. 7. Visit the elderly. 8. Pick up letters. 9. Write a note of encouragement to a teenager. 10. Invite a widow to dinner. 11. Be polite. 12. Take a neighbor flowers. 14. Bake something for a friend. 15. Listen. 16. Watch someone's children. 17. Ask, "What can I do for you?" 18. Invite someone new for coffee. 19. Make a new employee feel welcome. 20. Smile at a stranger. 21. Be a Big Brother or Big Sister. 22. Help without being asked. 23. Compliment five people each day. 24. Offer to pick up a neighbor's mail. 25. Talk respectfully. 26. Donate to a nonprofit organization. 27. Send a gift anonymously. 28. Visit someone in the hospital. 29. Feed the birds. 30. Do for others what you would like them to do for you.

ALICE GRAY, DR. STEVE STEPHENS, AND JOHN VAN DIEST

TRANQUILITY

⑨ You can have peace in your heart with little if you are in the will of God; but you can be miserable with much if you are out of His will.

⑨ You can have joy in obscurity if you are in the will of God, but you can be wretched with wealth and fame out of His will.

⑨ You can be happy in the midst of sufferings if you are in God's will, but you can have agony in good health out of His will.

⑨ You can be contented in poverty if you are in the will of God, but you can be wretched in riches out of His will.

⑨ You can be calm and at peace in the midst of persecution as long as you are in the will of God, but you can be miserable and defeated in the midst of acclaim if you are out of His will.

BILLY GRAHAM
FROM "UNTO THE HILLS"

RULES OF CONTENTMENT

Allow ourselves to complain of nothing, not even the weather.

Never picture ourselves in any circumstances in which we are not.

Never compare our lot with that of another.

Never allow ourselves to wish that this or that had been otherwise.

Never dwell on the tomorrow; remember, that is God's and not ours.

E. B. PUSEV
ENGLISH THEOLOGIAN

WE ALL NEED...

TO BE LOVED   *...when lonely.*

TO BE PROTECTED   *...when afraid.*

TO BE COMFORTED   *...when hurting.*

TO BE FED   *...when hungry.*

TO BE TAUGHT   *...when confused.*

TO BE ENCOURAGED   *...when downhearted.*

TO BE FILLED   *...when empty.*

TO BE HEARD   *...when crying.*

TO BE FOUND   *...when lost.*

TO BE GIVEN HOPE   *...when all seems dark.*

DR. STEVE STEPHENS
PSYCHOLOGIST AND SEMINAR SPEAKER

20 WAYS TO SIMPLIFY

1. Eliminate ten things from your life.

2. Cut back on TV.

3. Escape to a quiet spot.

4. Set your own pace.

5. Get rid of clutter.

6. When you bring in something new, throw out something old.

7. Do only one thing at a time.

8. Say no at least once a day.

9. Enjoy the little things.

10. Take at least four breaks per day.

11. Determine what really matters.

12. Make peace with all people.

13. Tell the truth.

14. Appreciate beauty.

15. If you don't need it, don't buy it.

16. If you don't have time, don't do it.

17. Have a place for everything and
    put everything in its place.

18. Share your thoughts, feelings,
    and opinions with a friend every day.

19. Allow time to pray.

20. Thank God for what you have.

DR. STEVE STEPHENS
PSYCHOLOGIST AND SEMINAR SPEAKER

HAPPINESS

  ℱ Happiness comes from spiritual wealth,
not material wealth.

  ℱ Happiness comes from giving, not getting.

  ℱ If we try hard to bring happiness to others,
we cannot stop it from coming to us also.

  ℱ To get joy, we must give it.

  ℱ To keep joy, we must scatter it.

JOHN TEMPLETON
FROM "MORE OF...THE BEST OF BITS & PIECES"

LIFE IS HARD...BUT GOD IS GOOD

HE IS STRONG *in our weakness.*

HE IS COMFORT *when we're in pain.*

HE IS LOVE *when we need acceptance.*

HE IS PEACE *when we're haunted by fear.*

HE IS PROTECTION *when we're in trouble.*

HE HEALS OUR WOUNDS *when someone or something has hurt us.*

HE IS OUR JOY *when our hearts are grieved.*

HE IS OUR FRIEND *when we've been rejected.*

HE IS OUR POWER *when we need a miracle.*

SHERI ROSE SHEPHERD
FROM "FIT FOR EXCELLENCE"

THE GREATEST THINGS

The best day, today;

The best play, work;

The greatest puzzle, life;

The greatest thought, God;

The greatest mystery, death;

The best work, work you like;

The most ridiculous asset, pride;

The greatest need, common sense;

The most expensive indulgence, hate;

The most disagreeable person, the complainer;

The best teacher, the one who makes you want to learn;

The greatest deceiver, the one who deceives himself;.

The worst bankrupt, the soul who has lost enthusiasm;

The cheapest, easiest, and most stupid thing to do, finding fault;

The greatest comfort, the knowledge that
you have done your work well;

The most agreeable companion, the one who
would not have you any different than you are;

The meanest feeling, being envious of another's success;

The greatest thing in the world, love—for family,
home, friends, neighbors.

AUTHOR UNKNOWN

FOUR THINGS THAT
BRING GREAT PEACE

1.
Strive to do another's will rather than your own.

2.
Always prefer to have less than more.

3.
Always seek the lower place and be submissive in all things.

4.
Always wish and pray that God's will
may be entirely fulfilled in you.

THOMAS Á KEMPIS
FROM "THE IMITATION OF CHRIST"

THE POWER OF SILENCE

It makes room for LISTENING.

It gives us freedom to OBSERVE.

It allows time to THINK.

It provides space in which to FEEL.

It lets us broaden our AWARENESS.

It opens us to the entry of PEACE.

AUTHOR UNKNOWN

7

Marriage and Romance

Experiencing the best

12 ACTIONS FOR
A HAPPY MARRIAGE

Ask

Listen

Accept

Respect

Risk

Encourage

Adjust

Forgive

Give

Love

Laugh

Comfort

DR. STEVE STEPHENS
PSYCHOLOGIST AND SEMINAR SPEAKER

THE FIVE LOVE LANGUAGES

1.
WORDS OF AFFIRMATION

Compliments, words of encouragement, and requests rather than demands all affirm the self-worth of your spouse.

2.
QUALITY TIME

Spending quality time together through sharing, listening, and participating in joint meaningful activities communicates that we truly care for and enjoy each other.

3.
GIFTS

Gifts are visual symbols of love, whether they are items you purchased or made, or are merely your own presence made available to your spouse. Gifts demonstrate that you care, and they represent the value of the relationship.

4.
ACTS OF SERVICE

Criticism of your spouse's failure to do things for you may be an indication that "acts of service" is your primary love language. Acts of service should never be coerced but should be freely given and received, and completed as requested.

5.
PHYSICAL TOUCH

Physical touch, as a gesture of love, reaches to the depths of our being. As a love language, it is a powerful form of communication—from the smallest touch on the shoulder to the most passionate kiss.

GARY CHAPMAN
FROM "THE FIVE LOVE LANGUAGES"

BETWEEN A HUSBAND AND WIFE

❧ We provide emotional, physical, and spiritual safety.

❧ We promise unconditional love and acceptance.

❧ We say in a hundred ways, "We belong together, here!"

❧ We provide for, and are sensitive to, each other's needs.

❧ We're loyal to each other—against all rumor and criticism; in the face of failure; in spite of disappointments.

DAVID AND HEATHER KOPP
CONDENSED FROM "UNQUENCHABLE LOVE"

A REGRET-FREE MARRIAGE

1.
Refuse to divorce.

2.
Make your mate's happiness a priority.

3.
Avoid hurtful words with your mate.

4.
Build memories with your mate.

ROBERT JEFFRESS
FROM "SAY GOODBYE TO REGRET"

QUESTIONS TO ASK
BEFORE YOU SAY "I DO"

1.
How does he treat his parents?

2.
Can you accept her for who she is if she never changes?

3.
What sort of people does he spend his time with?

4.
Does she have any addictive tendencies?

5.
Is he trustworthy?

6.
What is her reputation?

7.
What do your family and friends think of him?

8.
What is her philosophy of life?

9.
What is his spiritual life like?

10.
Do you respect her?

11.
What are his strengths and weaknesses?

12.

What are her parents like?

13.

What is his track record with past relationships?

14.

Is she kindhearted?

15.

What does he expect of you?

16.

How does she handle money?

17.

How does he respond to stress?

18.

How does she spend her leisure time?

19.

What are his likes and dislikes?

20.

What are her plans and dreams for the future?

~✦~

DR. STEVE STEPHENS
PSYCHOLOGIST AND SEMINAR SPEAKER

21 THINGS EVERY
COUPLE SHOULD KNOW

1. The qualities within your spouse that ignited your interest when you first met.

2. How to give your spouse a visible expression of love.

3. The importance of looking into your spouse's eyes while listening.

4. One compliment a day isn't too many.

5. Good memories are priceless no matter what they cost.

6. The importance of courtship after marriage.

7. How to make your spouse laugh.

8. The simple intimacy of holding hands.

9. A romantic location within walking distance from your home.

10. Unexpected gifts can bring great pleasure.

11. Marriages are built on small expressions of affection.

12. How to appreciate and accept the differences in your partner.

13. How to say, "I'm sorry."

14. How to agree more and argue less.

15. Being the right person is more important than trying
    to change your spouse into the right person.

16. How to make every anniversary a special celebration.

17. A growing marriage gets stronger and better over the years.

18. Guidelines for a great marriage won't work
    unless you apply them.

19. The triggers that hurt feelings.

20. The value of a hug.

21. Your spouse is priceless.

DOUG FIELDS
SELECTED FROM "365 THINGS EVERY COUPLE SHOULD KNOW"

NINE WAYS TO
E-N-C-O-U-R-A-G-E EACH OTHER

Express love.

Nurture your relationship.

Cooperate with each other.

Observe ways to creatively demonstrate love.

Understand, don't lecture.

Remember your blessings.

Accept each other.

Grow together.

Enjoy each other.

DUANE STOREY AND SANFORD KULKIN
FROM "BODY AND SOUL"

50 FUN THINGS TO
DO WITH YOUR SPOUSE

1. Look at picture albums. 2. Have a candlelight dinner. 3. Give each other fifteen-minute backrubs. 4. Make a date for a concert or a play. 5. Listen to your favorite recording. 6. Take a short walk. 7. Go window-shopping. 8. Tell each other two jokes. 9. Write a poem to each other. 10. Go to a movie. 11. Play charades. 12. Buy a plant. 13. Read a book, story, or article together. 14. Plan a trip to the zoo. 15. Sing some songs together. 16. Bake cookies together (clean up, too). 17. Make a surprise visit to someone. 18. Go bowling. 19. Make valentines for each other. 20. Read The Song of Solomon. 21. Play hide-and-seek. 22. Talk about favorite memories. 23. Go camping (campground or yard). 24. Go bicycle riding. 25. Have a wiener roast. 26. Call your spouse just to say "I love you." 27. Send flowers for no special reason. 28. Call and invite your spouse to lunch. 29. Put a love note where your spouse can find it. 30. Make popcorn or fudge. 31. Tell each other bedtime stories. 32. Go for a scenic drive. 33. Act out a play or skit with each other. 34. Plan a trip to the beach. 35. Spend a day in the city. 36. Surprise the other with dinner reservations. 37. Spend a night at a motel or hotel. 38. Play a favorite board game. 39. Spend an afternoon hiking. 40. Finger paint. 41. Go on a picnic. 42. Play racquetball or tennis. 43. Go out to breakfast. 44. Work in the yard together. 45. Wash the car together. 46. Have a pillow fight. 47. Make love by candlelight. 48. Take a class together. 49. Spend an evening in front of the fireplace. 50. Attend a sporting event.

DR. STEVE STEPHENS
PSYCHOLOGIST AND SEMINAR SPEAKER

THE TOP 10 MISTAKES COUPLES MAKE

1. AVOID CONFLICT.
Avoided conflict requires repression of anger, which leads to depression of feelings. A genuinely passionate partnership requires conflict, not terminal niceness or withdrawal.

2. AVOID EACH OTHER.
Occasional withdrawal is healthy. Habitual withdrawal (stonewalling) is death to partnership.

3. ESCALATE.
Conflict, skillfully handled, is one of the keys to a great relationship. Conflict out of control is an excuse for physical, verbal, or psychological abuse.

4. CRITICIZE.
Habitually speaking (or thinking) criticism is hard on a relationship. Criticism is usually a sign that the criticizing partner has some personal development work to do.

5. SHOW CONTEMPT.
Contempt is criticism escalated to outright mental abuse.

6. REACT DEFENSIVELY.

Fear is natural. Defensiveness naturally accompanies fear. Skillful partnering requires practicing techniques that allow you to drop the defensiveness despite your fear.

7. DENY RESPONSIBILITY.

When you deny responsibility for your part in the issue, you wind up blaming your partner and trying to change him or her.

8. REWRITE HISTORY.

Remembering mainly the negative experiences in a partnership is a predictor for future breakdown. All partnerships have difficult spots.

9. REFUSE TO GET HELP.

Partnership coaching (and willingness) works!

10. BELIEVE THAT CHANGING PARTNERS IS THE SOLUTION.

People may go through several partners while repeatedly avoiding the same basic issues.

NINE RULES FOR ROMANCE

1.
ONE DATE A WEEK

2.
HOLD HANDS

3.
WALK TOGETHER OUTSIDE

4.
SLOW DANCE TO MUSIC

5.
WATCH ROMANTIC MOVIES

6.
CANDLELIGHT DINNERS AT HOME

7.
WRITE CARDS AND LETTERS

8.
A WEEKEND GETAWAY

9.
TELL YOUR PARTNER WHAT IS ROMANTIC TO YOU

DAVID CLARK, PH.D.
PSYCHOLOGIST AND SEMINAR SPEAKER
FROM "MEN ARE CLAMS AND WOMEN ARE CROWBARS"

10 GREAT ROMANCE MOVIES

1.

AN AFFAIR TO REMEMBER

2.

BEAUTY AND THE BEAST (1940)

3.

CASABLANCA

4.

DOCTOR ZHIVAGO

5.

GONE WITH THE WIND

6.

ROMAN HOLIDAY

7.

SHADOWLANDS

8.

SOMEWHERE IN TIME

9.

THE PHILADELPHIA STORY (1940)

10.

WUTHERING HEIGHTS

COMPILED BY DAN MCAULEY
LONGTIME MOVIE BUFF

SIMPLE WAYS TO BE ROMANTIC

Shower.

Wear perfume/cologne.

Dress nicely.

Floss and brush.

Keep a supply of breath mints, gum, and mouthwash handy.

Hold hands as much as possible.

Whisper "sweet nothings" in each other's ear.

Leave little love notes around the house,
in lunch bags, in cars, in purses.

Call for no reason.

Exercise.

Eat healthy.

Kiss a lot.

Share your deepest desires and dreams.

Be spontaneous.

Put the kids down early, and eat supper late.

Invest in one of those "Romantic Love Songs" CDs.

Buy and burn some scented candles.

Stare into each other's eyes.

Stare into a fire together.

Share a blanket on the couch on a cold night.

Sit side by side on the couch.

Wink at each other.

Hug.

Reminisce about your courtship.

WOODS, HUDSON, DALL, LACKLAND
FROM "MARRIAGE CLUES FOR THE CLUELESS"

TIPS FOR THE
ROMANTICALLY CHALLENGED

1.
SHOWER HER WITH PRAISE.
Praise not only affects her,
it changes your perception of her.

2.
TRY NEW THINGS.
Boredom is a mortal enemy to relationships.

3.
ESTABLISH RITUALS.
Romantic rituals ensure that you are
spending quality time together on a regular basis.
If you wait until you are feeling spontaneous
or "in the mood" to be romantic, you
may end up waiting a long time.

4.
GET AWAY!
Don't make the mistake of thinking you can't
afford to take time away—you can't afford not to!

MICHAEL WEBB
CONDENSED FROM "NEW MAN" MAGAZINE

TALK ABOUT THESE THINGS

- ⸎ What do you think of when you imagine intimacy and closeness?

- ⸎ What is romance to you? Do you need romance to set the mood for sex?

- ⸎ What are the positive factors about our love life?

- ⸎ What brings you the most sexual fulfillment? What do you think brings me the most sexual fulfillment?

- ⸎ How often would you like to make love?

- ⸎ How much hugging and cuddling do you need before and after intercourse? (Define this in minutes if necessary.)

- ⸎ What are the fantasies you have been hoping to fulfill together?

- ⸎ What changes do we need to make to keep sex fresh and growing?

DAVID AND CLAUDIA ARP
ADAPTED FROM "LOVE LIFE FOR PARENTS" AND "10 GREAT DATES"

13 RULES FOR FIGHTING FAIR

1.

Make an appointment for the discussion.

2.

Face each other.

3.

Keep it limited to one issue.

4.

Keep it respectful.

5.

Keep focused on the present.

6.

Keep focused on understanding first,
being understood second.

7.

Keep focused on the problem, not the person.

8.

Avoid distractions.

9.

Keep it clean.

10.

Keep it tactful.

11.

Take a time-out if needed.

12.

Don't interrupt.

13.

Remember, *your* reality
isn't the only reality.

WARNING SIGNS THAT YOUR MARRIAGE NEEDS HELP

Enjoy spending times with others more than partner.

Easily irritated at spouse.

No sexual relations for one month or more.

Easily distracted when mate is talking.

Looking for excuses to stay away from home.

Impatient with partner.

Haven't gone out alone with spouse for a month or more.

Thoughts or threats of divorce.

Believe mate doesn't understand you.

Lack of trust.

Negativity, sarcasm, or criticism toward each other.

Not going to bed at same time (for reasons other than work).

Less communication now than one year ago.

Don't laugh together.

Arguing over the same issue over and over again.

Can't be honest with partner.

Don't enjoy spending time together.

Don't feel respected by spouse.

Bored by relationship.

Haven't given mate a gift in two months or more.

Wondering what it would be like to be married to someone else.

Haven't hugged or cuddled for a month or more
(without it leading to sexual relations).

Hard to forgive partner.

Don't know what to talk about when together.

Difficult to think of compliments for mate.

DR. STEVE STEPHENS
PSYCHOLOGIST AND SEMINAR SPEAKER

EIGHT STRATEGIES FOR THE SECOND HALF OF MARRIAGE

1.
Let go of past marital disappointments, forgive each other,
and commit to making the rest of your marriage the best.

2.
Create a marriage that is partner-focused
rather than child-focused.

3.
Maintain effective communication that allows you
to express your deepest feelings, joys and concerns.

4.
Use anger and conflict creatively to build your relationship.

5.
Build a deeper friendship and enjoy your spouse.

6.
Renew romance and restore a pleasurable sexual relationship.

7.
Adjust to changing roles with aging parents and adult children.

8.
Evaluate where you are on your spiritual pilgrimage.

DAVID AND CLAUDIA ARP
CONDENSED FROM "THE SECOND HALF OF MARRIAGE"

MARRIAGE ADVICE FROM 1886

Let your love be stronger than your
hate or anger.

Learn the wisdom of compromise, for it
is better to bend a little than to break.

Believe the best rather than the worst.

People have a way of living up
or down to your opinion of them.

Remember that true friendship is the
basis for any lasting relationship. The
person you choose to marry is deserving
of the courtesies and kindnesses you
bestow on your friends.

Please hand this down to your children
and your children's children: The more
things change the more they are the same.

JANE WELLS

8

Home and Finances

Managing your nest and your nest egg

PRINCIPLES FOR DEBT-PROOF LIVING

YOU MUST NEVER KEEP IT ALL
The first thing you must do when money flows
into your life is give some of it away.

YOU MUST NEVER SPEND IT ALL
Always pay yourself before anyone else. Always.

THERE ARE ONLY FIVE THINGS YOU CAN DO WITH MONEY
Give it, save it, invest it, lend it, and spend it.
Notice where spending comes in that lineup: last.
Spending should never be the first thing you do with your money.

PAY CASH
Paying cash requires making some lifestyle changes and
sacrifices, but it will keep you from drowning in a
sea of red ink on your journey to financial freedom.

NO DEBT NO MATTER WHAT
Unsecured debt is like cancer. At first it is not life-threatening
because it involves only a cell or two. But it never stays tiny.

DEVELOP A STRATEGY
Without a plan for getting there, reaching your goal of financial
freedom will remain a dream. A plan turns a dream into a goal.

MARY HUNT
ADAPTED FROM "DEBT-PROOF LIVING"

10 WAYS TO STRETCH
YOUR DOLLARS

1.

Reduce credit-card expense. The goal is really to eliminate credit-card expense. But if you have debts, they may as well cost you as little as possible. Switch to credit cards with the lowest interest rate you can find.

2.

Keep your car after it is paid off. Studies have shown that the cheapest car you can own is the one you already have.

3.

Trim your spending by 2 to 3 percent. It's a small enough amount that you might not even notice the difference.

4.

Save a portion of each increase in income. Try to maintain your existing lifestyle even when your income increases.

5.

Set up your own forced savings plan with money automatically withdrawn at regular intervals from your checking account and deposited in another account.

6.

Use Christmas Clubs or Vacation Clubs to save for large expenses. Money is deducted from your paycheck or bank account each pay period for a year.

7.

Pay cash as often as possible. Studies have shown that people who pay primarily with cash spend less money. It's harder to part with cash than to pull out a credit card.

8.

Give yourself an allowance. Rather than spend everything that's left after giving, saving, and debt paying, limit yourself and your spouse to a weekly allowance that's enough to have fun while still being financially responsible.

9.

Start an empty-wallet policy. If you have allowance money left at the end of the week, save it. I go a step further. Every night I empty my spare change into a big coffee jar.

10.

Don't window-shop. If you do, don't take any money with you, especially a credit card. Even without money, window-shopping is dangerous because it creates desire.

RAY LINDER
ADAPTED FROM "MAKING THE MOST OF YOUR MONEY"

ADVANTAGES TO PAYING CASH

§ Paying cash keeps you focused.

§ Paying cash promotes contentment because it
adds meaning and value to the things you do buy.

§ Paying cash lets you own things, not merely acquire them.

§ Paying cash adds meaning and value to the thing
purchased.

§ Paying cash makes spending difficult and uncomfortable.
And that is exactly the way it should be.

MARV HUNT
FROM "DEBT-PROOF LIVING"

TIPS FOR STAYING WITHIN YOUR BUDGET

DON'T BUY ANYTHING ON IMPULSE.

PAY OFF CREDIT CARDS EACH MONTH.
Charge items only for convenience.

TAKE YOUR LUNCH AND SNACKS TO WORK.
Avoid vending machines.

BUY IN BULK; USE COUPONS.

IF YOU SMOKE, QUIT.
Quitting is good for your health and your budget.

ENTERTAIN AT HOME INSTEAD OF GOING TO A RESTAURANT.

PUT SOME MONEY INTO SAVINGS EVERY PAY PERIOD.
If your company or bank has an automatic savings plan, sign up.

SELECTED FROM "ABOUT...CREATING A BUDGET," A LIFE ADVICE® PAMPHLET
PUBLISHED BY METLIFE'S CONSUMER EDUCATION CENTER

THE SEVEN PILLARS OF
FINANCIAL INDEPENDENCE

THE FIRST PILLAR: AN ATTITUDE OF GRATITUDE

Central to financial freedom is a sincere spirit of thankfulness to God for every big and small blessing in your life. From this heart of gratitude comes the natural, joyful overflow of sharing with your community, church, and worthwhile endeavors around the world.

THE SECOND PILLAR: A COMMITMENT TO HEALTH AND VITALITY

Good health is vital (a) to help avoid big medical expenses down the road and (b) to the fitness, energy, and vitality you will want in order to truly enjoy an active, fulfilling life style.

THE THIRD PILLAR: FREEDOM FROM DEBT

Break and stay free of those *Buy Now, Pay Forever* habits that rob your future as you pay for your past. When you get rid of consumer debt for good, you're liberating thousands of dollars that you can set aside for your future.

THE FOURTH PILLAR: DISCIPLINED SAVINGS

As your consumer-debt load lightens, you'll be able to direct more dollars toward savings for the future. Some of that money should fund a contingency reserve of two to six months' living expenses to help handle life's surprises. Your major savings commitment, however, should be for the long term—so you'll be financially free as you enter your retirement years.

THE FIFTH PILLAR: INVESTING FOR GROWTH

Even the most diligent savers will cheat themselves if they leave all their funds in "safe" places such as bank accounts or certificates of deposit. For long-term retirement savings, put your money to work more aggressively in investments averaging 10 to 12 percent or better annually. You'll be pleasantly surprised at the results over time!

THE SIXTH PILLAR: ASSET PROTECTION

Invest a few dollars now for some "safety nets" to guard against losing what you're working so hard to build. These include important insurance coverages such as adequate life, health, auto, homeowners/renters, and liability coverage. (Warning: Some policies are excellent values while others are wastes of good money. Choose carefully.)

THE SEVENTH PILLAR: MAKING YOUR MONEY LAST

As adults grow older their most prevalent financial fear is: "Will I have enough to 'make it' when I retire? Will I have to move in with my children or depend on the government?" We don't want to merely "survive" financially—we want to thrive! By combining smart planning, savvy investment choices, and systematic withdrawals of funds, we can have all the money we need for as long as we'll need it.

DAN BENSON
FROM "THE NEW RETIREMENT: HOW TO SECURE FINANCIAL
FREEDOM AND LIVE OUT YOUR DREAMS"

DEBT TRAP WARNING SIGNS

1.
You are living on credit.

2.
You pay your bills late.

3.
You are not a giver.

4.
You are not a saver.

5.
You dream of getting rich quickly
and living an extravagant lifestyle.

6.
You worry about money.

7.
You overspend your checking account.

MARY HUNT
CONDENSED FROM "DEBT-PROOF LIVING"

MOST COMMON WAYS TO
MISUSE CREDIT CARDS

§ Buying luxuries or nonessentials with credit cards. (Paying for vacations, entertainment, clothes, jewelry, or eating out on credit must be avoided.)

§ Paying the minimum amount due, rather than the entire bill, at the end of the month. (Failing to pay off the credit card bill in full each month is the most common first step toward the debt trap.)

§ Assuming that if we have the credit to buy it, we can afford it. (This is far from the truth.)

§ Accepting a new credit card without paying off the old. (Transferring the credit card balance to a card with a lower interest is wise, but make sure you cancel your old card.)

§ Using a credit card to purchase things that would normally be purchased with cash. (Buying groceries on credit, for instance, is a sign that you are falling into the debt trap.)

BOB RUSSELL
FROM "MONEY: A USER'S MANUAL"

HOW TO BUY A NEW CAR

BEFORE GOING TO A DEALER, DETERMINE YOUR PRIORITIES

- Consider the advantages of buying a new car over a used car—warranties, latest engineering features, and a car without an unknown maintenance history.

- Price and financing—Retail price and dealer costs are published in automobile magazines and on the Internet. Determine in advance the maximum you want to spend and don't budge from that figure.

- Safety and Reliability—Check out safety and crash test results in automobile and consumer magazines.

- Personal Preference—Weigh the advantages and disadvantages of your model choice. Sport Utility Vehicles are durable and offer good visibility but often have less comfort and lower gas mileage. Sports cars have higher insurance costs.

- Extras—There is substantial dealer profit on extras, and they quickly raise the price of your vehicle.

- Decide on at least two makes and models that interest you—Having two choices will help you negotiate more objectively.

READY FOR THE DEALER

🕉 Test drive the two models at the top of your list—Observe handling, visibility, braking, readability of dash instruments, quality of air and radio, comfort of seats, leg room, and storage space.

🕉 Remember the best times to deal—Dealers are usually more willing to deal the last few days of the month. Another good time is just before or after new models come out. Watch for dealer discounts and rebates.

🕉 Show that you are an informed buyer—Let the dealer know you have his invoice cost and that you will buy where you can get the best deal. Negotiate your best price without a trade-in. After you have your price, ask what they will offer you on a trade. Know the approximate value of your car by checking the prices for similar cars in your local newspaper ads.

🕉 Remember—regardless of what the salesman says, a deal is not a sale until it is in writing and signed by both the buyer and the seller.

🕉 It's worth it—Outside of buying a home, a new car is the largest purchase the average family makes. Careful research and intelligent decisions can save thousands of dollars.

HOLT BERTELSON
THE NEW CAR CZAR

HOW TO BUY A USED CAR

1.

Decide how much you can afford to spend before you start shopping. Don't go over that amount.

2.

Determine the value of the car you are considering. Check auto ads or contact lending institutions and ask for the wholesale and retail value. Low mileage, appearance, options, and mechanical conditions are all factors.

3.

Dealer or private party? Your best price is usually through a private party, but a dealer's price may include a warranty or dealer protection. Whenever you buy a newer car, find out if the manufacturer will transfer the unused warranty.

4.

Drive the car in traffic and freeway conditions. Look for problems with steering, vibrations, acceleration, shifting, brakes, engine noise, exhaust, alignment, electrical, ventilation, fluid leaks, and comfort. Look at the car in the daylight.

5.

Demand maintenance records, repair history, and a mechanic's check-up when buying from a private party or "as is" from a dealer. The money you spend on a mechanic can make the difference between buying a gem and a lemon. Ask the seller to put a statement in writing that the odometer has not been changed.

6.

Dicker for your best price. Start with the wholesale value and work up rather than starting from the asking price and working down.

7.

Don't pay cash to a private party unless you get a receipt. Be sure the legal owner signs the release on the car registration form. Don't delay in notifying your car insurance agent.

AL GRAY
CAR COUNSELOR FOR FAMILY AND FRIENDS

CHECKING CURBSIDE APPEAL
WHEN SELLING A HOME

- § Are the lawn and shrubs well maintained?

- § Are there cracks in the foundation or walkways?

- § Does the driveway need resurfacing?

- § Are the gutters, chimney, and walls in good condition?

- § Do the window casings, shutters, siding, or doors need painting?

- § Are garbage and debris stored out of sight?

- § Are lawn mowers and hoses properly stored?

- § Is the garage door closed?

SELECTED FROM "ABOUT...SELLING A HOME," A LIFE ADVICE® PAMPHLET
PUBLISHED BY METLIFE'S CONSUMER EDUCATION CENTER

QUESTIONS TO ASK
BEFORE GETTING A PET

ᔍ What kind of pet do I want?

ᔍ Can I afford the cost of purchasing a pet?

ᔍ Can I afford the cost of caring for a pet (food
and grooming, regular health checks, illness)?

ᔍ Do I have time to care for a pet?

ᔍ Do I have the proper environment for the pet?

ᔍ What type of extra housing or equipment
will I need for the pet?

ᔍ How will my children handle a new pet?

ᔍ How will other pets in my household react to a new pet?

ᔍ Does anyone in the household have allergies?

SELECTED FROM "ABOUT...CHOOSING AND CARING FOR A PET," A LIFE ADVICE® PAMPHLET
PUBLISHED BY METLIFE'S CONSUMER EDUCATION CENTER

QUALITIES OF A GREAT BABY-SITTER

Shows maturity and common sense

Follows your instructions

Respects your property and rules

Commands your child's obedience

Ensures your child's safety

Responds appropriately to an emergency

Displays love

Plays with your child

Listens to your child

Sets good boundaries

Disciplines in a way you feel comfortable with

Manages their own anger, stress, and frustration

Introduces games and play ideas appropriate to your child

Supports and models your values

Keeps the place picked up

Has good references

TAMI STEPHENS
MOTHER OF THREE

WHAT YOUR BABY-SITTER
NEEDS TO KNOW

- Where you will be
- How you might be contacted
- Where a first-aid kit is and how to use it
- Phone numbers to use in an emergency
- Address and cross streets of residence
- Location and use of fire extinguisher
- What and when the children are to eat
- Acceptable television channels and shows that may be watched
- What forms of discipline you wish them to use
- When the children should go to bed
- Bedtime routines and rituals
- Any fears the children have
- Important family rules that must be obeyed
- Expectations as to the children's manners, behaviors, obedience, and tidiness
- Any special allergies or medical problems
- When you will return

TAMI STEPHENS
MOTHER OF THREE

COP'S VACATION CHECKLIST

✓ Discontinue mail and newspaper.

✓ Ask a neighbor or friend to check for packages, flyers, etc.

✓ Ask a neighbor or friend to set out and bring in garbage can.

✓ Have someone check the house each day.

✓ Give key and alarm code to neighbor or family member.

✓ Ask local police or sheriff's department for drive-by checks.

✓ Arrange care for animals.

✓ Leave telephone number where you will be in event of problems.

✓ Set lights on timer.

✓ Arrange to have yard work done.

✓ Turn off water if on extended vacation.

✓ Set heat thermostats.

✓ Close gates, bring toys in, put tools and valuables away.

✓ Put jewelry and money in safe or safety deposit box.

✓ Check refrigerator and freezer doors,
  making sure they're closed.

✓ Walk through when you leave—check lights and
  windows, unplug appliances, and turn off computer.

✓ Lock all doors as you walk out.

✓ Take a final look at the house to see
  if you forgot anything.

KEN MCCLURE
RETIRED POLICE OFFICER

SIX EASY WAYS TO ORGANIZE YOUR KIDS' CLUTTER

A certain degree of clutter is an unavoidable side effect of family life. Here are some tips to help limit the mess in your household.

1. **Create a clutter cache.** If your kids persist in scattering their belongings, collect and place them in a box. Set some ground rules. For example, if your children need an item immediately, they can redeem it by paying a small fine. Otherwise, once each month, let them sort through the box, deciding what to keep and what to discard or give away.

2. **Obtain a large plastic bin for each child.** (Bins that fit under the bed are ideal.) When papers come home from school, allow the student to decide which to keep and which to throw away. A full bin is the limit.

3. **Color-code children's belongings.** Large families especially find this an effective organizational tool. Toothbrush, towel, duffel bag and sheets can be purchased in each child's chosen color. Color-coding makes for easy identification of belongings that need to be put away. It also eliminates some of the bickering over what belongs to whom.

4. *Cut down on paper clutter* by recording pertinent information on a calendar as soon as the birthday or invitation or sport information flyer arrives in the mail. Some families use different color markers for each child's events.

5. *Be selective with purchases.* For example, bypass school book fairs and visit the public library. If your child finds a book he really likes, then purchase it to place on a shelf with his favorites.

6. *Install lockers* (often available secondhand) in the laundry room, garage, or basement. Assign one to each child for the storage of sports equipment, school backpacks, coats, etc.

FAITH TIBBETTS MCDONALD
FROM "VIRTUE" MAGAZINE

22 ITEMS TO ALWAYS CARRY IN YOUR CAR

1.

Jumper cables

2.

First-aid kit

3.

Flashlight

4.

Work gloves

5.

Chains in inclement weather

6.

Fire extinguisher

7.

Flares or reflector triangles

8.

Help sign

9.

Jack (if car is not equipped with one)

10.

Tool kit

11.

Rags

12.

Ice scraper

13.

Tire gauge

14.

Spare tire

15.

Cell phone if driving alone

16.

Container of water

17.

Map

18.

Owner's manual

19.

Car registration

20.

Insurance information

21.

Notepad

22.

Pen or pencil

～⌒⌐

AL GRAV
A MAN KNOWN FOR BEING PREPARED

CREATE A FAMILY CRAFT BOX

Old shirts for smocks
Old shower curtains for drop cloths
Magazines
Safety scissors
Crayons
Notebooks
Sketchpads
Construction paper
Clothespins
Scrap cloth
Paintbrushes
Glue
Lunch bags
Yarn
Empty food cartons
Colored pencils
Photographs
Popsicle sticks
Tissue paper
Cotton balls
Paint
Newspapers
Twist-ties
Anything else you can find

CONDENSED FROM TRICIA GOYER
FROM "HOMELIFE" MAGAZINE

9
Teens

Shaping the future

10 GIFTS FOR YOUR TEENS

1.

The gift of time.

2.

The gift of respect.

3.

The gift of hope.

4.

The gift of caring for their friends.

5.

The gift of parameters.

6.

The gift of flexibility.

7.

The gift of understanding.

8.

The gift of other adult friends.

9.

The gift of loving our mates.

10.

The gift of a consistent role model.

SUSAN ALEXANDER YATES
CONDENSED FROM "HOW TO LIKE THE ONES YOU LOVE"

HOW WELL DO YOU KNOW
YOUR TEENAGER?

§ Who is your teen's best friend?

§ What color would he/she like for the walls
in his/her bedroom?

§ Who is your teen's greatest hero?

§ What embarrasses your teen the most?

§ What is your teen's biggest fear?

§ What is his/her favorite type of music?

§ What person outside the immediate family has
most influenced your teen?

§ What is his/her favorite school subject?

§ What is his/her least favorite school subject?

§ What has your teen done that he/she feels most proud of?

ॐ What is your teen's biggest complaint about the family?

ॐ What sport does your teen most enjoy?

ॐ What is his/her favorite TV program?

ॐ What really makes your teen angry?

ॐ What would your teen like to be when he/she grows up?

ॐ What chore does your teen like least?

ॐ What three foods does your teen like most?

ॐ What is your teen's most prized possession?

ॐ What is his/her favorite family occasion?

ॐ What activity did your teen enjoy most last weekend?

MIRIAM NEFF
CONDENSED FROM "FAMILYLIFE TODAY"

HOW TO MOTIVATE YOUR TEEN

❦

Teens feel motivated to do right when they have a sense that their parents trust them.

❦

Teens feel motivated to do right when they feel respected by their parents. That is, encouragement works better than put-downs.

❦

Teens feel motivated to do right when their parents live the standard they are being asked to live.

❦

Teens feel motivated to do right when they are given the moral reasons why.

❦

Teens feel motivated to do right when parents are willing to acknowledge their own mistakes instead of make up excuses.

❦

GARY AND ANNE MARIE EZZO
FROM "REACHING THE HEART OF YOUR TEEN"

KIDS WHO RESIST PEER PRESSURE HAVE...

An internal compass of right and wrong.

A fear of God.

General respect for parental and other authority.

A good relationship with their parents.

Self-control, including a willingness to say no to temptations.

Self-esteem.

Self-contentment.

An unwillingness to bend the rules.

A willingness to pay the price when they do make bad choices.

Wisdom to resist tempting environments.

DON S. OTIS
CONDENSED FROM "TEACH YOUR CHILDREN WELL"

FIVE SECRETS OF PARENTING TEENS

1.
CARE ABOUT WHAT MATTERS TO THEM

All teenagers need is the assurance that you have taken notice of their lives, that you have made a special effort to take interest in the things that matter to them. Make their interests your interests.

2.
EMBRACE MOMENTS OF PERSONAL PAIN

Most of the time, heartbreak in a teenager's life seems pretty trite to us. But when painful times hit, it's an open door for you to build trust and respect with your teenager.

3.
PREPARE TO BE TAKEN FOR GRANTED—IT IS WELL WORTH IT

The task of making boys and girls into men and women is not for the feeble at heart. Accept the fact that raising kids means long days and sleepless nights with rare instances of gratitude.

4.
STAY STEADY

More than anything else, teenagers are looking for people who will go the distance with them. They need you to pass the test of time and be there.

5.
PRACTICE MODELING

Whether we realize it or not, our kids are working their lives after ours. Count on it—they take note of everything we do and everything we say.

TED HAGGARD AND JOHN BOLIN
FROM "CONFIDENT PARENTS, EXCEPTIONAL TEENS"

HOW TO RAISE SEXUALLY PURE KIDS

Love them.

Provide them two loving role models.

Teach them who they are.

Teach them moral values.

Keep them active in church.

Help them select their friends.

Warn them about the joys and dangers of sex.

Provide them with clear guidelines for dating.

Teach them moral boundaries.

Help them make a formal commitment to virtue.

Teach them to purify their minds.

Teach them how to say NO!

Watch for signs of sexual involvement.

Provide good reading material that supports your values.

Surround them with prayer.

TIM AND BEVERLY LAHAYE
ADAPTED FROM "RAISING SEXUALLY PURE KIDS"

FOUR WAYS TO STAY SEXUALLY PURE

1.

DON'T PULL DOWN

2.

DON'T PULL UP

3.

DON'T UNZIP

4.

DON'T UNBUTTON

ROBERT JEFFRESS
FROM "SAVING GOODBYE TO REGRET"

TEENS

QUALITIES OF A GOOD TEEN FRIEND

Trustworthiness
Can you trust him when you are not around?

A sense of moral rectitude
Are his actions governed by absolute right or wrong?

The ability to defer gratification
Does your friend regularly resist an impulse?

Respect for authority
Does your friend respect his
parents and other adults?

Honesty
Can you trust him to tell you the truth?

Willingness to forgive
Does he find it easy to let go of the
wrong things others have done to him?

An even temper
When he doesn't get his way,
does he become angry or sullen?

Open-mindedness
Can he handle it when you disagree?

An inquiring mind
Does he strive for personal improvement?

DON S. OTIS
FROM "TEACH YOUR CHILDREN WELL"

TEEN GROUP-DATING IDEAS

- ❦ Plan a theme party.

- ❦ Go to a park and participate in outdoor activities.

- ❦ Make a video.

- ❦ Have a campfire/bonfire.

- ❦ Participate in a scavenger hunt (gather items, make a video, or make an audio recording).

- ❦ Play board/table games.

- ❦ Attend or participate in athletic contests.

- ❦ Participate in a trivia challenge.

- ❦ Play Clue (with real characters)

- ❦ Work 3-D puzzles.

- ❦ Cook out.

- ❦ Coordinate a bike adventure.

- ❦ Serve others through a ministry project.

JIMMY HESTER
CONDENSED FROM "HOMELIFE" MAGAZINE

HOW TO TEACH RESPECT

SET AN EXAMPLE.

How do you speak about others in your teen's presence? Determine to model respectful attitudes and actions to the youth in your life.

EXPOSE YOUR TEEN TO ETHICAL STANDARDS.

Whether at the dinner table, on the ride home from school, or on a field trip, make your kids aware of their duty to respect all human beings and help them think through why it's important to show an additional measure of respect to parents, elders, teachers and religious and civic authorities.

DEMAND RESPECT FROM YOUR TEENS.

Many parents allow their teens to speak rudely and act indifferently toward one or both parents. While it's certainly wise to pick your battles with a child, you should at the very least expect—and demand—common courtesy and decency.

TREAT KIDS WITH RESPECT.

Don't "talk down" to young people. Don't insult them or call them names. Ask their opinions and listen when they respond. Help them to develop a healthy respect for themselves, and they will be better equipped to respect others.

INSIST THAT SIBLINGS TREAT EACH OTHER WITH RESPECT.

Differences and disagreements may be inevitable among brothers and sisters, but disrespect need not be tolerated. Draw the line at name-calling, insults, and cruel teasing.

CREATE TEACHING OPPORTUNITIES.

Take your teens out on "dates" to teach them how to treat members of the opposite sex with respect and how to accept respectful gestures.

TEACH YOUR TEENS PRACTICAL WAYS TO SHOW RESPECT FOR OTHERS.

Explain manners as ways of communicating respect. Brainstorm practical ways you and your teens can honor the God-given worth of other people.

CONGRATULATE KIDS WHEN YOU SEE OR HEAR THEM ACTING RESPECTFULLY.

Make active attempts to "catch" your teens being respectful (such as offering a chair to Grandma or politely greeting a teacher in the grocery store) and explain why you appreciate and value their behavior.

BOB HOSTETLER
CONDENSED FROM "HOMELIFE" MAGAZINE

WHEN YOUR TEEN FAILS

DON'T BLAME YOURSELF.

Parents cannot be in the physical presence of their teenagers twenty-four hours a day and control their behavior. As frightening as it may seem, your teenager must be given freedom to make decisions.

DON'T PREACH TO THE TEENAGER.

A teenager who has failed needs to wrestle with his own guilt, but he does not need further condemnation.

DON'T TRY TO FIX IT.

If you seek to remove the natural consequences of the teen's failure, you are working against your teen's maturity. Teens learn some of life's deepest lessons through experiencing the consequences of failure.

GIVE YOUR TEENAGER UNCONDITIONAL LOVE.

The wise parent will give love to the teenager no matter what the failure. The teenager needs to know that no matter what he has done, someone is there who still believes in him, who still believes that he is valuable, and who is willing to forgive.

LISTEN TO THE TEENAGER WITH EMPATHY.

Empathy means to enter into the feelings of another. Parents need to put themselves in the shoes of the teenager and try to understand what led to the failure as well as what the teenager is feeling at the moment.

GIVE THE TEENAGER SUPPORT.

Let the teen know that while you do not agree with what he has done and that you cannot remove all the consequences, you will stand by his side as he walks through the process of dealing with the consequences of this failure.

GIVE GUIDANCE TO THE TEENAGER.

The teenager cannot become a responsible adult without having freedom to grapple with his situation and make decisions regarding where he goes from here. Parents who learn how to give this kind of guidance will continue to influence their teenager's decisions in a positive direction.

GARY CHAPMAN
CONDENSED FROM "THE FIVE LOVE LANGUAGES OF TEENAGERS"

MINIMIZE MATERIALISM

§ Engage in activities that don't cost much. This reinforces that fun isn't always associated with money.

§ Teach your children and show them by your actions that people matter more than things.

§ Minimize the exposure to commercial content, including advertisements that appear in your newspaper.

§ Keep conversations about major purchases or financial struggles between adults. Children don't need the added stress of knowing about or worrying over financial pressure.

§ Beware of "fiction wishing." Don't say, "Wouldn't it be great if we had…?"

§ Encourage the deferral of gratification. Encourage your kids to save money in order to purchase something they want instead of just going to the store and buying it for them. Let them know they can't have everything they want and have to make choices.

ੵ Reach out to people in need by volunteering time or services. Visit those in hospitals, nursing homes, or orphanages.

ੵ Encourage your children to save, recycle, reuse, give away, and take care of the material items they have.

ੵ Avoid the temptation of comparing what you or your children have with what others have.

ੵ Explain the difference between functionality and extravagance. For example, designer clothes may not always be better.

ੵ Reject the dress-for-success mentality.

ੵ Talk about the fact that happiness or contentment are rarely the result of what we have. Help your children see that it is what's inside a person that counts, not how many things he or she has.

DON S. OTIS
CONDENSED FROM "TEACH YOUR CHILDREN WELL"

TEENS

WARNING SIGNS THAT MY CHILD IS HEADED FOR TROUBLE

My child may be headed for trouble if he or she...

Becomes lonely, quiet, or moody.

Just seems depressed.

Has very low self-esteem.

Begins having difficulty sleeping.

Seems negative about everything.

Begins to isolate himself or herself.

Is often angry and abusive.

Changes his or her eating habits.

Becomes argumentative and lies to me.

Begins fighting at school and at home.

Begins receiving poor grades.

Begins violating curfew times.

Is arrested for shoplifting.

Drops out of once-loved activities.

Gets caught drinking or taking drugs.

Refuses to go to church anymore.

Becomes lazy and procrastinates regularly.

Dates/befriends kids against my wishes.

Becomes sexually active.

Changes his or her appearance.

Stops making eye contact.

DR. GREG CYNAUMON
ADAPTED FROM "HELPING SINGLE PARENTS WITH TROUBLED KIDS"

WARNING SIGNS OF TEENS HEADED FOR VIOLENT BEHAVIOR

§ Grades in school tumble suddenly

§ Personality shifts from outgoing to withdrawn

§ Fascination with violence, death, blood, and gore, including violent movies, video games, and music laced with violent lyrics

§ Intense interest in guns and bombs

§ Talking about "getting even" or "settling a score" with some group at school

§ Spending time on Web sites that focus on violence or how to build or obtain weapons

§ Changes in clothing and hairstyle, including tattoos and paraphernalia associated with gangs or neo-Nazi groups

MARK A. TABB
CONDENSED FROM "HOMELIFE" MAGAZINE

10 COMMANDMENTS FOR TEENAGERS

1.

Live with eternity in mind.

2.

Life is more than friends, money, and material things.

3.

Use your words well.

4.

Use your time well.

5.

Respect your mom and dad.

6.

Value people.

7.

Discipline your sexuality.

8.

Earn your own way.

9.

Tell the truth.

10.

Be grateful for what you have.

TED HAGGARD AND JOHN BOLIN
CONDENSED FROM "CONFIDENT PARENTS, EXCEPTIONAL TEENS"

10

Family Life

Learning and caring together

CHILDREN LEARN WHAT THEY LIVE

IF CHILDREN LIVE WITH CRITICISM, THEY LEARN TO CONDEMN.

If children live with hostility, they learn to fight.

If children live with ridicule, they learn to be shy.

If children live with shame, they learn to be guilty.

If children live with encouragement, they learn confidence.

If children live with tolerance, they learn to be patient.

If children live with praise, they learn to appreciate.

If children live with acceptance, they learn to love.

If children live with approval, they learn to like themselves.

If children live with honesty, they learn truthfulness.

If children live with security, they learn to have
faith in themselves and others.

If children live with friendliness, they learn the
world is a nice place in which to live.

DOROTHY LAW NOLTE
LIBRARIAN

TEACHING THE ABCS
TO YOUR CHILDREN

A lways be on time.

B e a model of honesty.

C are about their hurts.

D o acts of kindness.

E very day give plenty of hugs and kisses.

F orget past offenses.

G ive occasional "token gifts" of love.

H ave a happy disposition—"a merry heart."

I nvest quality time.

J ump for joy when they bring home good grades.

K eep looking for the good and positive.

L isten to their cares and woes and excitement.

M ake adjustments for physical pain.

N ever criticize in front of their peers.

O nly say words that edify.

P ut on the heart of patience.

Q uietly discipline in private.

R ecognize each child is creatively, uniquely different
and specially gifted.

S pend time reading to them and listening to
them read.

T ake care of yourself.

U nderstand the age-appropriate behavior of each child.

} oicing—teaching them to share facts, thoughts,
ideas, dreams, opinions, intuition.

W elcome their friends.

X -ray to the need of the heart.

Y esterday doesn't have to dictate today.

Z oom in on good behavior.

GLENDA HOTTON, M.A.
COUNSELOR

HELPING YOUR CHILD SUCCEED

ぅ   Help children choose their own goals.

ぅ   Help children imagine the positive results of achieving their own goals and the negative results of not reaching their goals.

ぅ   Remember the power of praise.

ぅ   Expose children to a variety of activities.

ぅ   Expect children to do things right.

ぅ   Believe your children can achieve great things.

ぅ   Help children develop a more positive self-image.

ぅ   Reward your children.

ぅ   Use the ol' "You can do it, can't you?" principle.

ぅ   Be persistent.

ぅ   Be enthusiastic.

ぅ   Develop strong inner convictions.

GARY SMALLEY
FROM "THE KEY TO YOUR CHILD'S HEART"

EVERY PARENT SHOULD ASK...

◈ What gives my child joy?

◈ Who is my child's hero?

◈ What does my child fear most?

◈ What activities give my child energy?

◈ Which activities wear my child out?

◈ If my child got to choose this year's vacation, where would he or she want to go?

◈ If my child could pick one activity for me to do with him or her, what would it be?

◈ What music does my child like?

◈ Other than going to school or sleeping, what does my child spend the most time doing each week?

◈ What does my child want to be when he or she grows up?

DR. JOHN C. MAXWELL
FROM "BREAKTHROUGH PARENTING"

25 WAYS TO HELP YOUR CHILD DO BETTER IN SCHOOL

1. Talk positively about school.

2. Develop a relationship with your child's teacher.

3. Attend open house functions.

4. Help out at your child's school.

5. Read with your child.

6. Take your child to the library.

7. Discuss current events.

8. Turn off the TV.

9. Discuss movies, concerts, and books.

10. Discuss your child's homework.

11. Travel with your child.

12. Explore nature with your child.

13. Help your child learn to manage money.

14. Discuss report cards and school reports.

15. Praise your child's progress.

16. Subscribe to periodicals.

17. Use good grammar.

18. Create environments for conversation.

19. Provide good nutrition and sufficient rest.

20. Strengthen your child's memory.

21. Invite interesting adults into your home.

22. Play games and work puzzles.

23. Choose toys that teach well.

24. Provide opportunities for your child to teach.

25. Be your child's biggest school fan.

JAN DARGATZ
CONDENSED FROM "52 WAYS TO HELP YOUR CHILD DO BETTER IN SCHOOL"

13 WAYS TO GET YOUR CHILDREN TO READ

1.
Model reading by having everyone in
the family reading regularly.

2.
Read to your children daily, beginning at birth.

3.
Choose early reading material carefully;
colorful, fun, and age-appropriate.

4.
Show esteem for books by setting aside
shelves or areas just for books.

5.
Purchase some special books such as pop-up books
and books autographed by authors and illustrators.

6.
Buy books on tape; better yet, have a
grandparent read books onto tape.

7.
Subscribe to magazines that keep children's
attention and feed their interest.

8.
Respect children's right to choose what to read,
but also introduce books they may not read on their own.

9.
Regularly visit libraries and bookstores.

10.
Always have good books in the car and take them into
restaurants, offices, etc., for "waiting times."

11.
Set aside part of a child's allowance for a book purchasing fund.

12.
Visit Web sites of children's authors.

13.
Unplug the television.

DORIS HOWARD
LIBRARIAN

FAMILY LIFE

KIDS ONLINE

- ✦ Never fill out questionnaires or give out personal information.
- ✦ Never agree to meet in person with anyone without parental presence.
- ✦ Never enter a chat room without parental supervision.
- ✦ Never tell anyone where you will be or what you will be doing without parental permission.
- ✦ Never respond to or send e-mail to new people you meet online.
- ✦ Never go into a new area online that will cost more money without parental permission.
- ✦ Never send a photo over the Internet or by mail to anyone you meet online without parental permission.
- ✦ Never buy or order products online without parental permission.
- ✦ Never respond to belligerent or suggestive contact that makes you feel uncomfortable.
- ✦ Always tell your parents when you see something that upsets you, whether you saw it on purpose or by accident.

DONNA RICE HUGHES
FROM "KIDS ONLINE"

SHOWING RESPECT FOR YOUR CHILD

§ Accept your child. Respect his developmental ability. Don't compare him to someone else.

§ Allow and accept your child's feelings, even anger. Remember, your child has a right to feel his feelings.

§ Share your own feelings with your child.

§ Don't expect more of your child than you do of yourself.

§ Show patience with problems.

§ Discipline in private.

§ Don't complain about your child or about the burdens of parenting in front of your child.

§ Show an interest in his friends. Invite his friends to your house.

§ Respect your child's need for privacy.

~~~

RON HUTCHCRAFT
FROM "FIVE NEEDS YOUR CHILD MUST HAVE MET AT HOME"

FAMILY LIFE

25 WAYS TO ENJOY YOUR FAMILY

1. Eat dinner together as a family for seven days in a row.
2. Take your wife on a dialogue date.
3. Read your kids a classic book.
4. Memorize the Twenty-third Psalm as a family.
5. Give each family member a hug for twenty-one days in a row (that's how long the experts say it takes to develop a habit).
6. Pick three nights of the week in which the television will remain off.
7. Pray for your spouse and children every day.
8. Plan a vacation together.
9. Take a vacation together.
10. Sit together as a family in church.
11. Take a few hours one afternoon and go to the library as a family.
12. Write each member of your family a letter sharing why you value them.
13. Take each of your children out to breakfast (individually) at least once a month for a year.
14. Help your kids with their homework.
15. Put together a picture puzzle (five hundred pieces or more).

16. Encourage each child to submit to you his most perplexing question, and promise him that you'll either answer it or discuss it with him.

17. Tell your kids how you and your spouse met.

18. Call your wife or husband from work just to see how they're doing.

19. Compile a family tree and teach your children the history of their ancestors.

20. Get involved in a family project that serves or helps someone less fortunate.

21. Spend an evening going through old pictures from family vacations.

22. Praise your spouse and children—in their presence—to someone else.

23. De-clutter your house.

24. Become a monthly supporter of a Third World child.

25. Give each child the freedom to pick his favorite dinner menu at least once a month.

TIM KIMMEL
SELECTED FROM "LITTLE HOUSE ON THE FREEWAY"

THREE WAYS TO KEEP
FAMILY BOUNDARIES

1.
SIMPLIFY THE RULES.

Begin by prioritizing what's essential to you and your family: Everyone is kind to one another, everyone puts dirty clothes in the hamper, everyone takes turns helping in the kitchen. By eliminating the rules that don't matter, you'll have more energy to follow through on those that do.

2.
ENFORCE SAFETY AND HEALTH RULES AND DON'T COMPROMISE.

Everyone washes up before dinner, everyone wears a seat belt in the car, everyone puts his or her toys away when finished playing.

3.
BE CONSISTENT.

If you make a rule, stick with it whether it's the weekend or the busiest day of your week. Your kids will appreciate the boundaries and in the long run, their behavior will reflect it.

DR. MARY MANZ SIMON
CONDENSED FROM "CHRISTIAN PARENTING TODAY" MAGAZINE

TIPS TO CUSTOM-FIT
YOUR PARENTING

HANG OUT WITH YOUR KIDS.

You'll learn who shares, who exhibits a big imagination, and who must be active in order to be happy.

OBSERVE YOUR CHILD'S REACTION TO STRESSFUL SITUATIONS.

What frustrates him? What makes him laugh? How does he respond to teasing? Is he tenderhearted or tough?

DISCOVER TALENTS.

Try lessons in piano, art, or karate, and see what develops: an athletic ability or a creative spirit?

OBSERVE YOUR CHILD'S NATURAL SPEED
AND CAPACITY FOR LEARNING AND PERFORMING.

Can she handle four things at once, or only one thing at a time? Does she finish projects on time or is she consistently late?

WHAT BRINGS OUT YOUR CHILD'S INQUISITIVE NATURE?

If bugs and spiders mesmerize your daughter, buy her an ant farm. She could be a budding entomologist!

DOTTIE G. BACHTELL
FROM "TODAY'S CHRISTIAN WOMAN" MAGAZINE

THE 10 COMMANDMENTS
OF GRANDPARENTING

1.
Thou shalt not freak out when thy grandchild, to whom thou has just given a one-half interest in Mt. Rushmore plus two Oreo cookies, refuses to speak to thee on the telephone.

2.
Thou shalt permit thy grandchildren to have other grandparents before thee on certain holidays.

3.
Thou shalt honor the father and mother of thy grandchildren, and thou shalt not substitute thy judgment for theirs.

4.
Thou shalt open the doors of thy home and thy heart to thy grandchildren without screaming "Don't touch," for thou knowest that the visit of thy grandchildren shall soon end.

5.
Thou shalt remember thy family history and teach it diligently unto thy grandchildren.

6.

Thou shalt refrain from exalting the roles of thy grandchildren,
remembering always that thy friends also have grandchildren.

7.

Thou shalt not commit effrontery; thou shalt answer
the questions of thy grandchildren with dignity and respect.

8.

Thou shalt not steal thy grandchild's witticism
and pass it as thine own.

9.

Thou shalt not covet thy neighbor's grandchild for his or
her good grades, sweet disposition, or gentle manner.

10.

Thou shalt love thy half-grandchildren, thy step-grandchildren,
thy somewhat grandchildren as surely as thou lovest thy
natural grandchildren, for it is the heart, not the bloodline,
that truly makes thee a grandparent.

DR. LARRY KEEFAUVER
FROM "HUGS FOR GRANDPARENTS"

FAMILY LIFE

GOOD TIMES WITH GRANDPARENTS

⚜ Allow your child to spend time alone with the grandparents. A connection between them is best forged on a one-to-one basis.

⚜ Don't expect your parents always to agree with the way you are raising your children.

⚜ When your parents give advice, attempt to listen graciously, even if you decide not to heed it.

⚜ Keep your children on the sidelines of any conflict. Don't let them feel they are driving a wedge between their parents and grandparents.

⚜ Let everyone take an occasional break. A trip to the grocery store or a walk with the kids might be the thing everyone needs when tension starts to mount.

⚜ Keep communication open. Allow room for discussion on parenting styles and the role grandparents play in the lives of their grandchildren.

CYNTHIA SUMNER
FROM "MOMSENSE"

GOLDEN MOMENTS IN A CHILD'S DAY

THE WAKE-UP:

It is important for a child to have some parent-love in the first conscious moment of her day.

THE SENDOFF:

Horses, Olympians, and children run a good race when they get off to a good start. As often as possible, you should be there for breakfast and your child's departure to school.

THE RECEPTION:

If you want to get a real reading on how the "game" went, you have to be there when the "player" comes off the field. Your presence when your child comes in the door says "I love you." Your responsibility at the "reception" is mostly to hug, to listen without judgment, to notice your child is home, and to just be available.

THE DEBRIEFING:

This may come right after The Reception. Kids need to debrief their day—not to be interrogated but to report, celebrate, evaluate, or explode. Again, your role is to listen. Your undivided attention communicates that you care.

THE HAPPY ENDING:

If "all's well that ends well," it's good for a parent to be there at the end of the day. It's a time for an "I love you," an "I'm sorry," or a "thank you." It puts a period on the end of the day.

RON HUTCHCRAFT
FROM "FIVE NEEDS YOUR CHILD MUST HAVE MET AT HOME"

PRINCIPLES OF PARENTING

DEFINE YOUR PRIORITIES.

What's really important to you? Don't spin your wheels on the unimportant things—save your energy for the important issues.

MAKE YOUR LIFE AN EXAMPLE FOR YOUR CHILDREN.

It must be just as much "Be what I am" as it is "Do what I say." Discipline is for parents first. That is why it is so hard.

STUDY YOUR CHILD.

Training your child requires studying him. Know your child. Talk with him. Ask him questions.

BE CAREFUL NOT TO CRUSH YOUR CHILD.

We must never crush his will through verbal or physical intimidation. Our ultimate goal is to train him to choose right for himself, from the heart, even when we aren't around.

TEACH YOUR CHILD TO CONTROL HIMSELF.

Hearing "no" and surviving the frustration that automatically comes with it gives kids strength. It builds endurance and helps them control their frustrations and impulses.

REQUIRE OBEDIENCE.

Say yes whenever you possibly can. But when you say no, mean it. If you must discipline, make the pain of the discipline outweigh the pleasure of disobedience or it will be meaningless to your child.

TEACH RESPECT FOR OTHER PEOPLE AND FOR PROPERTY.

Respect starts in the home. By learning respect at a young age, children see that people and things should not be targets for their wrath.

TEACH HARD WORK.

From a very early age, a child should be a helping member of the family unit. This requires patient, creative, structured teaching. First, you do it for him. Then, you do it together. Finally, he does it himself.

GIVE MANY REWARDS.

Punishment teaches what not to do. You want to teach your child that good and pleasure go together, just as surely as sin and pain. Reward kindness, good deeds, and cheerful obedience.

FORGET GUILT TRIPS.

We all make mistakes, children and parents alike. Children would rather live with a parent who makes an occasional mistake than with one who never cares enough to discipline them at all.

JANI ORTLAND
CONDENSED FROM "FEARLESSLY FEMININE"

STARTING YOUR CHILD
ON GOOD HEALTH

Keep safety in mind every minute.

Don't keep handguns at home.

Talk about drugs and sex.

Cut back on television.

Learn CPR.

Stop smoking.

Tell children you love them.

LORAINE STERN, M.D.
CONDENSED FROM "WOMAN'S DAY" MAGAZINE

BUILDING RELATIONSHIPS
WITH YOUR MARRIED KIDS

ॐ Build the relationship with each couple.

ॐ Visit each couple, but not too often.

And don't stay too long.

ॐ Resist the urge to give advice.

ॐ Tolerate small irritations.

ॐ Be interested in your children's professions,

hobbies, and activities.

DAVID AND CLAUDIA ARP
FROM "THE SECOND HALF OF MARRIAGE"

10 BEST INDOOR GAMES EVER

1. CHARADES

Each person selects a movie or song title, then has to get others to guess it by acting it out. No words allowed!

2. PING PONG

With two cheap paddles and one ball, you can play on your dining room table. You can even create your own rules, like allowing shots to bounce off the floor or walls.

3. BLOW HOCKEY

Make goals on each end of your kitchen table by placing two pieces of tape a foot apart. Divide into two teams, drop a ping pong ball onto the table, bend over, and start blowing. You score by blowing the ball through your opponent's goal.

4. PILLOW FIGHTS

If you don't occasionally have a gentle pillow fight with your kids, you're missing out on one of the most fun times of all. I suggest one rule: No hitting on the head. Anyone who violates that rule must sit out the rest of the fight.

5. PAPER PLANES

Help your kids fold paper airplanes and see whose goes the farthest. Then place a target on the rug and see how close everyone can come to landing on it.

6. FICKLE FEATHER

Have everyone kneel in a circle and pull a bedsheet taut, holding it in place with your chins. Place a feather on the sheet and try to blow it away from your side. Score a point for each time it drops on your side—fewest points wins.

7. TABLE HOCKEY

Position one person on each side of your dining room table, then drop a tennis ball in the middle. Players bat the ball to try to send it past an opponent. If it goes off your side, you're assessed a point. The ball must *roll* off the edge—no throwing. Low score wins.

8. BALLOON BLAST

Divide a room into halves with string, make two teams, and bat a balloon around. The purpose is to keep the balloon from falling on your side.

9. BALLOON SOCCER

Take off your shoes and use a balloon as a soccer ball, marking out two "goals" in your living room. No hands allowed—but have plenty of extra balloons ready!

10. FOLLOW THE LEADER

One person leads the family in funny actions (hop on one foot, rub your belly, etc.). Everyone else must follow him exactly.

JERRI AND PATTI MACGREGOR
CONDENSED FROM "FAMILY TIMES"

11
Family Love

Bonding together

A PARENT'S COMMITMENT

❧ We are committed to help them be successful
  in whatever they want to do.

❧ We will be committed to them after they
  are married.

❧ We will be committed to them no matter whom
  they marry.

❧ We will be committed to them no matter what
  happens during their marriage.

❧ We will be committed to their mates and to
  their children.

❧ We will always be available to listen.

❧ Should they get into trouble, we will be there
  to help.

GARY SMALLEY AND JOHN TRENT
FROM "LEAVING THE LIGHT ON"

25 SIMPLE WAYS TO TELL YOUR CHILD "I LOVE YOU"

1.

Make a pledge to love your child.

2.

Meet your child's basic needs.

3.

Use loving nicknames.

4.

Read with your child.

5.

Make something together.

6.

Keep your child's secrets.

7.

Keep a special place for memories of your child.

8.

Get down on your child's level.

9.

Find something to do for mutual fun.

10.

Just tell them "I love you."

11.

Give hugs and kisses.

12.

Be willing to let go.

13.

Leave surprise notes and messages.

14.

Give your child heirloom items.

15.

Have a listening ear.

16.

Send a card.

17.

Apologize when you need to.

18.

Take time to play with your child.

19.

Take your child with you.

20.

Have a "date" with your child.

21.

Display your child's photograph.

22.

Help your child build a collection.

23.

Set rules.

24.

Pray for your child.

25.

Protect your child.

JAN DARGATZ
CONDENSED FROM "52 SIMPLE WAYS TO TELL YOUR CHILD 'I LOVE YOU!'"

HOME RULES

Always be honest.

Count your blessings.

Bear each other's burdens.

Forgive and forget.

Be kind and tenderhearted.

Comfort one another.

Keep your promises.

Be supportive of one another.

Be true to each other.

Look after each other.

Treat each other as you treat your friends.

But most important
Love one another deeply from the heart.

SELECTED FROM THE HOLY BIBLE

A PARENT'S DAILY PRAYER GUIDE

MONDAY:

Ask God to place a protective, solid hedge around your children.

TUESDAY:

Pray that your children would use godly wisdom in selecting
friends and peers who will make a positive difference in their lives.

WEDNESDAY:

Pray that your children would stay pure in their thoughts and deeds.

THURSDAY:

Pray that they will be caught if they
wander into cheating, lies, or mischief.

FRIDAY:

Pray that they will be alert and thinking clearly as they attend school
and extracurricular activities, and as they take exams.

SATURDAY:

Pray for the spouse each child will marry someday.

SUNDAY:

Ask God to help them live their lives for Him.

~~~

DON AND SUE MYERS
CONDENSED FROM "REAL FAMILYLIFE" MAGAZINE

WAYS TO MAKE YOUR
MOM FEEL SPECIAL

1. Create a song to honor your mom.

2. Leave little thank-you notes in unusual places.

3. Ask your mom to tell you about experiences she had when she was a little girl.

4. Hug your mom and tell her, "I love you."

5. Offer to help Mom around the house in addition to your "job list."

6. Pray for your mom often.

7. Make a bookmark and put it in a book she is reading.

8. Say "I love you" each day to your mother.

9. Cut out magazine pictures of activities your mom likes to do and make a poster collage.

10. Make a banner with a slogan telling her about a special talent you appreciate, such as "My Mom's a Champion Pie Baker!"

11. When you pray as a family, thank God for your mother and ask Him to bless her in special ways.

12. Make a greeting card with a personal message. Write three things you love about your mom.

13. Talk with Mom about happy experiences you've shared.

CHARLOTTE ADELSPERGER
CONDENSED FROM "FOCUS ON THE FAMILY 'CLUBHOUSE'"

WAYS TO HONOR YOUR DAD

§ Seek his wisdom.

§ Honor his legacy.

§ Explore his family history.

§ Show him respect.

§ Express love.

§ Celebrate Father's Day.

§ Remember his birthday.

§ Honor his wife.

§ Pray for him daily.

§ Build a memory book.

§ Respect his preferences.

§ Surprise him with a special gift.

§ Take him fishing.

JOHN VAN DIEST
FATHER OF THREE, GRANDFATHER OF NINE

FAMILY LOVE

AFFIRMING YOUR CHILDREN

PRAISE SELECTIVELY.

Indiscriminate praise doesn't motivate; it only confuses. When your child i
disruptive or disrespectful, resist the myth that says children learn obedience
by flattery. Praise only when behavior or character reflects your desires.

PRAISE IMMEDIATELY.

Delayed praise has less meaning than immediate praise. When you praise a
child hours after a good choice was made, he may not remember the action
Catch your little ones "in the act" of doing something praiseworthy, and ther
respond immediately.

PRAISE SPECIFICALLY.

When you praise your child, assign your praise to noticeable acts or attitudes
"I like the way you shared your toy!" "What a good job you did making your
bed today!" "Look at you. You remembered to brush your teeth all by yourself!"

PRAISE INTENTIONALLY.

Look for ways to praise your child. When your daughter brings you a finger
painting, look carefully for something you like in it (maybe the colors are mostly
mud-like, but notice the smudge of bright yellow). Single out what you like and
then display the piece on the refrigerator or a bulletin board. When you're going
about your daily chores and you notice your toddler occupying himself with a
puzzle, tell him how proud you are of his choice to play alone sometimes.

ELISA MORGAN AND CAROL KUYKENDALL
FROM "WHAT EVERY CHILD NEEDS"

MESSAGES THAT LAST A LIFETIME

"I belong."
Those hours in your arms give your baby the
message, "I am loved. Somebody's there for me."

"I'm special."
It is never too early to begin affirming
your baby and letting her know how
valuable she is in God's eyes and in your heart.

"I trust."
Because in his distress you comfort him,
your baby learns…that you will
respond and are worthy of his trust.

"I can."
Applaud your baby's milestones. Show
your joy as he stretches his little body and his mind.

WILLIAM SEARS, MARTHA SEARS, JOYCE WARMAN, ET AL.
FROM "PARENT PROJECT: TOOLS FOR GODLY PARENTING"

10 GIFTS TO GIVE YOUR CHILDREN

1. LOVE

Every child wants love, and it's so easy to love a child.

2. DISCIPLINE

No parent likes to come home to the role of disciplinarian, yet that's exactly what your child needs from you—the strong, sure limits you provide.

3. A GOOD EXAMPLE

The most important messages you convey to your children are the unspoken ones.

4. RESPECT

A child needs your respect in order to develop self-respect.

5. A GOOD SELF-IMAGE

Love and respect enhance a child's self image, but try not to over-praise or hover. Compliments for a job well done are great, but when praise is undeserved, a child knows it, and that can undermine her self-image.

6. GOOD HEALTH HABITS

Start early to guard his health with preventive healthcare visits. Take care of yourself too: always brushing your teeth, exercising, and eating healthful snacks are the surest ways to install in your child the value of taking good care of his own body.

7. TIME TOGETHER

Even though life is busy and complicated, make sure your child knows that she comes first. You need to be available to her at mealtimes, on weekends, and for school functions. Bathtime and bedtime rituals are also important, as is sharing sports, music, and fun.

8. MOTIVATION FOR LEARNING

All parents who are concerned about learning naturally model that drive for their children, but the danger is in pushing them beyond their limits.

9. SENSE OF HUMOR

Laugh with your children so they can see the light and joyful side of things. Humor may not come easily when you're feeling stressed, but try not to be too serious. Laughter gives us balance.

10. PEER RELATIONSHIPS

From the second year on, a child needs playmates. Through play with children his own age or slightly older, he learns about compromise and empathy; he develops new skills, interests and responsibility to others.

T. BERRY BRAZELTON, M.D.
CONDENSED FROM "FAMILY CIRCLE" MAGAZINE

FAMILY LOVE

MAXIMIZE YOUR GRANDPARENTING SKILLS

Love each child equally.

Give gentle hugs and hold hands.

Be good listeners.

Read and tell good stories.

Know basic first aid.

Be supportive of the child's parents.

Look for teachable moments.

Have a cheerful attitude.

Tell children positive traits you see in them.

Remember birthdays and special occasions.

Initiate fun ideas and activities.

Play table games.

Keep regular contact by visits, phone calls, and letters.

Pray regularly.

Spoil a little but not too much.

JOHN VAN DIEST
GRANDFATHER OF NINE

I REMEMBER GRANDMA AND GRANDPA BECAUSE...

They read to me and let me read to them.

They liked my turtle and tree house.

They told interesting stories from their childhood.

They helped me with hard jobs.

They liked spinach!

They saw things I didn't (like good things about my brother).

They taught me how to save, give, and spend money.

They had special names for me.

They gave me their full attention.

They had rules to live by, and I knew what they were just by being with them.

They sent "snail mail" cards.

They thought I was special.

PAT VAN DIEST
GRANDMOTHER OF NINE

TRAITS OF A LOVING FAMILY

A LOVING FAMILY...

- ♪ Communicates and listens.
- ♪ Affirms and supports each other.
- ♪ Teaches respect for each other.
- ♪ Develops a sense of trust.
- ♪ Has a sense of play and humor.
- ♪ Exhibits a sense of shared responsibility.
- ♪ Teaches a sense of right and wrong.
- ♪ Has a strong sense of family in which rituals and traditions abound.
- ♪ Has a balance of interaction among members.
- ♪ Has a shared religious core.
- ♪ Respects the privacy of one another.
- ♪ Values service to others.
- ♪ Fosters table time and conversation.
- ♪ Shares leisure time.
- ♪ Admits to and seeks help with problems.

DOLORES CURRAN
FROM "TRAITS OF A HEALTHY FAMILY"

FOUR FOUNDATION STONES
OF PARENTAL LOVE

1.

Meeting the emotional and
nurturance needs of your child

2.

Giving loving training and
discipline to your child

3.

Providing physical and emotional
protection for your child

4.

Teaching and modeling anger
management for your child

DR. ROSS CAMPBELL
FROM "RELATIONAL PARENTING"

KEEP COMMUNICATION
OPEN WITH YOUR CHILD

- 🔥 Ask your child what his or her favorite song is, listen to it, go over the words, discuss what they mean, and ask what makes the song a favorite.

- 🔥 Break through superficial conversation by asking some probing questions: "What's going well in your life? What's not going well? What changes would you like to make? What is the biggest challenge you're currently facing?"

- 🔥 Ask your child to pick a new sport, hobby, art project, or interest for the two of you to develop together.

- 🔥 Keep a journal of family highlights and special accomplishments throughout the year. Review it together on December 31.

- 🔥 Help your child develop a set of lifetime goals.

- 🔥 Share some of the struggles you had when you were your child's age (this may require some digging in your memory!). Then ask your child what his or her struggles are.

- 🔥 Ask your child to pick three places within driving distance that he or she wants to visit, and make a plan to see them during the next year.

- 𝄞 Take your child to work or the place you volunteer for a day.

- 𝄞 Adopt a grandparent in a nursing home.

- 𝄞 Ask your child about his or her heroes. Write a letter to the person and see if you get a response.

- 𝄞 Tell your child your family history while he or she records it on cassette tape or videotape.

- 𝄞 Research the meaning of your child's name and point out the character traits that parallel the name.

- 𝄞 Write your child a letter saying what in your life you enjoy, what you don't, how you have succeeded, where you made mistakes, and what you hope he or she can learn from your life.

- 𝄞 Serve at a soup kitchen together.

- 𝄞 Play board games or cards with your child. Use this time to find out what's going on in his or her life.

STEPHEN ARTERBURN AND JIM BURNS
CONDENSED FROM "PARENTS GUIDE TO TOP 10 DANGERS TEENS FACE"

SIX QUESTIONS TO GET
YOUR KIDS TALKING

1.

What's one thing I could pray
for you about this week?

2.

If you could be anything when
you grow up, what would you be?

3.

What's one thing you really appreciate
about your best friend?

4.

If we could go anywhere on vacation,
where would we go and what would we do?

5.

What's your favorite thing for us to do as a
family that doesn't involve spending money?

6.

What's one thing I could work on that
would make you feel even more loved?

JOHN TRENT, PH.D.
FROM "CHRISTIAN PARENTING TODAY"

GIVING LOVE TO CHILDREN

GIVE THE CHOICE OF LOVE.
Commit to love because it is right, not because it feels good.

GIVE THE WORDS OF LOVE.
We all need regular verbal assurance, but children need it the most.

GIVE THE TOUCH OF LOVE.
Research has confirmed the human need for physical touch.
The need to be held and cuddled is especially critical for babies.

GIVE THE ENCOURAGEMENT OF LOVE.
"Put courage into" those little people by letting them
know that you are their best fan and cheerleader.

GIVE THE COMFORT OF LOVE.
In times of pain or sadness, love offers healing comfort.

GIVE THE LAUGHTER OF LOVE.
Laughter sets a pleasant mood, a bright tone.
Make merriment a daily dose of love in your home.

GIVE THE DISCIPLINE OF LOVE.
Discipline establishes boundaries for children,
making them feel safe and secure.

DONNA OTTO
FROM "THE GENTLE ART OF MENTORING"

BOLSTERING YOUR
CHILD'S CONFIDENCE

NOTICE AND AFFIRM WHEN THEY DO WELL:

"Your words showed understanding. I'm proud of the way you cared for your friend."

FIND STRENGTHS RELATED TO EVERY WEAKNESS:

"You ran hard after that soccer ball!" rather than "Why can't you learn how to kick the ball properly!"

DOWNPLAY CRITICISM. WHEN YOU HAVE TO CRITICIZE, FOCUS ON THE ACTION RATHER THAN THE CHILD:

"Being late makes it hard to trust you," rather than "You're always late! I'll never be able to trust you again!"

POINT OUT SOMETHING POSITIVE ABOUT FRUSTRATIONS:

"Even though you were late, you did call. That shows consideration and a sense of responsibility."

HELP CHILDREN SOLVE THEIR OWN PROBLEMS:

"How might we master this lateness problem? I know it's as frustrating for you as it is for me." Together with your child, list several possibilities and implement one.

GUIDE YOUR CHILDREN IN EVALUATING THEIR ACTIONS. ASK:

"What went well in your plan?" "What might we have done even better?" "What action would you change if you could do it again?"

KAREN DOCKREY
FROM "PARENTING: QUESTIONS WOMEN ASK"

12
Wisdom

Learning from the experience of others

SEVEN LESSONS FOR LIVING

1.
Don't waste.

2.
Work hard.

3.
Don't cut corners.

4.
Have fun doing things.

5.
Be strict but caring.

6.
Tackle problems head-on.

7.
Pray.

GRANDMA SINCLAIR, GRANDMOTHER OF DAVE THOMAS (WENDY'S)
FROM "WELL DONE!"

LESSONS FROM AESOP'S FABLES

Avoid solutions that are worse than the problem.

It is great art to do the right thing at the right time.

Example is more powerful than reproach.

Honesty is the best policy.

He who is discontented in one place will seldom be happy in another.

Do boldly what you do at all.

The worth of money is not in its possession, but in its use.

Those who seek to please everybody, please no one.

The memory of a good deed lives on.

Happy is the man who learns from the misfortunes of others.

He who wishes evil for his neighbor brings a curse upon himself.

Do not attempt too much at once.

AESOP
ANCIENT STORYTELLER

WISE SAYINGS MY MOTHER TAUGHT ME

A thing of beauty is a joy forever.

It's always darkest just before the dawn.

Big oaks from little acorns grow.

God never gives more than you can bear.

This, too, shall pass.

Can't never did anything.

Nothing ventured, nothing gained.

A man is known by the friends he keeps.

Still waters run deep.

All the flowers of tomorrow are in the seeds of today.

NOLA BERTELSON
MOTHER AND GRANDMOTHER

A FATHER'S ADVICE

§ Make God and people your top priority.

§ Stop and smell the roses.

§ Keep your promises.

§ Persevere. Life is tough. Period.

§ Express yourself.

§ Remember that God molds our character through discomfort, through challenge.

§ Choose your friends wisely.

§ Let your actions speak louder than your words.

- ❧ Remember your roots.

- ❧ Laugh, often and loud.

- ❧ Learn to discern right from wrong.

- ❧ Don't be afraid to say you're sorry.

- ❧ Pray.

- ❧ Read. Read. Read.

- ❧ Humility is a greater virtue than pride.

BOB WELCH
ADAPTED FROM "A FATHER FOR ALL SEASONS"

DO GOOD

Hate evil.

Cling to what is good.

Devote yourself to brotherly love.

Honor one another.

Be joyful.

Share with those in need.

Practice hospitality.

Rejoice with those who rejoice.

Mourn with those who mourn.

Avoid pride.

Do what is right.

Live at peace with one another.

Seek not revenge.

Do not be overcome by evil.

Overcome evil with good.

ST. PAUL
ADAPTED FROM ROMANS 12:9–21

LIFE

Life may change,
but it may fly not;

Hope may vanish,
but can die not!

Truth be veiled,
but still it burneth;

Love repulsed,
but it returneth!

PERCY BYSSHE SHELLEY
POET

10 RULES TO LIVE BY

1.

Count your blessings.

2.

Today, and every day, deliver more
than you are getting paid to do.

3.

Whenever you make a mistake or
get knocked down by life,
don't look back at it too long.

4.

Always reward your long hours of
labor and toil in the very best
way, surrounded by your family.

5.

Build this day on a foundation
of pleasant thoughts.

6.

Live this day as if it will be your last.

7.

Laugh at yourself and at life.

8.

Never neglect the little things.

9.

Welcome every morning with a smile.

10.

Search for the seed of good in every adversity.

OG MANDINO
FROM "A BETTER WAY TO LIVE"

KIDS SAY THE WISEST THINGS

- If you want someone to listen
to you, whisper it.

- You can't be everyone's best friend.

- All libraries smell the same.

- Sometimes you have to take
the test before you've finished studying.

- Silence can be an answer.

- Ask where things come from.

- If you throw a ball at someone,
they'll probably throw it back.

- Don't nod on the phone.

- Say grace.

- The best place to be when
you are sad is in Grandma's lap.

PHIL CALLAWAY
FROM "WHO PUT THE SKUNK IN THE TRUNK?"

THE WISDOM OF ABRAHAM LINCOLN

§ You are only what you are when no one is looking.

§ Character is like a tree, and reputation is like a shadow.
The shadow is what we think of it; the tree is the real thing.

§ I have simply tried to do what seemed
best each day, as each day came.

§ To sit by in silence, when they should protest,
makes cowards of men.

§ It often requires more courage to dare to do right,
than to fear to do wrong.

§ Those who deny freedom to others deserve it not for
themselves. And, under a just God, cannot long retain it.

§ The better part of one's life consists of his friendships.

§ It is more important to know that we are on God's side.

§ A good laugh is good for both the mental and physical digestion.

§ You cannot help men permanently by doing for
them what they could and should do for themselves.

§ Nearly all men can stand adversity, but if you
want to test a man's character, give him power.

§ Let minor differences and personal preferences,
if there be such, go to the winds.

ABRAHAM LINCOLN
16TH PRESIDENT OF THE UNITED STATES

10 SECRETS TO AGELESS LIVING

1.

Never let age get in the way of life.

2.

Stay curious, explore, discover,
and continue to learn new things.

3.

Play, have fun, be happy, and maintain
a zest for life by being vital.

4.

Keep the brain and the body busy;
stimulate the mind, eat healthy, exercise.

5.

Smile, laugh, maintain a sense of humor,
and always stay young at heart.

6.

Have a positive attitude, outlook,
and be optimistic to overcome challenges.

7.

Believe in yourself by having faith,
hope, spirit, value, meaning, and purpose.

8.

Stay connected, engaged, creative,
and useful by continuing to contribute.

9.

Find fulfillment, peace, serenity, and self-esteem
by giving back—volunteer.

10.

Enjoy and cherish healthy relationships
with loved ones, friends, and family.

KELLY FERRIN
FROM "WHAT'S AGE GOT TO DO WITH IT?"

PRACTICAL WORDS
OF A PHILOSOPHER

Be gracious.

Know your chief asset and cultivate it.

Never exaggerate.

Do nothing to make you lose respect for yourself.

Have strength of spirit.

Work with good tools.

Keep in mind the happy ending.

To jog the understanding is a greater feat than to jog the memory.

Know how to refuse.

Be alert when seeking information.

Forestall evil gossip.

Be generous in action.

Have a just estimate of yourself.

Attain and maintain a good reputation.

Do not make a show of what you have.

The shortest road to being somebody is to know whom to follow.

Prepare yourself in good fortune, for the bad.

Do not a business of the trivial.

Never cry about your woes.

Know the value of reconsideration.

BALTASAR GRACIAN
PHILOSOPHER

WISDOM

VANITY

It is vanity to seek material wealth that cannot last and to place your trust in it.

It is also vanity to seek recognition and status.

It is vanity to chase after what the world says you should want and to long for things you should not have, things that you will pay a high price for later on if you get them.

It is vanity to wish for a long life and to care little about a good life.

It is vanity to focus only on your present life and not to look ahead to your future life.

It is vanity to live for the joys of the moment and not to seek eagerly the lasting joys that await you.

THOMAS Á KEMPIS
FROM "THE IMITATION OF CHRIST"

SEIZE THE DAY...

- ♪ When you have the choice between taking an escalator or the stairs, take the stairs.

- ♪ Place fresh flowers in the places where you live and work.

- ♪ Visit the Holy Land once in your life.

- ♪ Smile at babies.

- ♪ When you develop your film, get double prints. Give the duplicates away.

- ♪ Remember, there is time for love and a place for love. Any time, any place.

- ♪ Always go the extra mile...whether for a friend or mint chocolate ice cream.

- ♪ Whenever you look back on your life, be positive.

- ♪ If you seek wisdom over opportunity, opportunity will usually follow.

- ♪ Change is a process, not an event.

- ♪ Plan to be spontaneous.

- ♪ Whenever you look ahead, be optimistic.

- ♪ Enjoy each day as if it were your last.

BRUCE BICKEL AND STAN JANTZ
FROM "GOD IS IN THE SMALL STUFF: AND IT ALL MATTERS"

12 LESSONS WORTH REPEATING

1.

Be honest.

2.

Set goals and work quietly
and systematically toward them.

3.

Assign a task to yourself.

4.

Never give up.

5.

Be confident that you can make a difference.

6.

Don't ever stop learning and improving.

7.

Slow down and live.

8.

Choose your friends carefully.

9.

Be a can-do and will-try person.

10.

Try to live in the present.

11.

You are in charge of your own attitude.

12.

Always remember that you are never alone.

MARIAN WRIGHT EDELMAN
CONDENSED FROM "THE MEASURE OF OUR SUCCESS"

BE

Be understanding to your enemies,

Be loyal to your friends.

Be strong enough to face the world each day.

Be weak enough to know you cannot do everything alone.

Be generous to those who need your help.

Be frugal with what you need yourself.

Be wise enough to know that you do not know everything.

Be foolish enough to believe in miracles.

Be willing to share your joys.

Be willing to share the sorrows of others.

Be a leader when you see a path others have missed.

Be a follower when you are shrouded by the mists of uncertainty.

Be the first to congratulate an opponent who succeeds.

Be the last to criticize a colleague who fails.

Be sure where your next step will fall, so that you will not tumble.

Be sure of your final destination, in case you are going the wrong way.

Be loving to those who do not love you, and they may change.

Above all, be yourself.

AUTHOR UNKNOWN

FEAR AND FAITH

Fear imprisons.   *Faith frees.*

Fear troubles.   *Faith triumphs.*

Fear cowers.   *Faith empowers.*

Fear disheartens.   *Faith encourages.*

Fear darkens.   *Faith brightens.*

Fear cripples.   *Faith heals.*

Fear puts hopelessness   *Faith puts fear at*
at the center of life.   *the feet of God.*

PHIL CALLAWAY
FROM "WHO PUT THE SKUNK IN THE TRUNK?"

HANDBOOK OF WISDOM

If you don't have a Bible, GET ONE.

If you've got a Bible, READ IT.

If you read the Bible, BELIEVE IT.

If you believe the Bible, LIVE IT.

BRUCE AND CHERYL BICKEL AND STAN AND KARIN JANTZ
FROM "LIFE'S LITTLE HANDBOOK OF WISDOM"

Life-Changing Advice in a
Quick-to-Read Format!

With sales of over 700,000 copies, the Lists to Live By series has something for everyone—guidance, inspiration, humor, family, love, health, and home. These books are perfect gifts for all occasions.

For the Moments
That Matter Most

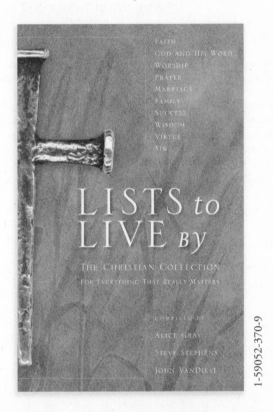

FAITH
GOD AND HIS WORD
WORSHIP
PRAYER
MARRIAGE
FAMILY
SUCCESS
WISDOM
VIRTUE
SIN

LISTS *to* LIVE *BY*

THE CHRISTIAN COLLECTION
FOR EVERYTHING THAT REALLY MATTERS

COMPILED BY
ALICE GRAY
STEVE STEPHENS
JOHN VANDIEST

1-59052-370-9

From the compilers of the popular Lists to Live By series come 200 powerful lists by some of the industry's top Christian speakers and authors. The lists are divided into thirteen easy-to-reference sections, with topics like virtue, prayer, faith, marriage, God and His Word, worship and praise, community, eternal hope, and family. Full of humor, insight, and practical advice, these lists will deepen faith, strengthen relationships, nurture hope, and build character.

www.multnomahbooks.com www.alicegray.com

Multnomah

Are You a Walk Out Woman?

There is an epidemic of women walking out on their marriages. In *The Walk Out Woman*, Dr. Steve Stephens and Alice Gray bring the expertise you need to uncover marital stressors and provide practical solutions to heal your relationship.

Are you a walk out woman? Find out! It could save your marriage.

"*For any man who wants to love his wife more deeply—and for any woman who is dying to be loved that way.*"
—NEIL CLARK WARREN, psychologist and founder, eHarmony.com

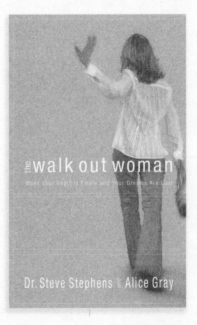

1-59052-267-2

The Stories for the Heart Series

compiled by Alice Gray

ACKNOWLEDGMENTS

More than a thousand books and magazines were researched and dozens of professionals interviewed for this collection. A diligent effort has been made to attribute original ownership of each list, and when necessary, obtain permission to reprint. If we have overlooked giving proper credit to anyone, please accept our apologies. If you will contact Multnomah Publishers, Inc., Post Office Box 1720, Sisters, Oregon 97759, with written documentation, corrections will be made prior to additional printings.

Notes and acknowledgments are shown in the order the lists appear in each section of the book. For permission to reprint a list, please request permission from the original source shown in the following bibliography. The editors gratefully acknowledge authors, publishers, and agents who granted permission for reprinting these lists.

SUCCESS

"Seven Favorite Quotations of Zig Ziglar" by Zig Ziglar, author and motivational teacher, condensed from *Christian Reader* magazine, May/June 2000. Used by permission of the author.

"Persistence" by Charles Stanley from *In Touch* magazine, January 2000, In Touch Ministries, Atlanta, GA. Used by permission of the author.

"Three Great Essentials" by Thomas Edison.

"20 Power Thoughts" from *Power Thoughts* by Robert H. Schuller. Copyright © 1993 by Robert Schuller. Reprinted by permission of HarperCollins Publishers, Inc.

"People Who Make a Difference Have…" by Charles R. Swindoll from *The Tale of the Tardy Oxcart*, Charles R. Swindoll, © 1998, Word Publishing, Nashville, Tennessee. All rights reserved.

"Thoughts That Hold Us Back" by John Van Diest, associate publisher. Used by permission.

"Effective Leaders" taken from *Things Only Men Know.* Copyright © 1999 by Preston Gillham. Published by Harvest House Publishers, Eugene, Oregon 97402. Used by permission.

"Don'ts for Decision Making" from *Healing the Hurting Heart* by June Hunt. Used by permission of the author. June Hunt is host of two international radio ministries, Hope for the Heart and Hope in the Night, located in Dallas, Texas. Author and speaker on biblical counseling, June communicates God's Truth for Today's Problems.

"Are You a Good Time Manager?" condensed from *Tyme Management*™ by Rutherford Publishing, Inc. The *Tyme Management*™ newsletter provides time management tips and suggestions to those in the workforce. For more information, visit www.rpublish.com. Copyright 2000 Rutherford Publishing, Inc. All rights reserved.

"Smart Goals Are…" by Alice Gray, Dr. Steve Stephens, and John Van Diest. Used by permission of the authors.

"Criticism Kills…" by Dr. Steve Stephens, Clackamas, Oregon. Used by permission of the author.

"Six-Step Recipe for Success" by Jeffrey Gitomer from *Women as Managers*, Vol. 98/No. 1, copyright © 1998, The Economics Press, Inc. Reprinted by permission. Copyright © 1998, *Women as Managers*,

The Economics Press, Inc., 12 Daniel Rd., Fairfield, NJ 07004-2565; Phone: 800-526-2554. FAX: 973-227-9742. E-mail: info@epinc.com Web site: www.epinc.com.

"Five Keys to Conversation" taken from *Confident Parents, Exceptional Teens* by Ted Haggard and John Bolin. Copyright © 1999 by Ted Haggard and John Bolin. Used by permission of Zondervan Publishing House.

"The Ten Commandments of Giving a Speech" by Steve Brown condensed from *How to Talk So People Will Listen*. Used by permission of Baker Book House, Grand Rapids, Michigan, © 1999.

STEPPING FORWARD

"Three Pillars of Learning" by Benjamin Disraeli.

"Seven Lessons to Learn" by John Van Diest, associate publisher. Used by permission of the author.

"Seven Important Choices" by Sheri Rose Shepherd from *7 Ways to a Better You*. Published by Multnomah Publishers, Inc., Sisters, OR, © 1999. Used by permission.

"Living Like There's No Tomorrow" by Jeff Herring from the *Oregonian* newspaper, Saturday, April 3, 1999. Reprinted with permission of Knight Ridder/Tribune Information Services.

"Seven Ways to Make Yourself Miserable" by Elisabeth Elliott from *Keep a Quiet Heart*. Copyright © 1995. Published by Servant Publications, Ann Arbor, Michigan. Used by permission.

"Life 101" by Phil Callaway from *Who Put the Skunk in the Trunk?* Published by Multnomah Publishers, Inc., Sisters, OR, © 1999. Used by permission.

"Goals for Authentic Growth" by Joe D. Batten from *New Man* magazine, March/April 1998. Used by permission.

"Five Ways to Start the New Year Right" by Liita Forsyth from *Virtue* magazine, January 2000. Used by permission of the author. Liita Forsyth has art directed three different consumer magazines and is currently an art director for Crossway Books in Wheaton, IL. She also maintains a home-based freelance design and illustration business where she lives with her husband and cat.

"Four Traits of Those Who Impact Our Lives" taken from *Growing Strong in the Seasons of Life* by Charles R. Swindoll. Copyright © 1983 by Charles R. Swindoll, Inc. Used by permission of Zondervan Publishing House.

"What Is Maturity?" by Dr. Steve Stephens, Clackamas, Oregon. Used by permission of the author.

"Vital Questions" by David Sanford, freelance writer. David Sanford is a lay pastor and vice president of publishing for the Luis Palau Evangelistic Association in Portland, Oregon. Used by permission.

"How to Put a *Wow* in Every Tomorrow" by Alice Gray, inspirational conference speaker, from her seminar, "Treasures of the Heart." Used by permission of the author.

"We Are Shaped By..." by A. W. Tozer.

"How to Lighten Up" by Ken Davis, author, adapted from the book *Lighten Up* published by Zondervan Publishing House. Used by permission of the author.

"The Optimist Creed" by Optimist International. Reprinted by permission of Optimist International, St. Louis, MO. An association of civic service clubs using the Optimist name.

VIRTUE

"A Balanced Life" from *God's Little Devotional Book,* copyright © 1995 by Honor Books, Inc., Tulsa, Oklahoma. Used by permission.

"Character and Conduct" by E. M. Bounds from *The Family Book of Christian Values,* copyright © 1995 by Christian Parenting Books.

"Good Character Is..." by St. Paul the Apostle.

"100 Positive Virtues" by Alice Gray, Dr. Steve Stephens, and John Van Diest. Used by permission of the authors.

"You Can Do It" taken from *The ABCs of Wisdom* by Ray Pritchard. Copyright © 1998, Moody Bible Institute of Chicago, Moody Press. Used by permission.

"Timeless Gifts" by Ruth Graham Bell. This article was taken from *Decision* magazine, January, 2000; © 1999 Billy Graham Evangelistic Association, used by permission, all rights reserved.

"Choosing Humility in an Arrogant World" by H. Dale Burke and Jac La Tour taken from *A Love That Never Fails,* Moody Press, copyright © 1999. Used by permission.

"Basic Manners That Teach Respect" by Bob Hostetler from *HomeLife* magazine, May 2000. Used by permission of the author. Bob Hostetler is an award-winning writer whose books include *Don't Check Your Brains at the Door* (coauthored with Josh McDowell). He lives in Hamilton, Ohio, with his wife, Robin, and two children.

"Why I Write Thank-You Notes" by Marilyn K. McAuley, copyright © 2000. Used by permission of the author. Marilyn is a freelance writer and copyeditor living in Vancouver, WA.

"The Secret List of Social Faux Pas" by Ann Platz and Susan Wales taken from *Social Graces.* Copyright © 1999 by Ann Platz and Susan Wales. Published by Harvest House Publishers, Eugene, Oregon 97402. Used by permission.

"A Virtuous Person..." by George Washington Carver.

"Three Basic Ingredients of Integrity" by Dr. Ross Campbell taken from *Relational Parenting,* Moody Press, copyright © 2000. Used by permission.

"George Washington's Rules of Civility" by George Washington.

"34 Things We Must Respect" by Dr. Steve Stephens, Clackamas, Oregon. Used by permission of the author.

"Seven Sacred Virtues" by Marilyn vos Savant from *Parade* magazine, December 5, 1999. Reprinted with permission from *Parade* and Marilyn vos Savant, copyright © 1999.

"Scout's Law" by Boy Scouts of America condensed from the *Boy Scout Handbook.* Used by permission.

FRIENDSHIP

"Why Friends Are Important" by Dr. Steve Stephens, Clackamas, Oregon. Used by permission of the author.

"10 Rules for Getting Along with People" by Norman Vincent Peale from *Time Talk.* Used by permission.

"A Friend Is One Who..." by Glenda Hotton, M.A., C.D.C., M.F.T., counselor specializing in women's issues of trauma, abuse, relationships and substance abuse in private practice in Santa Clarita, California. Used by permission of the author.

"Friendship Words" by Emilie Barnes and Donna Otto taken from *Friends of the Heart* by Emilie Barnes and Donna Otto. Copyright © 1999 by Harvest House Publishers, Eugene, Oregon 97402. Used by permission.

"The Four Promises of Forgiveness" by Ken Sande from *The Peacemaker*. Used by permission of Baker Book House, Grand Rapids, Michigan, © 1991.

"The Fine Art of Friendship" by Dr. Ted W. Engstrom condensed from *Christian Leadership Letter,* February 1986. Used by permission of the author.

"20 Questions to Ask a Friend" by Emilie Barnes and Donna Otto taken from *Friends of the Heart* by Emilie Barnes and Donna Otto. Copyright © 1999 by Harvest House Publishers, Eugene, Oregon 97402. Used by permission.

"Good Friends Are Hard to Find" by Patrick Morley taken from *The Man in the Mirror* by Patrick Morley. Copyright © 1997 by Patrick Morley. Used by permission of Zondervan Publishing House.

"Healthy Expectations of Friends" and "Unhealthy Expectations of Friends" by Glenda Hotton, M.A., C.D.C., M.F.T., counselor specializing in women's issues of trauma, abuse, relationships and substance abuse in private practice in Santa Clarita, California. Used by permission of the author.

"Antigossip Pact" by John Wesley and friends from *God's Little Devotional Book,* copyright © 1995 by Honor Books, Inc., Tulsa, Oklahoma. Used by permission.

"Proverbs on Friendship" by King Solomon selected from the Proverbs.

"10 Ideas for Staying Close When You're Far Away" by Emilie Barnes and Donna Otto taken from *Friends of the Heart* by Emilie Barnes and Donna Otto. Copyright © 1999 by Harvest House Publishers, Eugene, Oregon 97402. Used by permission.

"Fun Activities for Couple Friends" by Tricia Goyer from *HomeLife* magazine, October 1999. Used by permission.

"Being a Good Neighbor" by Tami Stephens, Clackamas, Oregon. Used by permission of the author.

HEALTH

"Stress Busters" by Alice Gray, Dr. Steve Stephens, and John Van Diest. Used by permission of the authors.

"Guidelines for Good Sleep" by American Academy of Sleep Medicine from an *AASM Wellness Booklet,* Rochester, MN. Used by permission.

"How to Keep Your Immune System Strong" by Terry Shintani, M.D., M.P.H. (nutrition Harvard University) is board certified in preventive medicine, director of integrative medicine at Coast Health Center, and author of *HawaiiDiet* (Pocket Books, 1999) and a book on "good carbohydrates" (Pocket Books, 2001).

"20 Ways to Relax" by H. Jackson Brown, Jr. condensed from *Life's Little Instruction Book* by H. Jackson Brown, Jr. and published by Rutledge Hill Press, Nashville, Tennessee. Used by permission.

"Why Laughter Is Healthy" by Dr. Steve Stephens, Clackamas, Oregon. Used by permission of the author.

"Warning Signs of Emotional Pain" by Sheri Rose Shepherd from *Fit for Excellence* (Lake Mary, FL:

Creation House, copyright © 1998, page 9). Used by permission.

"Don'ts for Emotional Fitness" by Sheri Rose Shepherd from *Fit for Excellence* (Lake Mary, FL: Creation House, copyright © 1998, page 10). Used by permission.

"Results of Anxiety" by Charles Stanley from *In Touch* magazine, January 2000, In Touch Ministries, Atlanta, GA. Used by permission.

"Avoid Getting and Doing Too Much" by Robert and Debra Bruce and Ellen Oldacre from *Standing Up Against the Odds* by Debra Fulghum Bruce and Ellen Oldacre, copyright 1999 by Concordia Publishing House. Used with permission under license number 00: 5-53.

"What Guys Need to Know about PMS" by J. Ron Eaker, M.D. condensed from *New Man* magazine, March/April 2000. Used by permission.

"Defusing Anger" by H. Dale Burke and Jac La Tour condensed from *A Love That Never Fails,* copyright © 1999, published by Moody Press, Chicago, Illinois. Used by permission.

"Top 10 Habits for Health and Vitality" by Dan Benson adapted from *THE NEW RETIREMENT: How to Secure Financial Freedom and Live Out Your Dreams* by Dan Benson. (Web site: www.NewRetirement.net) Copyright © 2000, Word Publishing, Nashville, Tennessee. All rights reserved. Used by permission of the author.

"Eating Healthy" condensed from *LifeWise* newsletter. Reprinted with permission, HOPE Publications, Kalamazoo, Michigan, (616) 343-0770.

"Guidelines for Choosing Healthy Foods" by Branda Polk condensed from *HomeLife* magazine, January 2000. Used by permission.

"Travel First-Aid Kit" by Kate Redd from *52 Ways to Make Family Travel More Enjoyable.* Reprinted by permission of Thomas Nelson Publishers from the book entitled *52 Ways to Make Family Travel More Enjoyable,* copyright 1994 by Kate Redd.

"Stay Active" by Amy Givler from *HomeLife* magazine, January 2000. © Copyright 2000 LifeWay Christian Resources of the Southern Baptist Convention. All rights reserved. Used by permission.

"How to Stop Smoking" by Amy Givler from *HomeLife* magazine, November 1999. © Copyright 1999 LifeWay Christian Resources of the Southern Baptist Convention. All rights reserved. Used by permission.

CONTENTMENT

"One Is Poor If He…" by Leroy Brownlow condensed from *A Psalm In My Heart,* © 1996 Brownlow Publishing. Used by permission.

"I Am Thankful For…" by Nancie J. Carmody from *Family Circle* magazine, November 16, 1999. Used by permission of the author.

"Joy for Today" by Goethe.

"If I Had It to Do Over Again" by John MacArthur taken from *The Family* by John MacArthur. Copyright ©1982, Moody Bible Institute of Chicago, Moody Press. Used by permission.

"Random Acts of Kindness" by Alice Gray, Dr. Steve Stephens, and John Van Diest. Used by permission of the authors.

"Tranquility" by Billy Graham from *Unto the Hills,* Billy Graham, © 1996, Word Publishing, Nashville, Tennessee. All rights reserved.

"Rules of Contentment" by E. B. Pusey.

"We All Need…" by Dr. Steve Stephens, Clackamas, Oregon. Used by permission of the author.

"20 Ways to Simplify" by Dr. Steve Stephens, Clackamas, Oregon. Used by permission of the author.

"Happiness" by John Templeton as cited in *More of…The Best of Bits & Pieces* (© 1997), published by The Economics Press, Inc., Fairfield, NJ 07004-2565; Phone: 800-526-2554. FAX: 973-227-9742. E-mail: info@epinc.com Web site: www.epinc.com.

"Life Is Hard…But God Is Good" by Sheri Rose Shepherd from *Fit for Excellence* (Lake Mary, FL: Creation House, copyright © 1998, page xi). Used by permission.

"Four Things That Bring Great Peace" by Thomas á Kempis from *The Imitation of Christ*.

MARRIAGE AND ROMANCE

"12 Actions for a Happy Marriage" by Dr. Steve Stephens, Clackamas, Oregon. Used by permission of the author.

"The Five Love Languages" by Gary Chapman from *The Five Love Languages,* copyright © 1992, published by Moody Press, Chicago, Illinois. Used by permission.

"Between a Husband and Wife" by David and Heather Kopp taken from *Unquenchable Love.* Copyright © 1999 by David and Heather Kopp. Published by Harvest House Publishers, Eugene, Oregon 97402. Used by permission.

"A Regret-Free Marriage" by Robert Jeffress from *Say Goodbye to Regret.* Published by Multnomah Publishers, Inc., Sisters, OR, © 1998. Used by permission.

"Questions to Ask Before You Say 'I Do'" by Dr. Steve Stephens, Clackamas, Oregon. Used by permission of the author.

"21 Things Every Couple Should Know" by Doug Fields taken from *365 Things Every Couple Should Know.* Copyright © 2000 by Doug Fields. Published by Harvest House Publishers, Eugene, Oregon 97402. Used by permission.

"Nine Ways to E-N-C-O-U-R-A-G-E Each Other" by Duane Storey and Sanford Kulkin from *Body and Soul.* Published by Multnomah Publishers, Inc., Sisters, OR, © 1995. Used by permission.

"50 Fun Things to Do with Your Spouse" by Dr. Steve Stephens, Clackamas, Oregon. Used by permission of the author.

"The Top 10 Mistakes Couples Make" written by Marty Crouch, copyright 1997 © Coach U. Used by permission.

"Nine Rules for Romance" by David Clark from *Men Are Clams and Women Are Crowbars.* Published by Promise Press, an imprint of Barbour Publishing, Inc., P.O. Box 719, Ulrichsville, OH 44683. Copyright © 1998.

"10 Great Romance Movies" by Dan McAuley. Used by permission of the author. Daniel McAuley is a retired school administrator and now teaches for a small private college.

"Simple Ways to Be Romantic" by Woods, Hudson, Dall, Lackland condensed from *Marriage Clues for the Clueless.* Published by Promise Press, an imprint of Barbour Publishing, Inc., P.O. Box 719, Ulrichsville, OH 44683. Copyright © 1999.

"Tips for the Romantically Challenged" by Michael Webb condensed from *New Man* magazine, March/April 2000. Used by permission.

"Talk About These Things" by David and Claudia Arp from *Marriage Partnership* magazine, adapted from *10 Great Dates* (Zondervan, 1997) and *Love Life for Parents* (Zondervan). David and Claudia Arp, founders of Marriage Alive, are educators, national speakers and seminar leaders, and authors of numerous books including *10 Great Dates* and *The Second Half of Marriage* (both Zondervan). Website: www.marriagealive.com. E-mail: TheArps@marriagealive.com.

"13 Rules for Fighting Fair" by Carol Clifton, Ph.D., psychologist. Used by permission of the author.

"Warning Signs That Your Marriage Needs Help" by Dr. Steve Stephens, Clackamas, Oregon. Used by permission of the author.

"Eight Strategies for the Second Half of Marriage" by David and Claudia Arp taken from *The Second Half of Marriage* by David and Claudia Arp. Copyright © 1996 by David and Claudia Arp. Used by permission of Zondervan Publishing House.

"Marriage Advice From 1886" by Jane Wells (1886).

HOME AND FINANCES

"Principles for Debt-Proof Living" by Mary Hunt, adapted from *Debt-Proof Living*, copyright © 1999. Published by Broadman & Holman Publishers, Nashville, Tennessee. Used by permission.

"10 Ways to Stretch Your Dollars" by Ray Linder, adapted from *Making the Most of Your Money*. Used by permission of the author. Ray Linder is a pastor, the CEO of Goodstewardship.com, and the author of three books including *What Will I Do With My Money?* (Northfield, 2000).

"Advantages to Paying Cash" by Mary Hunt, adapted from *Debt-Proof Living*, copyright © 1999. Published by Broadman & Holman Publishers, Nashville, Tennessee. Used by permission.

"Tips for Staying Within Your Budget" excerpted from *About…Creating a Budget*, a *LifeAdvice*® pamphlet produced by MetLife's Consumer Education Center (© 1996 Metropolitan Life Insurance Company, New York, NY). Used by permission. All rights reserved. To order a free copy of this booklet or any of the over eighty *LifeAdvice*® pamphlets, call 1-800-METLIFE, or visit our web site at www.metlife.com.

"The Seven Pillars of Financial Independence" by Dan Benson condensed from *THE NEW RETIREMENT: How to Secure Financial Freedom and Live Out Your Dreams*. (Web site: www.NewRetirement.net) Copyright © 2000, Word Publishing, Nashville, Tennessee. All rights reserved. Used by permission of the author.

"Debt Trap Warning Signs" by Mary Hunt condensed from *Debt-Proof Living*, copyright © 1999. Published by Broadman & Holman Publishers, Nashville, Tennessee. Used by permission.

"Most Common Ways to Misuse Credit Cards" by Bob Russell from *Money: User's Manual*, copyright © 1997. Used by permission of the author.

"How to Buy a New Car" by Holt Bertelson, Salem, Oregon. Used by permission of the author.

"How to Buy a Used Car" by Al Gray, Redmond, Oregon. Used by permission of the author.

"Checking Curbside Appeal When Selling a Home" excerpted from *About…Selling a Home*, a *LifeAdvice*® pamphlet produced by MetLife's Consumer Education Center (© 1996 Metropolitan Life Insurance Company, New York, NY). Used by permission. All rights reserved. To order a free copy of this booklet or any of the over eighty *LifeAdvice*® pamphlets, call 1-800-METLIFE, or visit our web site at www.metlife.com.

"Questions to Ask Before Getting a Pet" excerpted from *About…Choosing and Caring for a Pet*, a *LifeAdvice*® pamphlet produced by MetLife's Consumer Education Center (© 1996 Metropolitan Life

Insurance Company, New York, NY). Used by permission. All rights reserved. To order a free copy of this booklet or any of the over eighty *LifeAdvice*® pamphlets, call 1-800-METLIFE, or visit our web site at www.metlife.com.

"Qualities of a Great Baby-Sitter" by Tami Stephens, Clackamas, Oregon. Used by permission of the author.

"What Your Baby-Sitter Needs to Know" by Tami Stephens, Clackamas, Oregon. Used by permission of the author.

"Cop's Vacation Checklist" by Ken McClure, Clackamas, Oregon. Used by permission of the author.

"Six Easy Ways to Organize Your Kids' Clutter" by Faith Tibbetts McDonald from *Virtue* magazine, March/April 1998. Used by permission of the author.

"22 Items to Always Carry in Your Car" by Al Gray, Redmond, Oregon. Used by permission of the author.

"Create a Family Craft Box" by Tricia Goyer condensed from *HomeLife* magazine, January 2000. © Copyright 2000 LifeWay Christian Resources of the Southern Baptist Convention. All rights reserved. Used by permission.

TEENS

"10 Gifts for Your Teens" by Susan Alexander Yates condensed from *How to Like the Ones You Love.* Used by permission of Baker Book House, Grand Rapids, Michigan, © 2000.

"How Well Do You Know Your Teenager?" by Miriam Neff, B.A., M.A., Northwestern University, counselor in public high school, mother of four, author, and speaker, condensed from *FamilyLife Today* radio program. Used by permission of the author.

"How to Motivate Your Teen" by Gary and Anne Marie Ezzo from *Reaching the Heart of Your Teen.* Published by Multnomah Publishers, Inc., Sisters, OR, © 1997. Used by permission.

"Kids Who Resist Peer Pressure Have…" by Don S. Otis condensed from *Teach Your Children Well.* Used by permission of Baker Book House, Grand Rapids, Michigan, © 2000.

"Five Secrets of Parenting Teens" by Ted Haggard and John Bolin taken from *Confident Parents, Exceptional Teens* by Ted Haggard and John Bolin. Copyright © 1999 by Ted Haggard and John Bolin. Used by permission of Zondervan Publishing House.

"How to Raise Sexually Pure Kids" by Tim and Beverly LaHaye from *Raising Sexually Pure Kids.* Published by Multnomah Publishers, Inc., Sisters, OR, © 1998. Used by permission.

"Four Ways to Stay Sexually Pure" by Robert Jeffress from *Saying Goodbye to Regret.* Published by Multnomah Publishers, Inc., Sisters, OR, © 1998. Used by permission.

"Qualities of a Good Teen Friend" by Don S. Otis from *Teach Your Children Well.* Used by permission of Baker Book House, Grand Rapids, Michigan, © 2000.

"Teen Group-Dating Ideas" by Jimmy Hester condensed from *HomeLife* magazine, February 2000. © Copyright 2000 LifeWay Christian Resources of the Southern Baptist Convention. All rights reserved. Used by permission.

"How to Teach Respect" by Bob Hostetler from *HomeLife* magazine, May 2000. Used by permission of the author. Bob Hostetler is an award-winning writer whose books include *Don't Check Your Brains at the Door* (coauthored with Josh McDowell). He lives in Hamilton, Ohio, with his wife, Robin, and two children.

"When Your Teen Fails" by Gary Chapman condensed from *The Five Love Languages of Teenagers*, Northfield Publishing, a division of Moody Press, copyright © 2000. Used by permission.

"Minimize Materialism" by Don S. Otis condensed from *Teach Your Children Well*. Used by permission of Baker Book House, Grand Rapids, Michigan, © 2000.

"Warning Signs That My Child Is Headed for Trouble" by Dr. Greg Cynaumon from *Helping Single Parents with Troubled Kids*. Used by permission of the author.

"Warning Signs of Teens Headed for Violent Behavior" by Mark A. Tabb condensed from *HomeLife* magazine, November 1999. © Copyright 1999 LifeWay Christian Resources of the Southern Baptist Convention. All rights reserved. Used by permission.

"10 Commandments for Teenagers" by Ted Haggard and John Bolin taken from *Confident Parents, Exceptional Teens* by Ted Haggard and John Bolin. Copyright © 1999 by Ted Haggard and John Bolin. Used by permission of Zondervan Publishing House.

FAMILY LIFE

"Children Learn What They Live" by Dorothy Law Nolte excerpted from the book *Children Learn What They Live*. Copyright © 1998 by Dorothy Law Nolte and Rachel Harris. The poem "Children Learn What They Live" on page vi copyright © 1972 by Dorothy Law Nolte. Used by permission of Workman Publishing Co., Inc., New York. All rights reserved.

"Teaching the ABCs to Your Children" by Glenda Hotton, M.A., C.D.C., M.F.T., counselor specializing in women's issues of trauma, abuse, relationships and substance abuse in private practice in Santa Clarita, California. Used by permission of the author.

"Helping Your Child Succeed" by Gary Smalley from *The Key to Your Child's Heart*, Gary Smalley, © 1984, Word Publishing, Nashville, Tennessee. All rights reserved.

"Every Parent Should Ask..." by Dr. John C. Maxwell, Founder, The INJOY Group (Web site: www.injoy.com) from *Breakthrough Parenting*. Used by permission of the author.

"25 Ways to Help Your Child Do Better in School" by Jan Dargatz from *52 Ways to Help Your Child Do Better in School*. Reprinted by permission of Thomas Nelson Publishers from the book entitled *52 Ways to Help Your Child Do Better in School*, copyright 1993 by Jan Dargatz.

"13 Ways to Get Your Child to Read" by Doris Howard. Used by permission of the author.

"Kids Online" by Donna Rice Hughes from *Kids Online*. Used by permission of Baker Book House, Grand Rapids, Michigan, © 1998.

"Showing Respect for Your Child" by Ron Hutchcraft taken from *Five Needs Your Child Must Have Met at Home* by Ron Hutchcraft. Copyright © 1995 by Ron Hutchcraft. Used by permission of Zondervan Publishing House.

"25 Ways to Enjoy Your Family" by Tim Kimmel condensed from *Little House on the Freeway*. Published by Multnomah Publishers, Inc., Sisters, OR, © 1987, 1994. Used by permission.

"Three Ways to Keep Family Boundaries" by Dr. Mary Manz Simon condensed from *Christian Parenting Today* magazine, March/April 2000. Used by permission of the author. Dr. Simon is a nationally recognized speaker, bestselling author, and consultant on the children's marketplace. Dr. Simon also hosts the nationally syndicated daily radio program, *Front Porch Parenting*.

"Tips to Custom-Fit Your Parenting" by Dottie G. Bachtell from *Today's Christian Woman* magazine, March/April 2000. Used by permission of the author. Dottie G. Bachtell works for Marketplace Ministries as an Industrial Chaplain in Longview, Texas. She is a freelance writer, speaker, and homemaker. She and husband, Charlie, have two sons.

"The 10 Commandments of Grandparenting" by Dr. Larry Keefauver from *Hugs for Grandparents,* published by Howard Publishing. Used by permission. Larry Keefauver, D.Min., the senior editor of *Ministries Today* magazine and copastor of The Gathering Place Worship Center, Lake Mary, Florida, has authored *Hugs for Grandparents; Lord, I Wish My Husband Would Pray with Me*; and more than forty other books.

"Good Times with Grandparents" by Cynthia Sumner from *MomSense*, Spring 1996. Used by permission of MOPS International.

"Golden Moments in a Child's Day" by Ron Hutchcraft taken from *Five Needs Your Child Must Have Met at Home* by Ron Hutchcraft. Copyright © 1995 by Ron Hutchcraft. Used by permission of Zondervan Publishing House.

"Principles of Parenting" by Jani Ortlund condensed from *Fearlessly Feminine*. Published by Multnomah Publishers, Inc., Sisters, OR, copyright © 2000. Used by permission of the author.

"Starting Your Child on Good Health" by Dr. Loraine Stern, M.D. condensed from *Woman's Day* magazine, January 4, 2000. Used by permission of the author. Dr. Stern is an associate clinical professor at UCLA Department of Pediatrics, Fellow, American Academy of Pediatrics.

"Building Relationships with Your Married Kids" by David and Claudia Arp adapted from *The Second Half of Marriage* (Zondervan, 1996). Used by permission of the authors. David and Claudia Arp, founders of Marriage Alive, are educators, national speakers and seminar leaders, and authors of numerous books including *10 Great Dates* and *The Second Half of Marriage* (both Zondervan). Website: www.marriagealive.com. E-mail: TheArps@marriagealive.com.

"10 Best Indoor Games Ever" by Jerry and Patti MacGregor taken from *Family Times*. Copyright © 1999 by Jerry and Patti MacGregor. Published by Harvest House Publishers, Eugene, Oregon 97402. Used by permission.

FAMILY LOVE

"A Parent's Commitment" by Gary Smalley and John Trent from *Leaving the Light On*. Published by Multnomah Publishers, Inc., Sisters, OR, © 1991. Used by permission.

"25 Simple Ways to Tell Your Child 'I Love You'" by Jan Dargatz from *52 Simple Ways to Tell Your Child "I Love You."* Reprinted by permission of Thomas Nelson Publishers from the book entitled *52 Simple Ways to Tell Your Child "I Love You,"* copyright 1991 by Jan Dargatz.

"A Parent's Daily Prayer Guide" by Don and Sue Myers condensed from *Real FamilyLife* magazine, March/April 2000. Permission granted by Don Myers, director-at-large, Campus Crusade for Christ International.

"Ways to Make Your Mom Feel Special" by Charlotte Adelsperger. Portions of this article were taken from *Focus on the Family "Clubhouse"* magazine, May 2000; copyright by Charlotte Adelsperger, used by permission of the author.

"Ways to Honor Your Dad" by John Van Diest. Used by permission of the author.

"Affirming Your Children" by Elisa Morgan and Carol Kuykendall taken from *What Every Child Needs* by Elisa Morgan and Carol Kuykendall. Copyright © 1997 by MOPS International, Inc. Used by permission of Zondervan Publishing House.

"Messages That Last a Lifetime" by William Sears, Martha Sears, Joyce Warman, et al., condensed from *Parent Project: Tools for Godly Parenting*. Copyright © 1999 LifeWay Press, Nashville, Tennessee. Used by permission.

"10 Gifts to Give Your Children" by T. Berry Brazelton, M.D. Adapted from *10 Gift to Give Your Children*, copyright © 1998 by T. Berry Brazelton, M.D. Originally appeared in *Family Circle*. This usage granted by permission of Lescher & Lescher, Ltd.

"Maximize Your Grandparenting Skills" by John Van Diest. Used by permission of the author.

"I Remember Grandma and Grandpa Because…" by Pat Van Diest. Used by permission of the author.

"Traits of a Loving Family" by Dolores Curran from *Traits of a Healthy Family*; Harper San Francisco; 1985. Used by permission of the author.

"Four Foundation Stones of Parental Love" by Dr. Ross Campbell taken from *Relational Parenting* by Dr. Ross Campbell, Moody Press, copyright © 2000. Used by permission.

"Keep Communication Open with Your Child" by Stephen Arterburn from *Parents Guide to Top 10 Dangers Teens Face* by Stephen Arterburn and Jim Burns, a Focus on the Family book published by Tyndale House Publishers. All rights reserved. International copyright secured. Used by permission.

"Six Questions to Get Your Kids Talking" by John Trent, Ph.D. condensed from *Christian Parenting Today* magazine, March/April 2000. Used by permission of the author.

"Giving Love to Children" by Donna Otto taken from *The Gentle Art of Mentoring*. Copyright © 1997 by Donna Otto. Published by Harvest House Publishers, Eugene, Oregon 97402. Used by permission.

"Bolstering Your Child's Confidence" by Karen Dockrey from *Parenting: Questions Women Ask*. Published by Multnomah Publishers, Inc., Sisters, OR, © 1992. Used by permission.

WISDOM

"Seven Lessons for Living" by Grandma Sinclair taken from *Well Done!* by Dave Thomas. Copyright © 1994 by R. David Thomas. Used by permission of Zondervan Publishing House.

"Wise Sayings My Mother Taught Me" by Nola Bertelson, Salem, Oregon. Used by permission of the author.

"A Father's Advice" by Bob Welch taken from *A Father for All Seasons*. Copyright © 1998 by Bob Welch. Published by Harvest House Publishers, Eugene, Oregon 97402. Used by permission.

"Do Good" by St. Paul the Apostle selected from Romans.

"Life" by Percy Bysshe Shelley.

"10 Rules to Live By" selected from *A Better Way to Live* by Og Mandino, copyright © 1990 by Og Mandino. Used by permission of Bantam Books, a division of Random House, Inc.

"Kids Say the Wisest Things" by Phil Callaway from *Who Put the Skunk in the Trunk?* Published by Multnomah Publishers, Inc., Sisters, OR, © 1999. Used by permission.

"The Wisdom of Abraham Lincoln" by Abraham Lincoln.

"10 Secrets to Ageless Living" by Kelly Ferrin from *What's Age Got to Do with It?*, copyright © 1999, published by ALTI Publishing, San Diego, California. Used by permission.

"Practical Words of a Philosopher" by Baltasar Gracian.

"Vanity" by Thomas á Kempis from *The Imitation of Christ*.

"Seize the Day…" by Bruce Bickel and Stan Jantz adapted from *God Is in the Small Stuff: And It All Matters*. Published by Promise Press, an imprint of Barbour Publishing, Inc., P.O. Box 719, Ulrichsville, OH 44683. Copyright © 1998. Used by permission.

"12 Lessons Worth Repeating" by Marian Wright Edelman from *The Measure of Our Success* by Marian Wright Edelman © 1992 by Marian Wright Edelman. Reprinted by permission of Beacon Press, Boston.

"Fear and Faith" by Phil Callaway from *Who Put the Skunk in the Trunk?* Published by Multnomah Publishers, Inc., Sisters, OR, © 1999. Used by permission.

"Handbook of Wisdom" Bruce and Cheryl Bickel and Stan and Karin Jantz from *Life's Little Handbook of Wisdom*. Published by Barbour Publishing, Inc., P.O. Box 719, Ulrichsville, OH 44683. Copyright © 1992. Used by permission.